20.00

DATE DUE

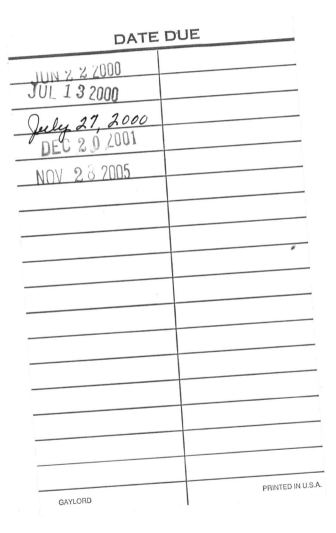

JUN 2 2 2000
JUL 1 3 2000
July 27, 2000
DEC 2 0 2001
NOV 2 8 2005

GAYLORD   PRINTED IN U.S.A.

The Cajuns:
Essays on Their History
and Culture

The Cajuns:
Essays on Their History
and Culture

U.S.L. History Series, No. 11

edited by

GLENN R. CONRAD

Center for Louisiana Studies
University of Southwestern Louisiana
Lafayette, Louisiana

THIRD EDITION

Library of Congress Catalog Number: 83-70981
ISBN Number: 0-940984-10-5

Copyright 1983
University of Southwestern Louisiana
Lafayette, Louisiana

Published by The Center for Louisiana Studies
University of Southwestern Louisiana

FOREWORD

The Louisiana Acadians, or Cajuns, have been a subject of curiosity ever since the first American and foreign travellers penetrated the wilds of Louisiana in the years following the Purchase. Later, as the fratricidal struggle of mid-nineteenth century sent new waves of "foreigners" into the bayou country of Louisiana, further descriptions and critiques of the Cajun were produced in the letters of homesick Union soldiers.

As the nineteenth century ended, the newspaper and magazine travel accounts became popular and scores of adventurous souls tramped across the Louisiana coastal plain in search of the "mysterious," "quaint," "effusive," or "gregarious" Cajun. Finally, in the twentieth century editors of glossy-paged popular magazines have periodically dispatched ultra-sophisticated reporters and photographic teams to capture in prose and on film the remnant of that "vanishing breed," the Louisiana Cajun.

This work is intended to announce to the world that the Louisiana Cajun is alive and well, that he is "up front" and "mainstream." If the Cajuns have appeared reticent in recent years, it is only an illusion prompted by their total involvement with social and cultural evolution and economic change.

The thirteen essayists seek here to tell the story of the Cajuns from the time of their exile from Nova Scotia to the present. They hope that their efforts will not only shed light on the romantic aspects of the Cajuns' past but also realistically portray the Cajun role in shaping contemporary Louisiana.

Glenn R. Conrad
Center for Louisiana Studies
University of Southwestern Louisiana
April, 1983

THE CONTRIBUTORS

BARRY JEAN ANCELET, a native of Lafayette, Louisiana, is of Cajun descent. He holds a B. A. in French from the University of Southwestern Louisiana, an M. A. in Folklore from Indiana University, and is a candidate for the *doctorat du 3e cycle* at the Université de Provence in Creole Studies. He is presently directing the Folklore and Folklife Program of the Center for Louisiana Studies. His research and publications have focused on the folk music and oral literature of French Louisiana's traditional culture.

VAUGHAN B. BAKER holds a Ph. D. in history from the University of Southwestern Louisiana. A native of Lafayette, Louisiana, Dr. Baker is descended from an Acadian family. She is the co-author of *Death of an Old World: Europe, 1914-45* and *Genesis of a New World: 1915-Present*. She has published several articles in the area of Louisiana history.

CARL A. BRASSEAUX, the descendant of an Acadian family, is a native of Sunset, Louisiana. He holds the *doctorat du 3e cycle* from the Université de Paris in North American Studies. Dr. Brasseaux is assistant director of U. S. L.'s Center for Louisiana Studies. His research and publications have focused on French colonial Louisiana. He is co-author of *The Courthouses of Louisiana*.

MALCOLM L. COMEAUX was born in Lafayette, Louisiana. A graduate of the University of Southwestern Louisiana, he received the M. A. degree from Southern Illinois University in Carbondale and was awarded a Ph. D. from Louisiana State University. All of his degrees are in the field of geography. Dr. Comeaux is presently associate professor of geography at Arizona State University in Tempe. His research centers on Louisiana and Arizona topics.

GLENN R. CONRAD is a native and resident of New Iberia, Louisiana. He was educated at Georgetown University and Louisiana State University. His areas of specialization are France and Louisiana. Professor Conrad is presently director of the Center for Louisiana Studies and is the author of many articles and books on Louisiana subjects.

GABRIEL DEBIEN, a native of France, spent a lifetime in the field of historical studies. He received the *doctorat-es-lettres* from the Université de Paris and taught at the University of Giza in Egypt and the University of Dakar in Senegal. Dr. Debien was the leading authority on the subject of the Acadians in the West Indies.

JAMES H. DORMON, professor of History and American Studies at the University of Southwestern Louisiana, holds a doctorate from the University of North Carolina and has done post-doctoral work in anthropology at the University of California as a National Endowment for the Humanities Fellow. He specializes in the study of American ethnic groups, and is author of *The People Called Cajuns: Introduction to an Ethnohistory.*

PERRY H. HOWARD is professor of Sociology at Louisiana State University. A native of Maine, he received his B. A. degree at Harvard and his M. A. and Ph. D. degrees at Louisiana State University. He is author of *Political Tendencies in Louisiana* and co-author or co-editor of other books on Louisiana politics. His main field of interest is political sociology. He has served as chairman of the sociology department at L.S.U.

HOSEA PHILLIPS is a native of Ville Platte, Louisiana. He received the M. A. in French from Louisiana State University and the doctorate from the Faculté des Lettres of the University of Paris. Dr. Phillips has taught at Northeast Louisiana University, the University of Chicago, and the University of Southwestern Louisiana. Before retirement from U. S. L., Dr. Phillips was Hébrard Honor Professor of French and Acadian Languages and Literature. He is the author of *Etude des parler français de la paroisse Evangeline (Louisiane)* and numerous articles in leading professional journals.

PATRICIA K. RICKELS is professor of English at the University of Southwestern Louisiana. She holds the Ph. D. from Louisiana State University and has done post-doctoral work in Afro-American Literature and Culture at Southern University. She is the author of numerous articles and books on the subject of Louisiana and American folklore.

R. WARREN ROBISON, Ed., professor-emeritus, is the founder and the former director of the School of Art and Architecture at the University of Southwestern Louisiana. He is co-author of *The Courthouses of Louisiana.*

ALEXANDER O. SIGUR, a native of Crowley, Louisiana, received the M. A. in history from Notre Dame Seminary (New Orleans) and a doctorate in canon law (JCD) from Angelicum University (Rome, Italy). Upon completion of his theological studies, Msgr. Sigur served for many years in predominately Acadian parishes. He has published articles in numerous ecclesiastical publica-

tions.   He is currently vicar of the Lafayette City Deanery and pastor of Our
Lady of Fatima Parish.

JACQUELINE K. VOORHIES holds the M. A. degree in Foreign Languages
from the University of Southwestern Louisiana.   An ardent student of the
Acadians, she has published numerous articles on the subject.   Her research has
led to the publication of *Some Late Eighteenth Century Louisianians, 1758-1796.* Mrs. Voorhies is a former instructor of French at U. S. L.

CONTENTS

The Cajuns:
Essays on Their History and Culture

THE ACADIANS:
MYTHS AND REALITIES

by Glenn R. Conrad

Early in the second half of the eighteenth century, Acadian exiles arrived in Louisiana to establish themselves and their progeny over a large portion of the southern half of the present-day state.[1] During the more than two centuries which have elapsed, these people, their life style, and that of their descendants have become a focal point of popular and scholarly misconception or preconception. The result has been a variety of published opinion about the Louisiana Acadian, or Cajun, which often polarizes in denigration or idealization. Critics usually cite the Cajun in terms of a well-inown litany beginning with accusations of "ignorant, stubborn, and self-centered" and ending with charges of Acadian xenophobia.[2] On the other hand, admirers have used such phrases as "warm and personal," "endowed with time-tested and respected values," and "culturally unique" to describe the Cajuns.[3] Indeed, so firmly implanted are these dichotomous notions of the Cajun and his lifestyle that not even the visual media has been capable of accurately portraying the culture and environment of the South Louisianian.

Seen by the scholar with a theory in search of facts or by the author or filmmaker after two weeks of research, the Cajun is usually cast in one of two lights. He is either depicted as an ignorant, cunning, superstitious swamp dweller, living in squalor in a moss-draped, reptile-infested wilderness which is truly a backwater of American civilization; or, he is interpreted as being a creature of simple virtue, somewhat religious, easily amused by bouree, beer, and quaint music and who occasionally blurts out (in his "unusual patois") unexpected words of wisdom. Regardless of the vision, the backdrop is always the timeless, changeless, "mysterious" bayou country of Louisiana.

An example of the misconceived or preconceived Cajun is to be found in Richard Ketchum's incredible article entitled "Cajun Country" which appeared in *The American Heritage Book of Great Historic Places*. The author states chat today's Cajun

> speaks an ancient French dialect which few outsiders can follow, mixing little with the modern world, they earn a living by fishing, boating, trapping, and by selling handwoven baskets and cloth. In a region of few roads, they live on simple wooden houseboats, dependent on the waterways and the pirogue. . . .[4]

1

Only rarely does one fine a balanced vision of the Cajun and his land such as that presented by John Lang in *U. S. News and World Report.*

> It's a place of enormous wealth and cruel hardship, where the sun draws bountiful crops from the rich soil and cooks the skin of a workingman's face to the color and coarseness of leather. There are boom towns linked by the smooth ribbon of I-10 and places where a man needs a boat to visit his neighbor. There are 300 millionaires in the Cajun hub city of Lafayette . . . and there are still those who live in the old way, trapping, netting crawfish, hunting to put meat on the table. Between the extremes are the great majority, whose dress, speech, habits and dreams are the same as Americans' anywhere.[5]

The many misguided representations of today's Cajun, his culture, and his land, Acadiana, spring largely from a shallowness of background information resulting from a hurried and haphazard investigation of the literature of the subject or from a brief encounter with a handful of South Louisiana residents.

Of all the stories about the Cajuns, of all the truths, half-truths, and untruths written about the Acadians and their descendants, certainly the most provocative, the most influential piece of literature has been Longfellow's *Evangeline.* As is well known, Longfellow did no on-the-spot research for his poem; het, its tone, the delicately told love story, the mood engendered through this fictionalized account of Acadia and Louisiana have served for over 125 years to create an image of the Cajun and his lifestyle which is largely mythical.

It is difficult to appraise the impact of Longfellow's poem in creating an enduring image, real or imagined, of the Acadians in Nova Scotia or Louisiana. If, however, citations to the poem in scholarly and popular works are an indication of the epic's influence, then it has played an important role in shaping the ideas of generations of Americans concerning the Acadians. The significance of the poem as an image-maker can be appreciated when it is understood that by 1980 there had been 290 printings of the work and over 250 books and articles dealing with the subject. With all of this activity, one cannot deny the extraordinary influence of Longfellow's poem.[6]

This influence has been demonstrated many times, but a few examples will suffice. Alcee Fortier, for instance, found it unnecessary to explain, when describing how Acadian families were separated, what was meant by his statement, "and many Evangelines never met their Gabriels." Another historian has claimed that "every student of literature has read Longfellow's beautiful poem . . . and generations will read and reread it." Finally, James Maxwell, writing in *Holiday* magazine, introduces an article on Acadiana by stating that he had read *Evangeline* as a seventh-grader, but had more or less forgotten the poem for many years until in later life he rediscovered it and was thereby prompted to make a trip to Cajun country, during which he "used Longfellow as our guide."[7]

Henry Wadsworth Longfellow
Creator of the Evangeline Myth

The point is, therefore, that Longfellow's mythical account of the Acadians has, on one hand, led many a film maker down the primrose path to romanticizing the Acadian and his Cajun descendants. On the other hand, critics of *Evangeline* have attacked the poor research of Longfellow and have condemned the romantic prose of his latter-day disciples, arguing that the canvas of the Cajun life style should not be painted in the soft pastels of simple virtue; rather, it should be set in the garish colors of ignorance, poverty, and bigotry.

Such an attack on the Louisiana Acadians is nothing new. Over two hundred years ago, Spanish Governor Antonio Ulloa declared that they were not only rebellious but downright ungrateful. Berquin-Duvallon, writing about the time of the Louisiana Purchase, charged that Cajuns were dirty and ignorant.[8] The fact is, however, that few detractors of Louisiana Cajuns have committed their criticisms to writing, and whenever this has been done, the barbs are usually buried in a flowing commentary on the beauty of Cajun country. Today's critic will also hide his derogation of the Cajuns behind a facade of badly conceived humor. Beyond the so-called humorous, writers in today's minority-conscious America usually are careful to mask their ethnic prejudices in moral platitudes.

So, to begin our investigation of this phenomenon of polarized opinion of the Cajun, let us revisit the master and examine but a few lines from the work which helped to create the Cajun myth. Early in *Evangeline*, Longfellow, in rapid succession, establishes the Acadian's three most important values: God, family, and land. After positioning Acadian mothers and daughters at spinning wheels in a scene of traditonal domesticity, the poet tells us that

> Solemnly down the street came the parish priest,
>   and the children
> Paused in their play to kiss the hand he extended
>   to bless them.
> Reverend walked he among them; and up rose
>   matrons and maidens
> Hailing his slow approach with words of
>   affectionate welcome. (Part I, Sec. I, lines 43-46)

To complete this blissful scene, the poet continues.

> Then came the laborers from the field, and
>   serenely the sun sank
> Down to his rest, and twilight prevailed. (lines 47-48)

Then, as though anticipating the Hollywood zoom out technique, Longfellow crowns the Acadian homelife scene with

Evangeline,
Heroine of Longfellow's Idyllic Epic

> Columns of pale blue smoke, like clouds of incense
>   ascending,
> Rose from a hundred hearths, the homes of peace
>   and contentment.
> Thus dwelt together in love these simple Acadian
>   farmers,
> Dwelt in the love of God and man. (lines 50-53)

Here, in essence, is the creation of the Acadian as the ideal man in an environment of love, virtue and contentment. Upon moving to the master's description of the Acadians' exile home, one finds:

> Beautiful is the land, with its prairies and forests
>   of fruit trees;
> Under the feet of a garden of flowers, and the bluest
>   of heavens
> Bending above, and resting its dome on the
>   walls of the forest.
> They who dwell there have named it the Eden of
>   Louisiana. (Part II, Sec. II, lines 859-862)

Is that not the stuff, surely refined for twentieth-century audiences, which went into Edwin Carewe's 1929 production of *Evangeline*, into Robert Flaherty's famous 1948 film, *Louisiana Story*, or, two decades later, into the National Film Board of Canada's *Les Acadiens de la Dispersion*? The Longfellow touch is also easily recognized in the work of numerous scholars and novelists from François Martin's *History of Louisiana* through Marshall Sprague's *So Vast So Beautiful a Land* to Harnett Kane, who has written concerning the Acadians:

> They were a quiet rural people, who wanted largely to be left alone. . . . They found themselves in a locale remote from other parts of the colony [Louisiana], and they rejoiced. They had, and still have, twin gifts of simplicity and humor, and they set to work to re-create everything as it was with them before—their small farms, their fields, their holdings of cattle, their meeting places for talk and song.[9]

Kane thus joins other romantics in seeing the Cajun life style as a re-creation of Longfellow's idealized Acadia. Critics, on the other hand, will not settle for this idyllic interpretation, which they consider to be romantic rubbish, and insist that today's Cajun, like the ghetto black and the reservation Indian, is a victim of his environment and must be dragged from the darkness of ignorance and isolation into the shining light of twentieth-century America.

At this point, then, it is easy to join the admirers or to side with the critics of the Cajun. But before doing so, should there not be an examination of whether there was ever a *distinct* Acadian way of life which could give rise to

The Myth Perpetuated:
Carewe's Company Filming *Evangeline*

A Romantic's view of the Cajuns:
"A quaint, virtuous people, spending a great deal of time
singing, dancing, praying and visiting. . . ."

the Longfellow myth and whether there has been a *distinctive* Cajun life style which has perpetuated some aspects of their ancestors' culture? The answer is affirmative in both cases.

In each area, Acadia and Acadiana, a distinctive culture grew from the seed that was the informal conspiracy of geographical isolation, illiteracy, and religion. As is well known, these three elements of a pre-industrial, agricultural society combined in instance after instance throughout Europe and North America to create communities simply structured, largely illiterate, and intensely religious, communities highly centered upon themselves and their set of values. With the coming of the industrial-transportation-communications revolutions of the nineteenth and twentieth centuries, these self-centered societies on both sides of the North Atlantic were increasingly overwhelmed by the wave of modern nationalism and thereby surrendered peculiar group activities and beliefs to become a part of the larger mainstream majority. So, by the early twentieth century, in the western world, only remnants of these groups could be found, the Negroes to a large degree, the Eskimos, the Indians, and smaller groups like the Cajuns and Amish.

In the case of the Acadians, the ancestors of today's Cajuns, one discovers that for a century after the establishment of Acadia, with only minor interruptions, the French settlers went about organizing a society which was founded on French tradition, but almost entirely superstructured by themselves.[10]   Divorced from the sea-lanes linking France with Quebec and Montreal, possessing few exportable items of great value to seventeenth-century France, the primary value of the Acadians seemed to be to enhance France's claim to an outpost on the southern flank of her far more important colony of Canada. Economically unimportant, of no practical political or military value except on rare occasions, the socially isolated Acadians developed a way of life centering on God, family, and the land.[11] Ignoring for the most part commercial and industrial pursuits, they acquired goods by barter or through an occasional sale to outsiders, the money from which they used to purchase manufactured necessities. Thus, during their first century in Nova Scotia these colonists learned to depend solely upon themselves. They grew accustomed to a farmer's and fisherman's way of life with their simple virtues and uncluttered social structures, but, at the same time, they began to develop a common characteristic of semi-isolated or isolated people: suspicion of outsiders.[12] Therefore,

by 1700, the descendants of the first settlers of Acadia, now in the third and even fourth generation, had developed new customs. United by traditions and habits imposed upon them by the circumstances which prevailed, they ultimately became a new people: the Acadians.[13]

Then, during the next half century in Nova Scotia, the Acadians added a further dimension to their cultural conditioning. Beginning in the last decade of the seventeenth century and continuing into the first half of the eighteenth, their pastoral isolation was reinforced by fear and violence. Midway between important French and English colonies, Acadia became, as frequently happens with buffer zones, the battleground for powerful neighbors. Thus, the Acadians, though dubbed "neutrals," became the prime victims of the contest.[14] As the turbulence and destruction of war passed through their homes and over their lands, they learned quickly not to associate themselves with one side or the other, for to do so was to invite the vengeance of both in the ebb and flow of war. Thus, as with the Jews in Hitler's Germany and Southern Negroes of the first half of the twentieth century, Acadians became apolitical and thus gave their social isolation a political dimension.

The traumatic experience of dispersion from their homeland of 150 years added yet another facet to the Acadians' growing desire for solitude. This desire was in consequence of the mental and physical injury inflicted upon them in the decade between 1755 and 1765. When the nightmare of persecution ended, Acadians reacted in much the same way as German Jews of a later date: while some sought to lose their identity in alien societies, and some returned to the scene of their persecution, others determined to forge a new life in a new land--their land.

"By far the largest number of Acadian exiles settled in Louisiana after the deportation of 1755,"[15] but more importantly is the fact that *they chose* Louisiana, that is to say, they had to make their way into this territory as best they could: British transportation did not include a trip to the Mississippi. But, why Louisiana? Why not Canada, France, or the Caribbean islands? It is to answer this question that one must go beyond the simplistic, romantic reasons put forward by Longfellow and his disciples.

To say that the Acadians chose Louisiana because of its French background, or because they thought it to be still a French colony, might be accepted as a plausible explanation for their self-imposed migration, but it is not a comprehensive explanation, for its fails to fully appreciate the tremendous driving force necessary to motivate a displaced, battered people out of the lethargy and complacency of accepting their lot in order to endure still further hardship to find a home for themselves in the world. Such motivation, more often than not, springs from an obsession to perpetuate a way of life, real or imagined, in a practical or idealized version of something remembered. It is, in a word, a desire to perpetuate a cultural identity. But the Acadians dispersed throughout the British Atlantic colonies were a numerically small group that, probably within a generation, would be swallowed entirely by Anglo-Saxon cultural predominance. Similarly, the desire to avoid cultural assimilation could account for the Acadians' refusal to settle on the French island of Saint-Domingue or even in

France itself. Such a train of reasoning, it seems, is far more realistic than the statement perpetuated for generations that they quit Saint-Domingue because of the tropical climate, or that they left Poitou in France because they were removed from the French dole.[16] It becomes evident that the causes for their continuing travels were far more complex than heretofore stated, and that one clear reason the Acadians left Saint-Domingue and France was their heritage of private ownership of land and their democratic traditions which conflicted with the quasi-serf and slave systems of the mother country and the Caribbean island.

Continuing their search for the promised land, therefore, the Acadian refugees left Saint-Domingue and arrived unexpectedly at New Orleans in mid-February 1765. Although Louisiana had been ceded to Spain in 1762, its administration was still being conducted by Frenchmen, principally Charles Aubry and Nicolas Foucault. So unexpected were the Acadians that Foucault, in reporting their arrival to officials in France, stated that "some people calling themselves Acadians and speaking French, have recently arrived here."[17]

Fearing that in the atmosphere of confusion surrounding the delayed Spanish possession of the colony there would be little they could do to accommodate the Acadians, Aubry and Foucault nevertheless met with the eight leaders of the first group of 231 refugees.[18] It soon became apparent to the officials that the primary occupations of these people were agriculture and husbandry, and that if placed on suitable lands quickly, they would have time to plant and harvest a crop that year as well as begin establishment of their herds.[19] Thus, between mid-February and early April, the Acadian leaders were apparently shown available lands for settlement because, in the end, *they chose* to establish themselves in the Attakapas district, the new Acadie.[20] The Acadians were then led to the Attakapas country by an army engineer named Andry who had been instructed by Aubry to decide, in concert with the Acadians, the exact spot where they would establish their village.[21] That spot and the subsequent village, is, of course, St. Martinville. In May 1765, Aubry commented that if Acadians continued to arrive in such large numbers, Louisiana would soon become a new Acadia.[22] His words were prophetic, for as Vernon Parenton, the sociologist, has pointed out, from the moment of the arrival "Acadians began in earnest to transform their new habitat into a second Acadie, in customs as well as in all phases of their culture."[23]

Even though government lands were available for settlement along the Mississippi above the German Coast as well as along the length of Bayou Lafourche (areas subsequently settled by Acadians arriving later), and even though these lands were much closer to New Orleans, they were apparently rejected by the initial group of Acadian leaders. It would be proper, then, to conclude that among their various reasons for selecting the semi-isolated area of the Attakapas, the refugee leaders were consciously seeking a place where they might preserve, protect, and project their Acadian way of life. There, on the plains of the Attakapas, virtually isolated from the mainstream of French-Creole life along the Mississippi by the vast, almost impenetrable Atchafalaya swamp, they envisioned a perpetuation of the quiet life with its simple values which they had known in Acadia.[24]

They found their Eden in the moss-draped, reptile-infested, subtropical region of South Louisiana, and felt confident that there they could devote their lives to God, family, and the land without interference from outsiders. And so they did for nearly two hundred years. There, they farmed, herded, fished, and trapped. Geography, language and occupation tended to reinforce the social isolation of these people and to protect their culture from changes introduced from outside.[25]

Not even the transportation revolution of the nineteenth century, largely manifested by the steamboat and the locomotive, could alter the lives and values of these simple folk. Towns which became linked by boat or grain were not inhabited by Acadians, for Acadians were never artists, craftsmen, or bourgeoisie. Acadian farm families cared little or nothing for the ideas or glitter brought by the rumbling machines to the markets of their region.[26] Indeed, it is proper to say that in Acadiana few nineteenth-century ideas penetrated beyond earshot of the steam whistle.

Thus, Cajuns entered the twentieth century possessing a language and culture more akin to that of seventeenth-century Nova Scotia than to that of their world on the brink of a technological revolution; a cultural identity which might have remained undisturbed had it not been for four factors: compulsory education, mass communication, the oil boom, and World War II.[27] Formal education, never high on the Cajuns' scale of values, became compulsory in 1916, and, to the chagrin of the family, Cajun children were not only taught in English, but were forbidden to speak French on the playground.[28] The coming of radio, motion pictures, and television, also exclusively in English, but entertaining and therefore appealing, particularly to the younger generation, further undermined not only the Cajun language but also the Cajun's distinctly pastoral life style. Concurrent with the new ideas broadcast by the mass media was the discovery of large oil deposits in South Louisiana.[29] The exploitation of these deposits for a mechanizing America brought English-speaking geologists, technicians, drillers, and roughnecks into Acadiana, and if the Cajun wanted part of this action and the material rewards accompanying it, he quickly associated himself with the life style of the newcomers. Finally, Cajun cultural isolation was undercut by compulsory military service, really beginning with World War II. Young Cajuns were forced out of their cultural milieu, confronted with the twentieth-century world, and told to make their way.

By 1945, then, the walls of Cajun cultural isolation had been breached.

An Acadian Town
as pictured by the Romantic (above) and the Realist (below).

For the outsider acquainted with the romance of Longfellow and his disciples, the exposed fortress of Acadiana is seen to be inhabited by a quaint, virtuous people, spending a great deal of time singing, dancing, praying, and visiting in a world of legendary bayous, undulating moss and exotic cuisine. For the outside critic, Acadiana reveals only an ignorant, superstitious people whose sluggish bayous symbolize the backwaters of their life style. And so, since the cultural isolation of the Cajuns began to crack and crumble in the 1930s and 1940s, the romantic has sought to capture on film, in verse, or prose, the mythical Acadian of Longfellow's *Evangeline*. The always present obstacle to achieving this goal, however, is that the twentieth century keeps getting in the way. On the other hand, the critic works ceaselessly and sincerely to rid the Cajun of the twin curses of apparent ignorance and poverty and thereby propel him from the symbolical backwater bayous into the mainstream of American life.[30] For this person the major obstacle is two hundred years of frustrating cultural conditioning.

Strangely enough, neither Cajun admirer nor critic seems to realize that when the walls of Cajun cultural isolation came crashing down, the inhabitants of Acadiana, seeing the outside world, became, as frequently happens with culturally isolated groups, not fearful of change and strangers but rather culturally curious about the outside world. Thus, the person who brings balance into his vision of today's Cajun sees his subject in the light of reality, that is, he sees him leaving not a picturesque little shack, but a modern, air-conditioned bungalow, stepping into a Ford, Chevrolet, or Datsun, not a rickety little buggy or a pirogue, driving to his children's graduation from high school or college, joining them thereafter for a feast of jambalaya, crayfish pie, and filé gumbo, stomping with them to the music of a Cajun band playing on a Saturday night, rising next morning to attend church services, and spending the rest of the day talking, visiting, and playing with several generations of his kinfolk. This may not be Hollywood, and it may not sell magazines or newspapers, but it is a more realistic view of today's Cajun.[31]

NOTES

1. Some primary source materials relating to the dispersion and the subsequent establishment of the Acadians in Louisiana are: Thomas B. Akins, ed., *Acadia and Nova Scotia, Documents Relating to the Acadian French and the First British Colonization of the Province, 1714-1758* (1869; reprint ed., Cottonport, La., 1972); France, Archives Nationales, Archives des Colonies, subseries C 13a, particularly vols. 45 and 46, and subseries F 3, vol. 243; Spain, Archivo General de Indias, Papeles Procedentes de Cuba, scattered reports of various officials to the Spanish governor.

Among secondary sources, probably one of the earliest accounts of the dispersion is found in Guillaume-Thomas Raynal, *Histoire philosophique et politique des établissements et du commerce des Européens dans les deux Indes*, 4 vols. (Geneva, 1780), IV, 219-229. Among sympathetic accounts of the Acadians, their way of life in Acadia, and their subsequent dispersion is that of E. Rameau de Saint-Père, *Une Colonie féodale en Amerique: l'Acadie (1604-1881)*, 2 vols. (Paris, 1889), and Emile Lauvrière, *La Tragedie d'un peuple*, 2 vols. (Paris, 1924). Although Lauvrière's work has been cited as one of great erudition and has won the Grand Prix Gobert de l'Académie française (see Shelby T. McCloy, «French Charities to the Acadians, 1755-1799,» *Louisiana Historical Quarterly*, XXI (1938), 657, note 7), there are noticeable errors of date, and therefore of fact, in the section on Louisiana (vol. II, 189-203). Pro-British accounts of the Acadians and their dispersion can be found in: Thomas C. Haliburton, *An Historical and Statistical Account of Nova Scotia . . .* , 2 vols. (Halifax, 1829), especially vol. I, chap. IV, 135-198; James Hannay, *The History of Acadia from Its First Discovery to Its Surrender to England . . .* (St. John, N. B., 1879). Hannay's chapter (XVI) on «The Acadian People» is of value for the census reports presented and for his evaluation of Acadian character. Also pro-British in tone is John Entick's *The Present State of the British Empire . . .* , 4 vols. (London, 1774).

Also of importance to the history of the Acadians is Francis Parkman's *A Half Century of Conflict*, 2 vols. (Boston, 1892), especially chapter XXII and appendix C; also Parkman's *Montcalm and Wolfe*, 2 vols. (Boston, 1892), I, chapters IV and VIII. A recent account of the Acadian dispersion is Bona Arsenault's *History of the Acadians* (Quebec, 1968). Of lesser value are Henry E. Chambers, *Mississippi Valley Beginnings . . .* (New York, 1922), pp. 131-146; François-Xavier Martin, *The History of Louisiana . . .* (1827-1829; reprint ed., New Orleans, 1963), pp. 180-194, *passim*; Charles Gayarré, *History of Louisiana*, 4 vols. (1856-1864; reprint ed., New Orleans, 1954), II, 115-122.

The best one-volume treatment of the wandering Acadian exiles is Oscar W. Winzerling's *Acadian Odyssey* (Baton Rouge, 1955).

For a discussion of the geographical area of French Louisiana, see Peveril Meigs, III, «An Ethno-Telephonic Survey of French Louisiana,» *Annals of the Association of American Geographers*, XXXI (1941), 243-250.

By far one of the best bibliographies is that compiled by Professor Pearl M. Segura, formerly of the University of Southwestern Louisiana, entitled *Acadians: A Bibliography*.

2. Gentler expressions of supposed Cajun xenophobia are often found among statements similar to that of Bern Keating: «The estimated quarter of a million French-speaking dwellers of the Louisiana coastal marsh do not accept strangers easily.» Bern Keating, «Cajunland, Louisiana's French-Speaking Coast,» *National Geographic*, CXXIX (March, 1966), 135.

3. The diversity of opinion regarding the Cajun is mentioned by Larry King in «Exploring Cajun Country,» *Holiday* (May, 1970), 70-71.

4. An early example of the distorted view of the Louisiana Cajun is to be found in Charles Dudley Warner's «The Acadian Land,» *Harper's New Monthly Magazine*, (February, 1887), 334-354. A more recent and profounder example of distortion is found in Robert Ketchum's article on «Cajun Country,» *The American Heritage Book of Great Historic Places* (New York, 1973), p. 181.

5. John S. Lang, "In Cajun Land, A Return to French Roots," *U. S. News and World Report*, LXXXIV, No. 19 (May 15, 1978), 31.

6. Manning Hawthorne and Henry Wadsworth Longfellow Dana, «The Origin of Longfellow.s Evangeline,» *The Papers of the Biographical Society of America*, XLI (1947), 201-202.

7. Alcée Fortier, *A History of Louisiana*, 4 vols. (New York, 1904), I, 157; George P. Bible, *An Historical Sketch of the Acadians: Their Deportation and Wanderings* . . . (Philadelphia, Pa., 1906), p. 5; James A. Maxwell, «The Evangeline Country,» *Holiday*, (December, 1960), 19.

Another popular writer emphasizing the influence of the poem, states that «the tragedies of separation and loss which followed the dispersal of the Acadians are known to virtually every schoolboy through Longfellow's Evangeline.» Keating, «Cajunland,» 361.

8. See Antonio Ulloa, «Observations sur le manifeste presenté par les habitants de la Louisiane au Conseil Supérieur,» AC, C 13a, 47:64-222. The remarks concerning the Acadians occur on folio 118; Pierre-Louis Berquin-Duvallon, *Vue de la colonie espagnole du Mississipi* . . . (Paris, 1803), pp. 51-64.

9. Harnett T. Kane, *The Bayous of Louisiana* (New York, 1944), p. 11.

10. Concerning the social isolation of the Acadians, sociologist H. W. Gilmore has written:

In considering the present and past isolation of the Acadians it should be borne in mind that they were subjected to considerable isolation for a century and a half before they reached Louisiana. . . . The process of cultural inbreeding, therefore, reaches much farther back than the Acadians' residence in Louisiana.

H. W. Gilmore, «Social Isolation of the French Speaking People of Rural Louisiana,» *Social Forces*, XII (1933), 82.

This early isolation is also noted by Mrs. P. A. McIlhenny in «The Retention of Original French Culture Traits by the Acadians of Rural Louisiana,» (M. A. thesis, Tulane University, 1935), and by Robert G. LeBlanc, «The Acadian Migrations,» *Proceedings of the Minnesota Academy of Science*, XXX (1962), 55-59.

11. Gilmore notes that «important elements in this culture which the Acadians appear to have brought to Louisiana with them are 1) a devotion to the Catholic faith, 2) strong family ties of the patriarchial type, 3) numerous patterns of neighborliness, and 4) a strong attachment to the land.» *Social Forces*, XV (1936), 72.

Concerning the Acadians' family ties, Vernon Parenton has noted that

The Acadian and French-speaking families offer an outstanding example of highly integrated family organization. It is a very complex cumulative group held together by blood bond, territory, religion, language, and to a certain extent economic status. The strength of this kinship tie is very well exemplified by the wanderings of the Acadian exiles in their efforts to be reunited once more with parents and relatives.»

Vernon J. Parenton, «Notes on the Social Organization of a French Village in South Louisiana,» *Social Forces*, XVII (1938), 78.

12. The Acadian reaction to the stranger is described by Gilmore in «Social Isolation,» 82-83.

13. Arsenault, *History of the Acadians*, p. 58.

14. For a discussion of the social and cultural impact of the British occupation of Nova Scotia, see Gilmore, «Social Isolation,» 79. The political impact, seen through somewhat prejudiced eyes, can be found in Murphy, «Were the Acadians 'Rebels'?»

15. Arsenault, *History of the Acadians*, p. 169. For numbers and destination of the Acadian exiles, see Robert LeBlanc, «The Acadian Migrations,» 15-17.

16. The most recent reiteration of the climatic reasons for the Acadian departure from Santo Domingo (a statement originating with Charles Aubry in 1765) is that by Marshall Sprague in *So Vast So Beautiful a Land: Louisiana and the Purchase* (Boston, 1974), p. 189.

Robert LeBlanc concludes that the Acadians might have remained in France «had not the treatment they received there been little better than that received in the American colonies.» LeBlanc, «The Acadian Migrations,» 18. A realistic account of the Acadians in France can be found in McCloy, «French Charities.»

17. Nicolas Foucault, *commissaire-ordonnateur* of Louisiana, reported to the Duke of Choiseul-Stainville, minister of war and the navy, that some Acadian refugees had arrived from Saint-domingue in mid-February, 1765. See Foucault to Choiseul, February 28, 1765. AC, C 13a, 45:108.

18. Before the Acadian refugees departed New Orleans for their new homes in Louisiana, their number had increased to 231. See Charles Aubry, director general of Louisiana, to Choiseul, April 30, 1765. AC, C 13a, 45:21.

19. Aubry and Foucault to Choiseul, April 30, 1765. AC, C 13a, 45:22.

20. Foucault to Choiseul, February 28, 1765. AC, C 13a, 45:108. In addition to the two months lapse of time from their arrival to their departure for their new homes, which is suggestive of the fact that a site for their establishment was being selected, there is the statement of Foucault which confirms this activity: «Elles sont pauvre et dignes de pitié, en conséquence je n'ai pu me refuser a leur accorder la subsistance jusqu'à ce qu'elles ayant choisi des terres. . . .» *Ibid.*

Aubry states that he had planned to put the new arrivals on lands along the Mississippi River above the German villages, but that he did not do so because the land flooded, levees would have to be constructed and the work of clearing the land would have been a considerable task requiring many years during which time the government would have had to support the Acadians. Therefore, he states, «Je les ai laisser aller aux Attakapas, distance de 45 lieux de la ville, et placées à 15 lieux de fleuve sur la rive droite du Mississippi.» Aubry to Choiseul, April 24, 1765. AC, C 13a, 45:50.

Alcée Fortier (*History of Louisiana*, I, 152-155) supports the idea that the Acadians were allowed to choose their lands. Dudley LeBlanc, a father of the contemporary Acadian renaissance, states emphatically that the eighteenth-century settlers «were permitted to choose lands for themsleves.» Dudley LeBlanc, *The True Story of the Acadians* (Lafayette, La., 1937), p. 162.

21. Instructions of Charles Philippe Aubry and Denis Nicolas Foucault to Sieur Andry, April 17, 1765. AC, F 3, 242:290-292vo.

22. Aubry to Choiseul, May 14, 1765. AC, C 13a, 45:56.

23. T. Lynn Smith and Vernon J. Parenton, «Acculturation Among the Louisiana French,» *American Journal of Sociology*, XVIV (1938), 361.

24. Over one hundred years later, Charles Dudley Warner could write of the Cajuns' semi-isolation: «The Acadians are fond of their homes. It is not the fashion for the young

people to go away to better their condition. . . . They marry young and settle down near the homestead. . . . They are a self-supporting community, raise their own cotton, corn, and sugar, and for the most part manufacture their own clothes and articles of household use.» Warner, «The Acadian Land,» 353-354.

25. For a description of reinforced social isolation of the Acadians in Louisiana, see Gilmore, «Social Isolation,» 78-84. Gilmore opines that «it is doubtful that geographical, occupational, and language isolation have been as effectively combined to produce social isolation of [an] ethnic group anywhere else in America.» *Ibid.*, 82.

Warner, visiting Louisiana in the 1880s, wrote: «They came into a land . . . which [has] enabled them to preserve their primitive traits. In a comparative isolation from the disturbing currents of modern life, they have preserved the habits and customs of the eighteenth century.» Warner, «The Acadian Land,» 335.

26. The Cajuns «grow nearly everything their simple habits require, they have for over a century enjoyed a quiet existence, practically undisturbed by the agitations of modern life, ignorant of its progress.» Warner, «The Acadian Land,» 350.

27. Writing in 1949, Vernon Parenton stated that «Today, urbanizing influences are permeating the entire section. These include improved communication, mechanization of agriculture (with it concomitant social implications) and, particularly, mass media of education (radio, movies, newspapers) as well as increased contacts outside French-speaking Louisiana.» Vernon Parenton, «Integration of a Rural French-Speaking Section,» *Southwest Social Science Quarterly*, XXX (1949), 195.

28. Kane, *Bayous of Louisiana,* p. 14.

29. Although there is at present an attempt to retain bilingualism in Louisiana, the supporters of the project are not very confident of success. They point out that «strong outside influences such as television and a large influx of outsiders when oil was discovered are now even greater threats than the discredited official policy of monolingualism.» Roy Reed, *New York Times*, May 7, 1972, 71:1.

30. Roy Reed (*ibid.*) has pointed out that «zealous educators who believe that the United States should have only one language began systematically to try to destroy French here, as they tried to drive out Spanish among the Mexican-Americans of Texas.»·

31. Reed also concluded that Cajuns «may be the only happy minority in America.» *Ibid.*, May 9, 1972, 43:1.

THE ACADIANS IN SANTO DOMINGO:
1764-1789

by Gabriel Debien

Translated by Glenn R. Conrad

Introduction

This essay on the Acadians in the Antilles seeks only to present, in broad, outline, an episode of their exile, the details of which have been heretofore little known. It is a well-known fact, however, that on the morrow of the Seven Years' War many Acadians arrived in Saint-Domingue. It is equally well known that many remained in these places only a short time before departing for Louisiana. One cannot turn to Emile Lauvrière for the sources or details of this episode.[1] On the other hand, Moreau de Saint-Méry's work is more scholarly, but he treats only with the Acadians getting to Saint-Domingue and concludes his study with their early settlement at Môle Saint-Nicolas.[2] He mentions nothing of the many other Acadians who settled in different areas of Saint-Domingue, or those on Martinique, Guadeloupe, or Sainte-Lucie, all French islands at the time.

Arriving in company with the Acadians, or separately but simultaneously, were numerous Canadians. The French Antilles, or at least Saint-Domingue, had attracted many Canadian immigrants even before the Seven Years' War; indeed, a small but constant immigration had existed. It is unfortunate that the origins and vicissitudes of this movement have not been closely studied, nor has it been determined whether there was a connection between this Canadian immigration and that of the Acadians.

Research for this essay has sought to clarify dates, names, and circumstances concerning the Acadian immigration. It was hoped that it would be possible to determine where the Acadians settled, how many were present, their manner of living, and why they eventually left for Louisiana. The results of this research, however, do not answer all these questions. It is hoped, nevertheless, that the essay will serve as a guide for further scholarly investigation.

Although research for this essay was extensive, it was not always fruitful. There are really three centers of research for this topic:

(1) The parish registers of the Antilles deposited in the Outre-Mer section of the Archives Nationales. For Saint-Domingue the following registers were investigated: For the northern part of the island, those of Môle Saint-Nicolas, Jean-Rabel, Bombarde, Dondon, Grande Rivière du Nord, Limbé, Cap Français,

19

Plaine de Nord, Petite-Anse, Limonade, Fort Dauphin; in the west, those of Gonaives, Petite Rivière de l'Artibonite, Saint-Marc, L'Arcahaye, Mirebalais, Croix-des-Bouquets, Port-au-Prince, Léogane; in the south, those of Petite Gouâve, Jacmel, Les Cayes, and Jerémie. The census records provide a list of colonists, Acadians and Germans, at the Camp du Flore on Martinique, in the upper portion of St. Peter Parish.

(2) The correspondence of the minister of the marine and his office administrators to the Antilles (Archives Nationales, Colonies Series B, for the years 1763-1780). The correspondence from the colonial administrators to the minister, that is: Colonies C 7a (Guadeloupe), C 8a (Martinique), C 9a (Saint-Domingue), C 13a (Louisiana). Volumes 73 to 95 of *Colonies en général*, and volumes 132 to 155 of the *Historical Notes on Saint-Domingue* from the Moreau de Saint-Mery collection of manuscripts provide extracts of the correspondence of the administrators not found in Series C.

(3) At the Château de Ravel (Puy-de-Dôme) are some important papers of the Count d'Estaing who was governor of Saint-Domingue from 1763 to 1766, that is, at the time of the Acadians' arrival. These papers have been organized by J. C. Devos, archivist of the Archives de la Guerre, and he has prepared an inventory of them. There are many letters relative to the settlement of the Acadians at Môle Saint-Nicolas, copies of some of these letters can be found in the C 9 series. These documents, however, do not present a history of the Acadians in the Antilles. The administrative correspondence from Saint-Domingue sheds light on only a single episode concerning the Acadians, their establishment at Môle Saint-Nicolas. At present no document has turned up concerning the Acadians at the Camp du Flore on Martinique, at the Camp du Parc on Guadeloupe, nor for that matter on the subject of the Acadians' departure from the Antilles.

Because of their extensive gaps, the parish registers are often deceiving. Hundreds of acts relative to Acadian baptisms, marriages and deaths have been lost. The surviving registers of Môle Saint-Nicolas begin only in 1775 and go through 1789. Those of Jean-Rabel and Bombarde, neighboring parishes of Môle, are yet more incomplete, and the registers of Cap, where the Acadians must have been most numerous, cover a period of only a dozen years.

Some refugees were settled at Dondon and at Grande-Rivière du Nord in the barracks which were built just before the end of the Seven Years' War. The registers for these parishes reveal nothing about the Acadians.

At Mirebalais is found a series of acts from 1764 to 1790. These provide good information on the Acadians who were sent there simultaneously with those arriving at Môle.

It is important to note that in recording acts the priests were not always as precise as one might desire. Moreover, only on rare occasions did they record the place of origin of the parents or godparents of the child being baptized. The only real guide to the Acadians are the surnames which are easily recognizable as having originated in Acadia. It is assumed that all children whose godparents carry recognizable Acadian names were Acadians, but there are Landrys, Héberts, and LeBlancs who came to Saint-Domingue directly from France. Some errors, therefore, occur through speculation, and undoubtedly numerous baptisms of Acadians have been omitted because the name was not an easily recognizable Acadian name. Also counted as Acadians are those persons with French names who are recorded as being born in "New England." This term, for the French of Saint-Domingue, referred to all the English continental colonies.

No great significance can be attached to the titles "Mister," "Miss," or "Mrs." They were frequently used by some priests and not at all by others. In addition, extant records are not always exact copies of originals, but often only a hurried copy which omits titles and mutilates names and surnames.

A great many Canadian names appear in these eighteenth-century registers. At first the plan was to present these with the Acadian names. This idea, however, was abandoned, for its seems that the reasons for Canadian migration to Saint-Domingue were completely different from those of the Acadians.

Finally, this essay will deal only with a portion of the Acadian refugees in Saint-Domingue: those at Môle Saint-Nicolas and the adjoining parishes, Mirebalais and Croix-des-Bouquets. Those who settled in the towns of Cap, Port-au-Prince, Saint-Marc, and Léogane, as well as the Acadians who went to Martinique, Guadeloupe, and Sainte-Lucie, will comprise the subject of another work.

I

At the Time of the Treaty of Paris,
February 11, 1763

Canadians and some Acadians, primarily sailors, migrated to Saint-Domingue before the Seven Years' War. At Léogane, for example, are found five Acadians whose deaths were recorded between 1742 and 1754. Four of these died at the hospital; two were from Louisbourg, one from the "Northern Coast" of Acadia, one from Ile Royale, and one from Ile St. Jean. Only one was a sailor, although Guillaume Vaux is "frère de la côte," that is to say a *filibustier* (buccaneer), therefore, on occasion, sailor and pirate. All five were young; two, aged 19 and 25, are listed as "paupers," apparently survivors of shipwreck. The absence of any mention of occupation is indicative that they were not settlers on the island. In any case, reference to these Acadians is marginal at best.

Following the dispersion, not all Acadians were sent to "New England" and some who were sent there soon escaped. A Martinique official wrote to the Minister of the Navy and Colonies on April 20, 1756:

> You have undoubtedly been informed of the disaster which has befallen the French families so long established in Acadia. These are the families who, since the Treaty of Utrecht, have lived as neutrals, and the English government promised not to disturb them.
>
> The British sought to intimidate them and to disarm them by surprise at the beginning of this past summer, and in October they tried to force the Acadians to bear arms on their behalf. Unable to get the Acadians to acquiesce, even in the face of threats and violence, the British made them embark upon ships and dispersed them along the coasts of Pennsylvania, Carolina, and Virginia. It is estimated that the number of exiled persons, of both sexes and all ages, is approximately 12,000.
>
> On the eighth of this month, one of these families arrived at Saint-Eustache.[4] The English ship carrying this family also had on board 300 refugees from Annapolis Royale,[5] and had orders to transport them to New York. But, encountering contrary winds, the ship was forced off course and arrived at Antigua[6] at the end of last January. The governor of Antigua immediately sent the exiles to St. Christophe,[7] and the family which arrived here tells us that they stayed there from January 25 until the first of this month, at which time they found a shipowner who agreed to transport them to St. Eustache. The English authorities on St. Eustache gave them only one pound of [salted] beef, five pounds of flour, and two pounds of hardtack per person. They were able to survive only through the charity of various individuals.
>
> Once they had arrived in St. Eustache, the Dutch government eagerly sought for us to take them, for they did not want to feed them. These refugees numbered twenty-eight persons, an old man seventy-five years of age, his four sons, their wives, and nineteen children.
>
> These people ask to be sent to Louisbourg, and we will avail ourselves of the first opportunity to send them there. Messieurs Drucourt and Prévôt can settle them in their district on Cape Breton Island, or they can go to Quebec. While they are here, my lord, we will furnish them with all necessities. [8]

The records do not give the names of these people, nor is there any evidence that they were eventually sent to Louisbourg or Quebec.

Some Acadians arrived in France prior to 1762, but there is no certainty of their number. It appears that they settled primarily around La Rochelle and were supported by a royal subsidy. Before the Seven Years' War ended there were discussions about sending these people to Guiana [Cayenne], to settle the colony of Kourou; otherwise, they would be sent to the Antilles. On December 26, 1762, a circular expressing these intentions was addressed to the naval intendants and the port commissioners.

> Although the anticipated peace should reduce the royal subsidy to the families coming from Cape Breton Island and other places, it will, nevertheless, be continued during the winter. It is agreed that while awaiting the details of

the reduction, the poorest of these families should be presented with the idea of emigrating to Cayenne, Martinique, Sainte-Lucie, Guadeloupe or Saint-Domingue. They should be informed that the king will continue the present assistance to them as well as accord them other advantages.[9]

At the beginning of the preceding October, the Duke of Nivernais, the French ambassador in London, addressed a memoir to the Duke of Choiseul supporting the appeal of the Acadians in England for a French subsidy. It was understood that upon the conclusion of peace they would emigrate to French colonies.[10] In fact, the treaty of peace (Treaty of Paris, 1763) stated that the Acadians who had been deported at the beginning of the war to the English colonies in America or to England itself would have eighteen months to depart for a French colony. Everyone knew the reference to a "French colony" implied the French Caribbean possessions.

A large number of refugees, however, asked to be sent to France. In England alone there were 4,397,[11] who were waiting to leave. Only the persistent demands of the Duke of Nivernais resulted in their repatriation. In "New England" there were more than 6,000 Acadians.[12] They wanted to migrate to the Antilles, but they did not have the means to profit by the treaty provision which would let them go.

For all Acadian exiles three possibilities lay open:

(1) Since the early years of the century, New France had been in contact with the Antilles, especially Saint-Domingue which imported wood from Canada. The recorded deaths of sailors from Quebec and Montreal are numerous in the parish registers of the port towns of Saint-Domingue. Here, too, can be found the tombs of several merchants from the St. Lawrence area. Most of these sailors, coopers, carpenters, and merchants were young; few were accompanied by their wife and fewer still married wives in the colony. One finds, for example, the rare case of François Menage of Quebec who, on March 19, 1718, married Suzanne Grosille de Villemarceau at Croix-des-Bouquets. He was buried there on October 27, 1743, after having "died on his farm." The importation of wood from the Mississippi Valley into Saint-Domingue became an active enterprise only after the Seven Years' War. It is not surprising, therefore, that the Antilles, and not Louisiana, became the focal point of migration for the exiled Acadians as the Seven Years' War came to an end. Some residents of Louisbourg and of Canada, for instance, asked to migrate to Saint-Domingue as early as the spring of 1763. On May 24, 1763, the Minister of the Navy and Colonies wrote to Choquet:

You have acted properly by embarking the residents of Louisbourg and Canada who wish to go to Saint-Domingue on the *Amphitrion* and the ships from

La Rochelle. You also acted properly in sending to La Rochelle that group which seeks to go to Guadeloupe. They will be put aboard a ship destined for that place.[13]

(2) Some Acadian families sought to go to Louisiana where some of their relatives had migrated before the war. This was impossible because Louisiana had been ceded to Spain, and France did not want to strengthen a Spanish colony. Indeed, there were other plans being formulated.

(3) The Duke of Choiseul wanted these people to settle in Guiana. In light of this, he made the following proposal to the Acadians:

When the king promised assistance to the residents of North America who wished to go to Cayenne and the Antilles, it was only for the purpose of keeping these families within his Majesty's dominion, that is, to assist them in their migration. The king promised this royal assistance for two years for those families migrating to Cayenne and Sainte-Lucie,[14] but his Majesty cannot accord the same assistance to those who are seeking to go to St. Pierre or Miquelon, for they are only returning to the area from which they originally left.[15]

And to the French attaché in London, M. de l'Eguille, the minister wrote:

Versailles, December 26, 1763

I draw your attention, sir, to the fact that the king intends to send, during next February, the ship *Nourrice* and the *Neptune* to St. Pierre and Miquelon. These ships will embark the Acadian refugees and others for transportation to Cayenne. His Majesty has placed Gilbert in command of the *Nourrice*, and he is to report to Rochefort at once.[16]

The Acadians, however, had little enthusiasm for this project. It was for them nothing more than a further experience in their continuing exile. On the other hand, Gabriel Berbudeau, formerly a physician on Cape Breton Island, who was in La Rochelle with his wife and children, asked to go to the islands where he could practice his talents, because the situation in France was not to his liking.[17] Another Acadian refugee at Nantes, Lartigue, who was from Isle Royale, also asked to go to Cayenne. But those who let themselves be sold on the idea of going to Cayenne, which was portrayed as having a salubrious climate, fertile land and a rich future, perished there like flies, much as did the Alsatians and Germans who preceded the Acadians to Guiana.

The eyes of the Acadians were focused on the Antilles. The Duke of Choiseul also gave the Antilles a prominent place in his thinking. The war of revenge, of which the duke dreamed, required that the defenses of France's Caribbean islands be strengthened. Toward that end he could see two approaches: the augmentation of the white population which would be a reserve in the event of a colonial conflict, and the building of a large naval base on Saint-Domingue. It was thought that this naval base should be located at Môle Saint-Nicolas in the northern extremity of the island, a position which could command the narrow passage separating Saint-Domingue and Cuba, and which could dominate the sealanes from the Atlantic to the Caribbean.

In the end, the Duke of Choiseul encouraged the Acadians to go to the Antilles. Their migration to the islands was therefore partially planned and partially spontaneous.

Thus, in 1763 and 1764 more than 2,000 Acadians arrived in the Antilles. Some came from Louisbourg, others came from France after being repatriated from England. Above all, however,. they came from the English continental colonies. Mixed among their numbers were some Canadians. They went to Saint-Domingue, Martinique, Sainte-Lucie, and Guadeloupe. This essay, however, will concern itself solely with those who arrived in Saint-Domingue, particularly those who settled at Môle Saint-Nicolas and Mirebalais.

II
The Acadians at Môle Saint-Nicolas,
1763-1764

Upon debarking at Cap Français [today Cap Haitien] on the northern coast of Hispaniola, the Acadians were divided into two groups. One was sent to Môle Saint-Nicolas, located about one hundred miles northwest of Port-au-Prince, and the other group was settled at Mirebalais in the western portion of the island.

The project at Môle served a double purpose: to establish a fortified position overlooking a well-sheltered roadstead capable, if need be, of protecting the French fleet; secondly, to populate this part of the colony which was largely uninhabited. Plans were to establish a new system of colonization: small plantations worked mainly by white laborers.

At the end of 1763, three officers, Du Moulceau, Beauval, and Petit, conducted a reconnaissance mission to Môle Bay. They were to sound the bay, describe the climate, the water resources, and the quality of the soil. At the time, of course, there was still no plan to locate the Acadians in this area. The conclusions of the reconnaissance team remain unknown, but it would appear from their report that their judgements were based upon superficial evidence. Then, writing from Cap Français on January 24, 1764, the chevalier de Montreuil, commandant of the northern part of the island, and acting governor, outlined for the minister plans to establish a colony at Môle. He proposed to settle there some recently arrived Acadians.[18] But Montreuil was no daydreamer; he assured the minister that there would be little or no hope of permanently settling the Acadians unless they were given "absolute and incontestable rights to the land" granted them. The value of these concessions would be based upon previously granted land which had not yet been deforested. The royal decree of January 17, 1743, empowered colonial administrators to make such grants. A survey to be made, as soon as possible, would permit a grant of 10 *carreaux*[19] to each family. The Acadians could then be brought in as soon as possible.

At first the Acadians could be put to work constructing warehouses, a hospital, officers' quarters, and a road from the seashore to the vicinity of the raft in the Môle River. A commission as director general could be given to Moynet, who had already been appointed by the minister, and another commission, as assistant director, could be given to Chiconneau. A general practitioner, at least, could be assigned to the Acadian community. Two surveyors and Saltoris, the naval scribe, could be sent to divide the land among the Acadians.[20]

Tents, blankets, and hammocks could be distributed to some individuals, such as those received by the royal slaves, and by the thirty soldiers being sent with them. Only the Acadians, however, would receive clothing. No firearms would be distributed. While awaiting these preparations for their settlement, the Acadians could be employed on the corvée.

The instructions which Clugny, the intendant, and Montreuil jointly prepared for the director of the Môle project detailed that the Acadians camp near the sea, in the vicinity of a source of fresh water, and that they assist in unloading the construction materials. The surveyors, meanwhile, should draw up a plat of the land to be parceled out. If the amount of arable land along the river was insufficient, some suitable place in the vicinity would have to be found, always near a source of fresh water. The surveyors' plat, after being sent to Saltoris, would be shown to the Acadians who would draw lots for their lands. This would be done in the presence of the officers and the heads of families. Those who drew a parcel of land should be settled there immediately, together with their family. A general description of lands distributed would be sent to the intendant who would confirm title to the grantees. The instructions continued:

> With regard to these new colonists, it will be necessary to combine kindness with firmness, but they should not be maltreated. It will be necessary to punish by imprisonment those who refuse, without reason, to do their share of the work for the establishment of the base. Therefore, a building will be erected to serve as a jail and will be guarded by a sentinel. The commanding officer has orders to lend a helping hand to Saltoris, the naval scribe, and to the directors, Moynet and Chiconneau.[21]

Slaves necessary to double the number of Acadians were to be gotten from the plantations of Jean-Rabel,[22] the closest place to Môle. Nothing more, however, is said on this subject.

The Acadians' needs would be provided by the government; they would not be paid a salary.

The letters[23] which Saltoris wrote from Môle, sometimes to the intendant, sometimes to the governor and the intendant, concerning the colony which he was ordered to oversee, and which he directed for six months, afford an insight, at least twice a week, to the difficult beginnings of the colony. There were four hundred Acadians at Môle.[24]

No. 1, to the Intendant   Môle Saint-Nicolas
                                                           February 2, 1764

We have finally, happily arrived at Môle Saint-Nicolas after having been delayed at Cap Français for two days by contrary winds. We found there the two supply ships as well as the *François*, all destined for the new settlement.

As soon as we had anchored, we went ashore to select the best spot to set up our tents and huts. We found no area in which it was not necessary to clear the land of trees and brush. Then we penetrated the forest to the river in order to reconnoiter the countryside. Our settlement will be about one and one-half miles from the river. The water is quite good.

We are working hard to set up camp. Tomorrow all of our people will come ashore. We will next begin building the warehouses and the hospital, and unloading the ships.

Since we have no lime, and this is extremely necessary for the construction of our ovens, we are dispatching a schooner, belonging to M. Duval of Cap Français. The boat was on ballast in the harbor. We have written to M. Lavaud, a resident of the Borgne district[25] and begged him to be kind enough to send us one hundred barrels [of lime]. . . .

I shall be honored to send you additional reports on our operations.

Please forgive the crossed-out words, I am writing on a knee.

————

No. 2, to the Intendant   February 9, 1764

I have had the honor to inform you of our arrival at Môle Saint-Nicolas, and to give you an account of the beginning of our operations. We have pursued them until now with much success, especially since the weather has been favorable. But now the weather is threatening, and I shudder to think of it. We have so many things to do, and so little wherewithal, that if the gods abandon us, we are lost. We have built the warehouse, that is to say a shed which is fairly convenient and fairly strong and which will serve as a warehouse until one is built. We have also built a hospital, and we are all housed somehow or other. . . .

The chevalier de Rausanne[26] and I have announced a prohibition on hunting.[27] We have also prohibited fishing in the river so that the water will not be disturbed and will remain pure for drinking. For the same reason we had a basin dug one hundred feet beyond the river runoff to be used for a washing place.

I am extremely satisfied with the Acadians. I have not had to punish a single one. These are the best people on earth.

From time to time I have given them wine and tafia as a reward. The fact is that they could hardly continue this difficult work, exposed as they are to the hot sun, without their ration of spirits. I trust, therefore, that you will not object to me having done this on my own authority. These good people pester me for vegetables. Please sir, issue orders to have some peas, lentils, and beans, with which, together with a small amount of fish they catch, they will envigorate their blood, which has become sluggish as a result of eating too much salted meat.

It will also be quite necessary to establish here a butchery, not to operate on a day-to-day basis, but, at first, for the slaughter of cattle and sheep on occasion. At present we have many people ill with diarrhea and it is not only the water which causes their illness. Scurvy is surely a factor also.

We also have need of hardtack, salted meat, wine and tafia. We have only enough hardtack on hand to last 15 days.

It will also be necessary, in the future, to send two *cabrouets*,[28] well coupled, to transport the lumber from the seashore to the raft in the river, at the point where the store will be built, and later to transport the supplies and other things necessary for the new colonists.

M. Moynet has not yet arrived. Moreover, we still have not received any Negroes from the work force of Jean-Rabel and this fact prevents Messieurs Chiconneau and Buisson from operating.[29]

We have taken all of the timbers and planks off the *Campus*, and have kept only a small amount of this in reserve. We absolutely need all of this wood to build the different warehouses and hospital. This wood is, moreover, very good and not expensive.

No. 3, to the Intendant   February 11, 1764

Our fears of the approaching bad weather were fully justified. We have just endured a two-day storm. The launches from the *Francois* and the *Gramprey* were carried away and were wrecked on the coast. We have been inundated in our tents and huts. Many sacks of hardtack were turned into paste, but the sun reappears and our ill-fortune is forgotten. The weather, however, is still threatening.

I must say again, sir, that the Acadians are the best people in the world. Scarcely have we ever heard them complain during these cruel days. It is true that we have forgotten nothing to alleviate their distress, and that our situation appears to be no better than theirs. They therefore have not dared to complain. We are very fortunate that they have not complained and this is a favorable omen. I recommend them, sir, to your attention. . . .

The Acadians like and fear me. I constantly strive to understand what inspires in them these two feelings. I am yet to punish a single one, and all goes well.

Saltoris had to punish only two Acadians; one spent the night in jail and the other was incarcerated for four days.[30]

The greatest difficulty was presented by the lack of building materials, especially wood. The loss of the *Gramprey*'s longboat prevented the unloading of all the planks; therefore, five to six thousand planks were left on board to serve as ballast. Chiconneau had gone to Jean-Rabel to expedite the departure of the Negro work force. Moynet still had not arrived.

No. 4, to the Governor and Intendant   February 15, 1764

In the instructions which you gave me regarding the establishment of Môle Saint-Nicolas, it states that the surveyors should start their operations in the area of the raft in the river. Buisson therefore began this work day before yesterday with ten Acadians. The Negro work force from Jean-Rabel has still not arrived.

Yesterday afternoon Buisson told me that it will not be possible to settle colonists along a part of the river because from one knoll to another there is only a distance of 72 paces and that is largely occupied by the main road and riverbank. Moreover, the land is absolutely worthless.

I went to the place. We placed surveyor's markers between the two knolls and these confirmed Buisson's declaration. We then measured the length of the land which we judged to be of no value. We discovered that it was 1,500 paces and when this is compared with the width, it forms a farm of only 10 *carreaux*.

The ten Acadians who were helping with the survey were quite distressed. They imagined that all the land which we are to grant them was similarly of little worth.

We managed to reassure them by taking them beyond the point marked "B" on Buisson's plat, which I am enclosing.[31] We then climbed the knoll on the right of the ravine and discovered that beyond it is a beautiful stretch of land about seven miles deep and about two hundred paces wide watered by the river. Descending the knoll, we had them [the Acadians] examine the soil which is truly very good. This consoled them a little, but did not prevent them from returning to the demand which they had made many times: give them lands in the vicinity of our settlement [Môle]. They presented me with their request, which I am enclosing.[32] I told them that I would have to report their request to you.

I am taking the liberty to suggest that the Acadians' request seems justified to me, even though the land in question was granted to the Widow Blin Rouvigny about six months ago.

I am sure you must have been quite surprised, sirs, concerning the status of this concession. Surely someone has misinformed you concerning its location and its boundaries. It was your intention for at least six months to erect a settlement at Môle Saint-Nicolas, and you would not have begun that project by granting to an individual not only the land where the town is to be built, but also all the land around it for nearly a mile.

If the land was properly granted, the owner now has every right to make us clear out of the town. Our buildings, our huts, everything, is on this land.

Moreover, sirs, this concession contradicts your views on populating this area. One hundred *carreaux* of land will provide for ten families (I maintain that it will provide for twenty families, as I will point out below). The Acadian families are composed of 5, 6, 7, and 8 people. Taking the average of six per family, one thereby has sixty persons on a tract of land which at present is providing for only three or four people. We could have, sirs, 120 people on this same land if you annul the original concession and order this land to be divided among the Acadians, for in place of the ten *carreaux* which you have agreed to grant them, they will be content with only five. They, themselves, assured me of this.

There could be still another advantage accruing from such a division, when you order it. At the same time, sirs, instruct me to determine which Acadian families are headed by skilled men. I can find forty excellent carpenters who are most capable of all types of construction, both for land and for sea. I believe that these forty families can be placed all the easier on the lands immediately adjoining the town. If, moreover, there is insufficient land to give them 5 *carreaux* apiece, they will gladly accept three in preference to ten at a greater distance from the town.

The heads of these forty families are, without doubt, farmers, but farmers alone cannot establish the town. I think that at this particular time builders are at least as necessary as farmers. The remaining Acadian families will then be placed on the land first designated for their use.

Buisson has discontinued his operations on the river. He is actually trying to determine how much land would be involved if the concession were joined to the available vacant lands. He will either continue with this work or he will return to his work on the river, depending upon your instructions. I beg you, sirs, to send these instructions as soon as possible. . . .

For about a month four of Widow Blin Rouvigny's slaves have been working on the concession mentioned above.[33] They have reduced the value of the concession by two or three *carreaux* of wood; therefore, the indemnity which can be asked by Widow Blin Rouvigny would amount to very little.

No. 5. to the same   February 19

. . . I forgot to reassure you concerning the shortage of water which could occur as a result of the proposed division [of the Acadian families]. Certainly, only a portion of the Canadian [Acadian?] families will be settled along the river, but the great ease in digging wells is equivalent to this advantage of living along the stream. Thus, sirs, the consideration of lack of water must not impair your plans; moreover, I had the honor to indicate previously to the intendant that we have dug a pool about 150 paces from the raft in the river and that it serves as the public washing place. I noticed, however, that the pool did not fill rapidly; therefore, I decided to dig a ditch to the pool and this solved the problem. If we want to provide a large volume of water to an area, we will divert the river. We will survey a diversionary route so that it will connect with the town, and that will provide water for the settlers.

Nothing would be easier, sirs, to do than to dig this waterway, and I am morally certain that the river will flow through it. I went back up the river, about two miles, walking not on the banks but, with boots, in the stream. I discovered that the lack of strong current is primarily owing to the large number of obstacles in the river. Old fallen trees and rotten branches, to which is attached a kind of moss, fall into the river and block its current every step of the way. It is all of this debris which causes the raft. Removing these obstacles would reduce the meandering of the river to a single channel, and we would not lose a single drop of water.

There is still another reason to remove the raft. About where we plan to locate the first farmers, the land is flat and is only slightly inclined toward the river. It is, therefore, very soggy, but if the river bed was cleared, and the river given a rapid course, the surrounding land would be easily drained.

What are we risking? It is absolutely necessary that the river supply the town with water and that its waters empty into the sea. If the operation which I propose is not successful, then our only choice will be to dig a canal which is lined with masonry or flagstones. The construction of a canal, however, will involve the additional work of excavating the land.[34]

If you approve my plan for the river, sirs, I think that it will be necessary to change the order with regard to land distribution. It is most unlikely that you will be sending us additional help; therefore, we must use what we have. If we follow the instructions concerning land distribution, our people will begin to move out to their farms in the next few days. Once that occurs no amount of money or threats will make them return to work on the project. Moreover, we should give the surveyors sufficient time to divide the land properly before it is granted. Once the division is made, we will be able to proceed as you have ordered.

Until now, sirs, the work at Môle has cost the king nothing. I say nothing— a little wine, a little tafia, a few vegetables to supplement the diet, and about 100 *écus*—but our Acadians are unhappy. I do not think it will be possible to get them to work without paying them a salary.

When I was receiving instructions from the commandant-general,[35] I spoke to him about this matter. He responded that they would be given some clothing which would take the place of wages. Permit me, sirs, the liberty to say that such a substitution for wages will never satisfy these people. They are absolutely convinced that the king must feed and clothe them, at least in part, and no matter what I say, they will not be dissuaded of this idea. Please fix a price for their work. These are the best people in the world; they deserve your generosity.

It is also necessary, sirs, to establish wages for the carpenters who are presently working on the royal warehouses. These are excellent workers, quite capable at construction. It is essential that they remain in the colony [at Môle]. Permit me to recommend that the carpenters be paid 1 *écu* per day and their helpers 30 *sols* per day.[36]

No. 6, to the same   February 21

At four o'clock this morning a canoe arrived in the harbor with its owner, his crewman, and some young men. I questioned them as usual and asked that they show me their passports and travel permits. They replied that they had none and that they thought these items were not necessary.[37] Because of their attitude, I put them in jail.

I believed it necessary to employ such severity, sirs, because the four passengers were obviously dead drunk. They blurted out some fairly strong remarks, gave every appearance of being a bad lot, and therefore I had every reason to suspect them. Moreover, it takes only four men such as these to create an uproar and disorder in this settlement. We still have to deal with so many little things that we can never be too careful. I think, therefore, if it is agreeable, that I will send them to you so that you can mete out the justice which they deserve, once you have questioned them. Fortunately for us, the *Saint-Jean*, commanded by Le Molène, is in the harbor and leaves tonight for Cap Français. I will keep the canoe owner and his crewman in jail here until I receive your orders regarding them. They are young men, perhaps 20 to 22 years old, who innocently broke the law, it would appear to me.

Daily there appear here, sirs, all kinds of ships from different nations. Some say they stopped here because of bad weather, others claim they need water and wood, still others offer to sell us supplies. We have put up with this situation until now, sirs, because we have no orders, no instructions, from you regarding these matters. I think you should send instructions as soon as possible. . . .

It is strange that the officials at Môle had not received instructions regarding foreign ships before they left Cap Français. These ships would appear and offer to sell illicit merchandise for cash, not in exchange for colonial products.

No. 1, Response from the Intendant   Cap Français
                                                                    February 20, 1764

It has been reported to me, sir, that the storekeeper has refused to make some rations available to the children of the Acadians, and that he only gives them 12 ounces[38] of hardtack per day, and that there is no question of distributing tafia to them. When I recommended to you to employ economy in the distribution of rations, my intention was only that it be done with moderation. These people are not to be deprived of the bare necessities. Contrary to what appears to have been done, it is essential from the beginning to satisfy them and to see to it in all cases that this be done proportionately according to family size. I urge you to give this matter your fullest attention because without such encouragement, the Acadians will become disgusted and will refuse the work. I trust you will handle this matter with meticulous care and that you will give the children rations as you would to the others, without exception, as prescribed in the contract.

———————

No. 2, from the Intendant   Cap Français
                                                                    February 22, 1764

I have received your letters of February 8 and 11 (Nos. 2 and 3), but the first (No. 1) has not yet reached me.

I am pleased that you are satisfied with the Acadians and I trust that you will continue to be in the future. This will be likely, especially after a part of their work is completed and they can provide themselves with a few luxuries. I am sending out to you money and vegetables and another supply ship. Until these arrive, however, you can procure from Jean-Rabel, as far as possible, the things necessary to satisfy your people. I strongly recommend that you do everything necessary to encourage their work. Also, reassure them that they will be supplied with everything needed to get established. You understand, of course, that it is imperative to maintain order among the settlers. I trust that you will neglect nothing to fulfill these different goals. . . .

Bad weather has delayed the departure of supplies, but this is being expedited. The commanding officer at Môle has asked for a land grant. You can tell the surveyor to give him a certificate.

———————

No. 8, Saltoris to the Intendant   March 1, 1764

. . . I have addressed you on the subject of the ways which I believe necessary to bring water from the river to our encampment. On the same day I wrote to you, I told Buisson of my project. He found my proposal to be sound, and has offered to support it. I suggested that we determine the fall of the ground, and we discovered that the land falls at the rate of two inches per fathom [*toise*].[39] It was this fact, together with the necessity of going over a mile to get water, which caused us to undertake the project. We enlarged the ditch which he had begun and we had lengthened it to 300 *toises*[40] when M. Moynet arrived. At first he found the project useless because the water did not flow sufficiently, but I soon calmed his fears. I took six men and we went above the spot where the river is dammed with debris. I cleared away the debris for only 200 paces, and that sent sufficient water into the canal to wet the feet of those who were digging it. Today there is sufficient water in the vicinity of our encampment to turn a millwheel. What will it be like when we have removed all the debris from the river? Meanwhile, sirs, talk persists of paving the canal to the river. Frankly, I do not see the need for this, but if I am mistaken in my opinion, I think that it would be better to delay this work at least until the concessionaires have cleared the lands which they have been granted; otherwise, they will only be working blindly and will end up doing twice the amount of work.

The matter of water supply was settled first, for the administrators concluded that it was the most immediate problem. Problems dealing with the arable land were far more serious and were, almost from the beginning, next to insoluble. This was to become a tragic situation for the future of the colony. Shortly after the Môle project began, it became apparent that it would be impossible to find 10 *carreaux* of land for each family. The area had been only carelessly surveyed in December 1763. Moreover, the prime consideration was always the building of a major defense base at Môle, not the establishment of a farming community. In the minister's opinion, peopling the area would automatically follow. Thus, if the surveyors' findings were wrong, and if the arable lands near the river were insufficient and widely separated, no one can reproach Saltoris, for he had at no time concealed these problems.

But he did fail to mention other matters, above all the problem of supplies. The goods brought during the first month were mainly of a military nature and of little variety–hardtack, saltmeat and tafia. These items arrived regularly, but there was little or no flour, no green vegetables and no freshly butchered meat. Beginning only in March were cattle bought in Jean-Rabel for butchering, but the meat was reserved for the sick. Two cows were bought to provide milk for the children. Before the end of February complaints arrived at the intendancy.

No. 9, to the Intendant   March 3, 1764

. . . You have indicated reports to you that the storekeeper is mishandling his functions. There is some truth, sir, in what has been reported to you, but not one of the Acadians has ever complained about having been denied his rations. They would not be silent on such an important matter, for they are quick to complain about the smallest reduction in their rations. The report that the Acadians have complained is, therefore, false and calumnious.

As soon as I was informed of the suppression of the tafia ration for the children, and the reduction in the hardtack ration, I spoke to the storekeeper concerning these matters. He justified his actions by saying that the children did not drink tafia, nor could they eat their entire ration of hardtack. I reprimanded him for taking such action, and ordered him to supply the complete ration, conforming to the letter of our instructions. Since then, I have not heard a single complaint, and it appears to me that everyone is content.

You have in your possession, sir, my letter of the 8th of last month, in which you will find convincing evidence that instead of a reduction in the ration, it has actually been increased, and today's sick list, which is enclosed, is still further proof of this fact.

Without doubt, sir, it is most proper on your part to have an anonymous person here to report to you on all that occurs. This type of surveillance will certainly restrain everyone and things can only go better, but in your wisdom, sir, permit me to say that you should accord to this person only the degree of confidence which an informer merits. You should always be on guard concerning inaccurate reports, for what was his purpose in making these reports?

In the postscript to your second letter, sir, you authorized me to give a surveyor's certificate to M. Rausanne confirming the concession which he asked for. I went to speak to M. Rausanne concerning the concession and demonstrated to him the impossibility of granting him a tract of land. He accepted what I had to say in good faith, and I am sure he has no reason to be angry with what I had to say.

In my letter of the first of this month, I reported to you that the surveyor estimated that we had sufficient flat lands to give thirty families about 5 *carreaux* apiece. He has now discovered that there are only 45 *carreaux* of flat land in all. I discreetly discussed this matter with the Acadians and discovered that they would prefer a little plot of land near the town to a larger piece farther away. I told them of the problem and said that we could only grant one *carreau* to each family. Without hesitation they responded that they would gladly accept whatever is given them.

If the people who should know are so grossly in error when estimating flat lands, what must their estimations be like in hilly terrain?

I think, sir, that you should refrain from granting any lands until we are assured of a true value of the land and until we know of all the lands which have been granted until now.

No. 10, Saltoris to the Intendant   March 10, 1764

. . . The royal ship *Coureur*, commanded by Fontaine, has just arrived and is filled with a thousand good things. We are eternally grateful to you, sir.

Also on board this ship from Cap Français were two men and a woman, together with their belongings. They announced their intention to settle here. One of the men said he was a carpenter, the other described himself as a scribe. I asked them for their passports, their permissions to travel. At first they said that Fontaine had them, but he absolutely denied this. Because M. Martissan[41] had not mentioned these people in his correspondence, I will return them to Cap Français aboard the same ship which brought them here.

Please, sir, send no one here for the time being, that is until we can place the Acadians on their farms.[42] You can always replace them [as workers on the Môle project] with an equal number of newcomers who will always be easy to find.

Everything progresses well. The Acadians are angels. I will have the honor or demonstrating this fact in two days. . . .

. . . Send us no more hardtack. We have a large supply and our Acadians prefer flour because of the children. . . .

No. 11, Saltoris to the Intendant   March 12

In my letter of the 10th, I told you that the Acadians were angels. The hyperbole is undoubtedly strong, but I dub 'angels' men who have fewer of the faults of other men and many more virtues. Such are our Acadians. I want to begin a very serious study of their humor and character.

I was already convinced of their kindness, but the ceremony we recently had for them reinforced my conviction. This ceremony was for the 23 marriages which were to be blessed[43] or which were contracted among themselves. It took place on Monday before Ash Wednesday.

I had an arbor built, long and spacious in order that it could contain them all. Beneath this we set up some sawhorses upon which we nailed planks to serve as tables.[44] The sheets from our beds served as tablecloths and napkins. The hunt began on Saturday before the banquet, but we killed only one wild boar[45] and some wood pigeons. Happily, we got a calf from Plateforme,[46] and having fifty pigs in our barnyard, we had no troube stocking our table.

Everyone was at the table—men, women, and children—all mixed together. 'To your health, officer. To your health, commissary! To the health of the intendant! To the health of the king! Hooray!' We had every reason to frequently repeat these salutes.

They did not eat until each and everyone had given his toast. They danced, the old and the young alike, all dancing to a fast step. When the horseman has eaten oats, the horse runs better. In time, however, they grew tired, and at eleven o'clock we said good night and went to bed.

The next day the ceremony continued. We had about 400 at table, even mothers with children at the breast were there. Believe me, sir, there was not an ugly remark heard, neither was there indecency offered or made.

If 50 of the wisest men in France were to be selected, and if they were given a long party, where they would sing and dance and get drunk, would not someone have to leave because one of the wise men threw his glass and put out someone's eye. I will say that the Acadians are not just ordinary men, as of now I believe that they are something more.

It is, therefore, in all justice, sir, that I repeat what I have said: The Acadians are the best people in the world. Please forgive my lavish praise of them in connection with a party. We have drunk two and one-half barrels of wine, eaten a young calf, twelve pigs, 3 barrels of flour, and a large cheese. But how would one avoid this in light of twenty-three marriages and as many baptisms? The good days, our misery, our satisfaction. No, sir, you cannot be angry.

I attach, sir, a copy of the certificate of a blessed marriage. I do not know if you will find the form appropriate. We still have not recorded these matters in

the parish register. We await your orders on this subject.[47] The marriage cer-
tificates of the young men and young women are very simply drafted and also
remain unrecorded.

The blessing of the marriages and the baptisms provide evidence that the
Acadians of Môle had come directly from the English continental colonies.

The optimism voiced in the above report, as well as the satisfaction with
progress, was naturally for Saltoris' defense, for he knew he was being severely
criticized in government circles at Cap Français.

This happy event was immediately prepared by the intendant as a short
article for the *Gazette de Saint-Domingue* which had been recently established
at Cap Français.

> The new settlement which the Acadians formed at Môle Saint-Nicolas progresses
> as well as one can expect. Water is being brought into the area which is to be
> cultivated. There have been 35 marriages until now. The climate of this area is
> most healthful. Acadian industriousness, the satisfaction which they demon-
> strate the health which they enjoy, all give hope that these initial steps toward
> colonization will be followed by many happy developments.[48]

Similar sentiments of administrative satisfaction are found in the letter
which Clugny wrote to the minister on March 15.

> I had the honor to report to you in a joint letter with M. de Montreuil of
> the way in which we sent to Môle Saint-Nicolas the Acadian families who came to
> this colony for the purpose of establishing a settlement.
> I must detail, in particular, some of the precautions which I have taken
> to assure the subsistence of these new colonists, as well as the success of their
> enterprise.
> To accomplish the first point, I sent them some saltmeat, wine,[49] tafia,
> flour, hardtack, and anything else necessary to sustain life. I ordered that each
> person be given a ration composed of: one pound of flour, a half-pound of
> saltmeat, an eighth of a pint[50] of tafia. In the case of the officers employed in
> the service, the ration is a quart of wine instead of the tafia.
> Moreover, I have furnished all the tools required for these new settlements,
> using those which had come from France, even though the principal artillery
> officer claimed them for the future needs of the fortifications. But I believed
> that the pressing need of these people should prevail over other considerations.
> I also distributed tents to these people in order that they might have a shelter
> from the sun while they are awaiting construction of their homes on the lands
> which will be granted to them. . . .
> This settlement appears to me to merit close attention. I thought it neces-
> sary to place a breveted officer[51] in charge of the place; in consequence, I sent
> Sieur Saltory [*sic*] and placed him in charge of all the operations relating to the
> royal service. I placed under his command a storekeeper and a clerk.[52] It has
> been necessary to provide a priest, even though that kind is scarce here and not
> of the best quality, but the Acadian character is such that it would not be possible
> to leave them without spiritual guidance.

With that need satisfied, I am equally concerned for their temporal needs. Two doctors have been given the responsibility of looking after the health of these inhabitants[53] and have gone to Môle with all the remedies necessary for the establishment of a good hospital.[54]

Numerous colonists have asked for title to the land which they have been assigned, but M. de Montreuil has refused to sign an ordinance of reunion as we had agreed to do on the subject of some concessions granted in this area and which until now remain without effect.[55]

The return to the king's domain of land routinely granted, but not cleared according to prescribed terms, was always a delicate matter. Here the concessions had been only recently accorded; one could not expect them to have been improved already. The withdrawal of the grant would certainly have raised protests and would have probably resulted in lawsuits. But without the nullification of such grants the persons concerned with the Môle project faced serious problems. Nullification of the grants, however, was only a stopgap arrangement, for even such action would not provide sufficient land for each family to have 10 *carreaux*. Clugny, the intendant, and Montreuil, the acting governor, left office on April 24 with the arrival of Magon and the Count d'Estaing. The new administration immediately took up its duties, and on April 30 proceeded with the nullification of Mme Blin-Rouvigny's grant and all those which had been accorded at Môle, Henne Bay[56] [several miles south of Môle], and at the Springs.[57]

Contentment among the Acadians was not as widespread as Saltoris was inclined to report. The newcomers worked, but received nothing more than the government ration as compensation. The officials never realized that such an exchange was exploiting the goodwill of the Acadians. Protests could arise at any time and a storm ensue. One incident almost generated the tempest.

No. 12, Saltoris to the Intendant   March 16, 1764

I had the honor to bring to your attention in my letter of the 10th of this month the arrival of the royal ship *Bachelier* [No. 10 states the name of the ship was the *Coureur*] , commanded by Fontaine, three men and a woman who had come here to settle, but not having passports or permissions, I told them they had to leave by the same boat. One of these men, named Barbereau, and his shop boy asked me Wednesday for permission to return by land, and I granted their request. Thus, only the wife of Barbereau and a person named Aucoin will go by boat.[58]

I shall be eternally grateful, sir, if you do not permit Barbereau to settle here. There is not an indecent threat which he has not made to the Acadians about me. He has even boasted that he will return here by your orders and will chastise me for daring to send him away. It is most fortunate I did not hear about this before his departure. I would have had him spend a little time in jail. . . .

I would like to point out to you, sir, . . . that it would be dangerous to allow all sorts of persons to come to a new colony such as this one. I know that the islands were first populated by the vilest types from whom no one could expect morality or honesty, but we have here a completely different case, we do not fear the lack of settlers, and if you want, sir, before you leave,[59] to accelerate the unity of the settlement, to give it a steady foundation, as I have already said, one must take wise precaution. Leave, I beg you, to my zeal, to my attachment, the honor to advise you on this occasion.

There arrived at Môle a few days ago two Acadians from the eight or ten families which arrived some time ago from Port-au-Prince. They came to see the land and to ask me when all can come here to take their concessions. I told them that they must await your orders on this matter, and that those who would come without permission would be sent back immediately.

I love the Acadians with all my heart and I believe that they merit preference in all things because these people are the most honest, the most moral, the most tranquil, and there is not one who does not have the necessary abilities to contribute to a new settlement, but we are not ready to receive them. We do not have a spare tent nor an extra plank, and until those here have been settled, I believe it best to keep the others where they are. . . .

We have a good supply of hardtack. Our Acadians are disgusted with the stuff. Please be so kind as not to send any more, at least for some time.

I am returning to Cap Français, on board the *Bachelier*, the eight barrels of wine which it brought to us. These contain only vinegar which is impossible to give to convalescents to drink.

I had sixteen head of cattle brought from Jean-Rabel for the infirm. We will kill two per week unless I receive your orders to the contrary.

Some Acadians were compelled to denounce the dishonesty of the store-keeper, Courneuve, who, it seemed to them, was retaining a portion of their rations for his profit. Protests, therefore, were forthcoming. On March 17 the intendant wrote:

. . . I ask you to indicate to me whether there has been some breach of trust on the part of Sieur Courneuve, and based upon your report, I will make the decision whether or not to recall him.

I ask you to supply me with reasons for refusing to grant the concession demanded by M. de Rausanne, and why we should suspend delivery of the certificate.

You can reserve about five *carreaux* for the site of the town of Môle, and then distribute the remaining land to the Acadian families. Put as many families as possible on this land, and then put the remainder along the river or in its vicinity where there are springs. If the Acadians are content with one *carreau* per family, it will not be necessary to give them any more than this, but it will be necessary to have the lands selected by lot in order to avoid jealousies. I have written this also to M. Buisson. Whenever the partition of land is accomplished, you will send me your report with the dimensions of each plot of ground and the name of the occupant. Only when I have received this information will I grant the concession of land. Be quick to deliver this information, for, rather than grant this land on any other terms, I will take back all the lands formerly granted in this area, even those of Madame Rouvigny.

I will give the necessary instruction that the Jean-Rabel district furnish the public work force for the road linking Môle. They have spoken to me about the matter of feeding the negroes [on the work force]. It appears that it would only be right for you to feed these workers with some hardtack and saltmeat or salted cod.

The Acadians have informed me that when their pound of flour is measured out the weight of the sack is not deducted. It is only proper to give them the net weight of the ration which is due them.

I have written to M. Dutillet[60] to take the necessary steps to establish messenger service to carry the mail each week from Port-au-Paix[61] to Môle. In this way Môle will be linked to the rest of the colony.

I have been assured that one can find livestock, either at Jean-Rabel or at Port-a-Piment,[62] which can be bought for about 100 *livres*, each animal weighing about 250 pounds. Please see to it that a procurement system is established which will assure each of your colonists some fresh meat once or twice a week. I will pay the bill here for whatever arrangements you make in this regard or I can forward the necessary funds to you if the sellers prefer, that is, whenever their bill has reached a certain amount.

I propose to appoint a blacksmith. You are on the scene and are the best judge of the salary which should be paid to one who is there. . . .

I would, if I could, pay the salaries of the Acadians, but I have no orders to do so. I will report on this matter to the minister. I have no doubt that he will order this reimbursement. Please tell them this on my behalf. . . .

In his letter No. 13, dated March 18, Saltoris returned to the subject of Barbereau's return, and gave some additional details. The remarks which Barbereau made to the Acadians were tending "to inspire them with a spirit of independence, of revolt, and scorn for those who govern them."

I would still not know about it if the person named Orillon, who lodged with Barbeau for two or three days, had not put into practice the poor wretch's lessons in his actions toward M. Moynet and Sieur Thibault. Moynet and Thibault have been employed by M. Chiconneau to oversee the workers and keep an exact record of their day's work. There is no limit to the atrocious language which Orillon directs toward M. Moynet. 'I don't give a damn about you or your orders,' he has told him on several occasions.

Barbereau and Orillon were punished.

Meanwhile, all goes well, and the Acadians appear to me to be quite content with the justice which I meted out to one of their comrades. It is well known that he was always a bad person, whether in Acadia or here, and he has always discouraged his neighbors.

My intention was to return Orillon's wife and two daughters, but knowing that his family had always conducted themselves in a manner above reproach, the Acadians asked me to let the family stay. I said I would only on the condition that the father himself asked me in writing. This he did, as you can see, sir, by the copy of the letter attached.

I have the honor to send you the list[63] of all the people whom I have returned to Cap Français on the royal vessel. I think that they have been sufficiently punished by being driven from this settlement.

Meanwhile, a new group of Acadians arrived.

No. 14   March 24, 1764

Until now I have only worked with the lambs, but it appears now that I will have to tame the bulls. I do not wish to appear to be prejudiced concerning some of the people whom you have sent on the royal ship *Marie*, but I know them from Cap Français. They are a collection of the worst sort of humanity, having absolutely no morals, possessing a spirit of independence, and always ready to sound the tocsin on their leaders. What a difference between these people and my good Acadians here. I used to swear once every two weeks and all went wonderfully well.

I can see, sir, that it will be necessary to change the recipe. I will be forced to change my approach; in place of kindness, I will have to be severe. I will not, however, employ that tactic until I have exhausted all other means. It is a great satisfaction to reach one's goals while still remaining humane.

I have spent some time seeking to determine whether or not Sieur Courneuve was acting selfishly when he withheld a portion of the ration. I have been unable to verify any charge against him. Since the charge was made, I have almost always been present at the time rations were distributed and can assure you in good conscience that the sixteen ounces of flour per person has been delivered in full measure. I am not being unduly protective of Sieur Courneuve. In the beginning, for example, I had to reprimand him. I have cautioned him to forego his stern manner when dealing with the Acadians, and it has not been easy for him to do this, but at present I am satisfied with him in all regards. . . .

You asked me for reasons, sir, for not granting a concession to M. de Rausanne. Here they are: the concession which Rausanne wants is 10 *carreaux*. It is located above the first concession, being about 2.5 miles from the sea. The soil is excellent, but the cultivable land is so narrow that it will be necessary to furnish 1,200 paces frontage on the stream.

The property of the Acadians, located on the outskirts of the town, spreads out to this concession and goes up to the source of the river, a distance, I would say, of about 12.5 miles from the seashore.

Approximating that there are 15 miles from the seashore to the source of the river, I estimate that it is possible to place 100 families on this land, giving each of them 2 *carreaux*, not counting those who are located on the edge of town. I have seen most of this land, and I do not believe that my estimate can be far from correct.

If M. de Rausanne is given the land he asks for, he will take a piece sufficient to support 5 families. These 5 families are composed of 25 to 30 people and M. de Rausanne will only have an overseer on his concession. This will only hinder the growth of the population.

His concession will break up the continuity of the small farms. It will be a source of jealousy for the Acadians who will justifiably complain that one person has been granted a piece of land which was not granted to thirty people. The granting of the land will be an extremely dangerous thing to do and will cause trouble.

The Acadians are unaware of Rausanne's request, but I would not deserve your confidence, sir, if I did not say that I am fairly certain of their reaction when they learn of it.

I have asked M. de Rausanne to wait a while and he has agreed. I cannot guarantee that we will find a suitable piece of land for him to receive as a grant,

but if he break ς our chain, if he removes a single link, we will find it very difficult
to mend it.

You are undoubtedly surprised to learn that we have only 200 *carreaux* of
arable land in so large a district, and still further surprised, perhaps, by the proposal which I made to the effect that each family be accorded two *carreaux* of
land. But if they accept the two *carreaux*, if they follow their praiseworthy
manner of thinking everything out, they will prefer the two *carreaux* to a much
larger farm as soon as it becomes a question of separating the family (for these
people are like one large family). Would you consent, sir, to letting them have
fewer material rewards in order that they might secure a greater good—that of
inner satisfaction? The interests of this settlement, indeed those of the state,
will in no way be subverted by this arrangement.

The one hundred families placed along the river, occupying such a modest
piece of land, can only remain there as farmers. They will never engage in commerce, but they are in all ways the gardeners of the settlement.[64] This is not
contradictory, sir, to that which I previously told you about the Acadians who
live around the town. It is, in fact, six of one and a half-dozen of the other,
because some will be on the river and some will be in the back country. The
land in the back country is better for farming. The land on the river is better
located with reference to the town and those who live here will be artisans and
craftsmen.

I have already mentioned to you on many occasions that we will not lack
farmers for the settlement. We will place the poor at Plate-Forme, Henne Bay
at the Springs, and we will have many well-to-do ones to place on the poorer
lands. Whenever it is a question of something new, one can calculate geometri-
cally on the folly of men.

The settlement of Môle has a great potential for growth, but that is because
of its location rather than its productivity. Whatever is done, our land will never
be regarded as worth selling. It will be enough if it merely supplies the food
needs of the town. Undoubtedly, however, the town will become a commercial
center with many advantages. This is because of its location on the coast, particularly at the entrance to the Bahaman Canal,[65] on the sealanes to Cuba and
Jamaica. It is strategically located on the Inague Strait [Windward Passage].[66]
Saint-Eustache, one must remember, is only a barren rock in the middle of the
sea, but in time of war it becomes a great commercial center.

You have ordered me, sir, to reserve 5 *carreaux* of land for the site of the
town, but you failed to designate the spot where you wish it placed. I know
that there are differing opinions in this regard. Some people, who are quite
knowledgeable of the area, prefer the back of the bay; others, however, prefer
the cove to the north. The first base their opinion on the facility of building
fortifications at that spot; the second opinion is based largely on the excellence
of the site for commerce and as an anchorage. . . .

No. 15   March 27, 1764

I have received, on the *Marie*, all of the supplies designated for the king's
warehouse, as well as the people named on the closed list. Some of them, whose
names appear in the margin, have asked me to allow them to return to Cap
Français. I have allowed them to return, and I am also sending back Nicolas
Vaudois and Marie-Louise Dubois,[67] his wife. Indeed, sir, they have engaged in
bitter fighting on ten different occasions, night and day for a period of 48 hours,

and I was obliged to send the woman on board ship to prevent her from pestering her neighbors. She is a real devil; however, Salomon assured me that both have been whipped and branded at Louisbourg.

I trust, sir, that you will punish severely the man named Barbereau, about whom I complained in an earlier letter. The man is clearly a thief and has created a lot of trouble for us here with his outrageous talk.

Many sailors from the *Deux Amis*, commanded by Captain Bertrand Gretteau and calling at this place, have set about ten fires on the peninsula which pose a threat to most of the lumber on hand. A detachment of six men under the command of a corporal was dispatched to arrest the captain. Another detachment, under the command of Captain Salomon, was sent out to seize the ship and its crew, but as soon as the crew saw them coming, they set sail and escaped. But where did they go? The captain has had to pay a *portugaise*[68] for the detachment and for the Acadians who had gone on board his ship.

I try, sir, as much as I can to keep an eye on everything and I have not only required the doctor and the surgeon to provide me with a daily list of the sick and the nature of their illness, but also I have required that they send me a daily list of their needs and I personally supervise their distribution. During the time that Sieur Roux was surgeon only two people died, one of old age and the other of indigestion. Nevertheless, we have always had a large number of sick people and the remedies which they need have never amounted to one-sixth of that which the new surgeon, Sieur Chevalier, prescribes. I have complained about this matter since shortly after his arrival here, but he has always gone his merry way. He has not even wanted to talk about the matter until today, Monday, the day after the distribution of the fresh meat which we give to the sick three times a week and to the others twice a week. I have received 36 bills for meat, poultry, and other things. I swear, sir, this made me mad, but without saying a rude word to him, I ordered the former surgeon, in his presence, to stay here and resume his functions until we hear from you regarding this matter.

The Acadians asked me write to you on behalf of Roux. I told them this would present no difficulty, for I have the honor to communicate with you, and that I hope you will not want to take him away from us. I know, sir, that he has requested to leave. He begged me at the time to recommend his departure. I promised I would, but I did not do it, for I sensed the need we would have for him. He is a man who knows his art and who has, above all, mannerisms most gentle and most simple, as are needed by our Acadians. I hope, sir, that you will carefully consider my request. Sieur Roux has agreed to remain out of the goodness of his heart. I have promised him the honor of your kindness.

I do not have remaining a single *sol* of the 6,000 *livres* which you sent me. I am even ahead in some things, but I owe nothing. All the livestock which I have bought, all the poultry, all the workers are paid. The merchants do not want paper money. Therefore, sir, I beg that you be so kind as to send some specie. I will forward my list of expenses at the first opportunity.

Because I am quartered in an old tent and consequently exposed to being robbed at all times, I think, sir, that it will be necessary that I have a sentry. That will be possible without too much trouble, for M. de Rausanne just asked for 15 more men; thus, the detachment will not be too hard pressed to let me have this guard.

The Acadians, organized into a work force, worked steadily. "Our Acadians are always the same," wrote Saltoris to the intendant on April 2 (Letter 17). "I am, however, like a judge these days, but all goes well and even though I may have some as mad as dogs, I will be pleased as a king if everyone does his job."

There was not, however, a concurring view among those who directed the project. One can even speak of tensions arising. The areas of authority had never been sufficiently delimited, and assignments tended to overlap. Moynet had been long delayed in arriving at Môle. When he did come upon the scene, he accused Saltoris of assuming all authority. Saltoris, who was a special protege of the intendant, Clugny, wanted to become sub-commissioner. It does appear that Saltoris assumed a degree of authority beyond that which had actually been delegated to him.

Here is what he [Saltoris] thought of Moynet and Chiconneau.

No. 16   March 31, 1764

Until now I have said nothing to you about M. Moinet and M. Chiconneau because I did not think I knew them well enough. Now, however, I have been able to study them for two months and I believe it to be my duty to report to you on their abilities as well as their conduct.

M. Moinet, [*sic*], whom you have honored with the position of director-general of the settlement, is absolutely good for nothing. He gets drunk, smokes, and sleeps, but for this project he can do nothing. Here is a totally inept man, upon whom nothing makes an impression; a man whose sensitivities are either impaired or destroyed. Nevertheless, he is a very honest man and from a happy-go-lucky background.

If Moinet would content himself with doing nothing, no one would know that he is here, but when he is drunk (and when is he not?), he tells the colonists incessantly that he is their father and their leader and that they only have to ask him whenever they are in need of something. 'You will see Sunday,' he adds, 'that I am not just trying to impress you. I will make public, following mass, my titles and qualities.'

Indeed, he has asked M. de Rausanne and me many times for the drum to beat a ban. We have responded to him jeeringly that this is not done, but that he can attach a list of his virtues to his back and walk around the settlement.

M. Chiconneau, a malicious liar, is nevertheless a sober, untiring man, and he would be an excellent second in command under the direction of an enlightened individual. He never sees anything but the present situation. He never sees consequences.

He has lost the wood for a 100-foot hospital and for a chapel. . . .

M. Chiconneau, on the other hand, endlessly disputes Moinet's claim to precedence. He tries to persuade the Acadians of this, and overlooks nothing in trying to convince them in such a way that they do not know what to think. However, because Chiconneau has promised the workers twice what they are being paid, they are beginning to doubt his importance, and are turning a little more to M. Moinet. . . .

M. Chiconneau has been gone for eight days, and I do not know where he is, what he is doing, or when he will return.

Please send us a capable man, one who has proved himself; otherwise, we will be three months without warehouses, and those which we have built so hastily will not permit that long a delay. Every time it rains it causes us to lose some sacks of hardtack and other commodities. But, whoever you send, please do not give that person a commission as director or inspector general of the settlement. These titles are very broad in meaning. One does not know the limits of authority implied by them, and this generates a conflict of jurisdiction, a situation which is much more dangerous among those who think themselves independent, who never report and who always want to be first. . . .

All goes well.

Similarly, he was now "also as satisfied with the new arrivals as with the first arrivals."

At the end of May, many events began occurring which would upset the equilibrium of the Acadian colony: sickness, the arrival of important contingents, and toward the end of the year, the arrival of the Alsatians and Germans.

Saltoris never engaged in great detail concerning the health conditions of the colony. He sent to the intendancy, regularly one hopes, medical reports, but he did not refer to them in his reports and the medical reports are no longer extant. The number of people ill seems to have been quite numerous at the beginning, but none seems to have been seriously ill, except those who were infected with the fever of the new arrivals [malaria]. The search for fresh meat, the slaughtering of two beeves per week for the convalescents, suggest that the tent which served as the first hospital was usually filled.

The frame hospital was not yet built when Saltoris left. He went to Cap Français at the beginning of May to greet the Count d'Estaing, the new governor. When he returned, on May 15, he found "everyone sick with fever and scurvy," and he even fell ill with the "epidemic sickness."[69] The king's storekeeper, Courneuve, reported on May 31 that during the course of the three preceding weeks seventy people had died.[70] On June 10, there was not a single doctor at Môle.

Berthelot de Crosse, an officer who had served in Canada, was immediately dispatched to Môle with two doctors. "I have found," he wrote on June 10, "all the residents in a pitiable state, almost all being moribund. The air is putrid with the dead on the sand and by the saltwater which is standing on the land in the vicinity of where the largest number of Acadians are settled. There are entire families confined to bed, completely unable to assist one another."[71] Magon, the new intendant, reported on July 7 that of the 556 people comprising the colony, 104 were dead and 4 were dying.[72] But he failed to indicate when the colony counted 556 people and if the 104 dead were those who had arrived since February 2. The complaints, the cries of alarm, quickly spread from Môle to Cap Français. The new administrators were much better disposed to listen to these outcries than were Clugny and Montreuil. The new officials had to go by sea to Port-au-Prince, and therefore decided to profit from this circumstance by stopping at Môle to inspect the Acadians, inspect the state of affairs, and report to the government on the progress of the project. They arrived there [Môle], on July 7, 1764.[73]

D'Estaing, and Magon even more so, was furious with Saltoris for not having properly recognized the deplorable condition of the Acadians. They summoned Saltoris aboard their ship and Magon seriously reproached him, accusing him of being the Acadians' executioner, and of forbidding them to hunt while keeping a hunter on his staff. His superiors further accused Saltoris of having a butler and of pretending to be an intendant, of daily using milk in his coffee while sick children died of starvation owing to a lack of provisions.

It is difficult to know how much rumor was incorporated into these accusations, for many of the alleged misdemeanors had the ring of the joint complaints of Moynet and some of the Acadians. Saltoris was a harsh commander, the officials charged, and he had been wrong to prohibit hunting in an area where there was so little fresh meat. Moreover, his action left the people with no form of entertainment. In his defense, Saltoris stated that the chevalier de Montreuil had prohibited weapons, and that the white servant whom he had brought with him--at fifty *livres* per month--had been mistaken for a butler. But nothing would suffice in Saltoris' defense, and he received orders to leave Môle immediately.[74]

One cannot say whether Saltoris' recall was good or bad for the colony, but the visit of the governor had two advantages for the Acadians. The recrimination of the planters of Jean-Rabel that the workers were overburdened by the royal corvee, together with the complaints of the Acadian workers that they were not paid and were undernourished, caused d'Estaing to undertake relief measures. The project of the Acadians was augmented at first with 25 slave carpenters who were in the royal service and who had been bought at great expense.[75] If the provisions of the black code had been adhered to concerning their sustenance, their maintenance would have been a severe burden, but in place of those provisions, they gave them some plots of ground to cultivate. In August, 120 slaves, recently arrived from Angola--80 men and 40 women--were apprenticed to the royal carpenters.[76]

Saltoris was replaced by Salomon, captain of the *Marie* and formerly pilot for the port of Rochefort. He was, according to Saltoris, assigned without rank in the navy. He was also authoritarian, and under his command work on the project accelerated.[77] After July the number of sick was less numerous. A canal brought some water to the hospital, the site of the village was surveyed and platted by Buisson, the streets and a central square were laid out, the sites for a church, a lime kiln, and the governor's [commandant's] home were selected. The colonists drew lots for their lands. The colonists sought out all sources of fresh water in the area, they measured all the arable land and cleared the banks of the river to build the cabins and slave quarters. It was also decided that the crops upon which they would have to depend would have to be

Charles-Henri d'Estaing,
governor of Saint-Domingue

grown at Henne Bay, several miles from Môle. There, they would start by planting yams.

There remained in New England many Acadians who wanted to migrate to Saint-Domingue. French officials on the island were solicited by American "navigators" and merchants to be allowed to transport these would-be emigrants. All that was needed was authorization. The transportation of the Acadians would afford the English and Americans an excellent excuse to introduce into Saint-Domingue contraband merchandise and to export from the island goods reserved for the mother country—sugar, coffee, and indigo.[78] A Mr. Hanson, a New York merchant, well known at Cap Français, was officially selected to transport the remaining Acadians. A contract was signed June 24, 1764, which in essence stated: Hanson was to take as many Acadians as possible, 72 prefabricated houses of pine and oak, and planking for 32 cabins. The plans for these houses had been drawn by Acadian carpenters who themselves had come from New England. All this lumber would be bought with silver to be transformed into rum and molasses in the port which Hanson found to be the most advantageous.[79]

On June 26 d'Estaing issued a statement announcing to the Acadians still in New England that they could contact Hanson who would furnish them with supplies and the means to go to Saint-Domingue where they would be well received. They would receive a land grant, and the government would support them until such time as they could support themselves. Passage and food for the trip would cost 150 *livres*.

From September 23, 1764, to January 26, 1765, Hanson's ships transported 418 Acadians to Môle.

September 23, 24 on the *Freymaçon*, Captain Robert Simes, from New York.

September 26, 32 on the *Dauphin*, Captain Jean Briant.[80]

September 27, 24 on the *Lidie and Rachel*, Captain Licky.[81]

October 11, 32 on the *Rebecca*, Captain Guillaume Morton.[82]

October 14, 16 on the *Phebee*, Captain Lawrence.[83]

October 24, 16 on the *King George*, Captain Singlar.[84]

October 30, 43 on the *Amitié*, Captain Guillaume Whetten.[85]

November 19, 30 on the *Elisabeth*, Captain Palfrey.

December 8, 31 on the *Renard*, Captain David Monfort.[86]

December 10, 101 on the *Samuel*, Captain Zacharie Welsh.[87]

January 5, 1765, 8 on the *Robert*, Captain Holmes.[88]

January 17, 44 on the *Lucrèce*, Captain Saltonstall.[89]

The "List of English Ships" accounts for 307 Acadians debarking between September 23, 1764, and the following January 26, and the "List of the Acadians . . . ," accounts for 418. A letter mentions 421 which must have been the number embarking, 418 as the number debarking, three having died during the voyage.

A shipment of the wood and the transportation of the Acadians were subjects for prolonged arguments; first, because the wood did not correspond to the dimensions and quantity agreed upon, then, because Hanson had demanded from the Acadians passage money even after it was agreed that their passage and subsistence were to be borne by the king. The Acadians complained "that he [Hanson] had them pay more for their passage than they would have paid elsewhere."[90] Hanson assured them that their passage was a matter totally unrelated to his fee for transporting the lumber. Moreover, he claimed to have encountered heavy expenses because it was impossible to embark Acadians at New York. "The entire mission had been most delicate," because, in order that these families leave the colony after the month of July, the expiration date of the period of grace accorded them in the treaty, it was necessary for them to surreptitiously board the ship.

The delicacy of the mission, however, really centered on the fact that Hanson was engaged in smuggling. If he brought contraband into Môle, the wrong done was not great and officials closed their eyes to it. But he had brought into Cap Français such a quantity of New England flour, and had taken in return such quantities of indigo and sugar, that the local merchants had complained bitterly to the minister. D'Estaing was quite indignant concerning "the infamous charges of the merchants." He appeared to be conscious of the illicit commerce, and nobly warned the local merchants that foreign ships would have to be better inspected in the future. Hanson's ships were thus sent on to Môle, and thereafter he was excluded from the colony, but the matter remained unresolved for many years.[91]

The 400 Acadians who arrived in February 1764, together with the 120 who arrived on the *Marie* and the 418 brought by Hanson—the only documented figures—totalled about 950 and were concentrated at Môle. Of this number 290 died, the majority of these being infants and children. Others returned to Cap Français or deserted. At the end of 1764, there were at Môle 121 men, 130 women, 230 boys and 182 girls: 672 Acadians of whom we do not know how many were actually born there.

Moreover, a certain migration had begun in January when some families moved to Plateforme and to Henne Bay, districts considered no more fertile and larger than that at Môle.

Several thousand Germans had been recruited for the colony planned in Guiana. That enterprise ended in catastrophe, but new emigrants from the Rhineland continued to arrive every day at Rochefort and St-Jean d'Angély, seeking to migrate to America. Thus, 82 left for Martinique, 22 for Guadeloupe, and 18 for Sainte-Lucie in September.[92] Until then there had never been a question of Germans emigrating for Saint-Domingue, but the Germans came in such numbers that the French could not hope to send all to the Leeward Islands. On September 19 the minister wrote to d'Estaing:

> Be informed that you will receive some German emigrants at the end of this year or the beginning of 1765. Maybe you will find it difficult to place all these people on the land, and because the Germans are always better suited than others to the climate, they will be preferable to the Acadians who are good and true subjects, full of zeal and industry, but with a singular instability.[93]

About 2,470 Germans asked to migrate to Saint-Domingue rather than to Cayenne.[94] They were prepared to depart for that destination; thus, the French administrators did everything possible to prevent them going to Saint-Domingue. The experience with the Acadians at Môle had not been encouraging and had resulted in enormous delay.[95] Nevertheless, the officials were aware that in the neighborhood of the Acadians there was insufficient land for settlement purposes. What would it be like if they tried to settle thousands of new colonists in this area?

In November 1, 216 Germans debarked at Cap Français. Others arrived in December,[96] bringing the total to 2,558. Fortunately, they were not all sent to Môle. Many of the new arrivals were sent to Dondon and to Grande-Rivière du Nord, and there they remained unoccupied. These hilly areas were well drained and were thought to be good settlement sites. Some coffee bushes had already been planted in the area, and some Acadians had been settled there, but no one knows when and in what number.

In December 1764 and January 1765 there were 726 Germans in Môle. From that time onward they were always counted with the Acadians in the various censuses. Throughout 1765, then, it becomes increasingly difficult to follow the activities of just the Acadians.

Many Acadian families arrived from Dondon in January and February 1765, thus bringing the total number of Acadians at Môle to 794: 155 men, 143 women, 113 boys and 81 girls of marrying age, 288 children under 15, and 14 persons of advanced age.

In the course of the first four months of the year [1765], undoubtedly brought from New England by Hanson, there debarked 188 new colonists:

50 men, 12 women, 32 boys, 15 girls, 73 children, and 6 persons of advanced age, but they had only registered 14 children, and 6 old people, for a total of 126. Forty-three had departed: 14 men, 4 women, 16 girls, 2 boys, 5 children, and 2 elderly persons. The total loss of population was 169 people. Eight hundred and thirteen remained at the end of April.

One fact is most remarkable: the small number of births among the Acadians, a prolific people, after fourteen months at Môle. Their numbers grew very slowly, primarily because of high infant mortality.

Salomon, who had replaced Saltoris, did not perform the expected marvels. He lasted only as long as someone was there to notice him and report wonderful things to the intendant. He was never able to revive the enthusiasm of the Acadians. Moreover, it was reported that he was sampling the royal supplies, and very precise complaints soon appeared. As house construction languished, it became obvious that a new director was necessary.

At the time there was in Port-au-Prince a friend of the Count d'Estaing, the royal botanist, Aublet.[97] Damage to the ship which he had boarded in Cayenne had caused it to put into Saint-Domingue for long weeks of repair. Aublet had with him over 200 different plants for the Trianon gardens. The governor thought that Aublet could proceed with his mission in Saint-Domingue so he sent him to Mirebalais "to visit the Acadians in order to provide them with agricultural implements, conforming to the orders which I have received."[98] The governor asked Aublet to provide him with a report on the Acadians of the Mirebalais area.

The report which Aublet submitted upon his return appears well prepared. The value of the land at Môle was again discussed. D'Estaing sent him as an expert to determine what might be expected of the cultivation which had begun. Aublet would direct the colony, Salomon would come under his command. Petit, port captain at Cap Français, went with Aublet to inspect the construction work. First of all, however, Aublet had to settle the Germans (December 10, 1764).

D'Estaing readily admitted to himself that the plans to establish plantations at Môle had ended in defeat.

To (?)   Cap Français

Môle St-Nicolas continues to develop well. The botanist Aublet has established some villages and named landmarks along the coast. The colony will only progress if the king sends many Negroes here. The way is easy and will cost nothing. The proposal is attached to my letter.[99];

Aublet was able to accomplish very little more than his predecessors. His vindictive character, perhaps his "honest intransigence," made enemies for him at the end of a few weeks. He was a scatterbrain with no sense of administration. A protege of the governor, he was very anxious to please. Among the Germans, particularly those recently arrived, desertions multiplied, and he was blamed for these. In general, however, criticism of Aublet was widespread.

Kerdisieu-Tremais, the *commissaire-ordonnateur* of the navy in the north, and the man who had become the subdelegate of the intendancy, brought these criticisms to the attention of the minister.

Cap Français, July 1, 1765

Upon returning from Port-au-Prince to Cap [Français], M. Magon and I stopped at Môle St-Nicolas where Count d'Estaing had just been. I had indicated to these gentlemen a great desire to see this place. We found the population diminished by more than half through mortality and desertion, despite the precautions which the officials had taken. I realized that those who were still there were still exposed to the vexations and the most deplorable injustices from Sieur Aublet, and it is as a result of a definite proof offered Count d'Estaing or as a result of seeing it himself, that he has decided to name, under some pretext, someone to take Aublet's place. He has never seen a more extravagant man, or a man who is a greater enemy of order than Aublet. His knowledge as apothecary and botanist has not given him the slightest ability as an administrator. He does not even know how to write [as an administrator].[100]

Aublet had found it impossible to report on his expenses which were enormous. Kerdisieu could only be pessimistic about the future: the wooden houses would all have to be rebuilt within a few years. It was evident that the deforested land was too little to allow the colonists to survive on anything more than what the government furnished them. Moreover, commerce at this place would always be negligible. The governor's opinion of the situation at Môle paralleled that of Kerdisieu.

D'Estaing to the Minister   Cap Français, Sept. 21, 1765

I will no longer have the honor to report as extensively as I should, considering the importance of Môle Saint-Nicolas. A brief summary of what I have done, the actual state of affairs there, and what one might expect in the future, obliges me to restrict my comments to a few general reflections on this important, but expensive and difficult, project.

Upon our arrival [in Saint-Domingue], M. Magon and I were told that Môle was established. We were given to believe that there were several hundred Acadian cultivators and laborers, working contentedly and cherishing those who administered their affairs. Soon, however, some doubts began to be cast upon this most pleasant picture. I sought out the facilities of an Englishman named Hanson, the friend of some influential people at Cap Français, and a man made famous by his lucrative smuggling operations and by the supplies which he can furnish in time of war. The intendant and I drew up with Hanson the contract for the purchase of houses necessary to lodge the troops and officers of a bat-

talion and for the transportation of Acadians [still in the continental colonies]
to Saint-Domingue. . . . I had the honor, sir, to report this operation to you. . . .

The complaints of the colonists of Saint-Domingue, however, have begun to
surface. I was there [Môle] and I found some men bewildered, without shelter,
dying under bushes, abundantly furnished with hardtack and saltmeat which they
cannot eat, as well as tools which are of inferior quality. They curse an existence
so filled with discouragement that they despair. The commander, the scribe, and
the crowd of inexperienced administrators are all dying. The worst criminal
would prefer the galleys and the torture associated with that punishment rather
than stay in this horrible place. No one could believe that such a place exists.
The captain of a royal vessel, a man named Salomon, who is accustomed to risking his life for very little money, accustomed to the kind of cruelty necessary to
make active today the man who will truly die tomorrow, and to supply a certain
knowledge which serves to turn to account these places—it was this man whom I
believed had the strength and brutal audacity to hold out against odds which
would seem insurmountable to other men. He fulfilled my object of clearing the
land, of constructing a hospital, and of building the most rudimentary shelters.

The increasing number of Acadians, the arrival of the Germans, and your
orders, sir, convinced me at the end of several months to examine, as a result of
several trips to Môle, the progress of this establishment. Captain Salomon,
foreman, or rather foremost laborer, began, in this capacity, to build some ridicu-
lous structures—and to want to steal on a grand scale. I replaced him with a
botanist named Aublet, an outstanding man in his field. He was returning half-
dead from Cayenne. A fanatic for everything attached to his profession, he
proved to be as peculiar as he is learned. He was attached to me in Asia in much
the same way as he is now attached to M. de Bombarde. I wanted to know what
kind of soil existed at Môle and the type of cultivation which one could expect.
I persuaded Sieur Aublet, as soon as he was physically able, to succeed Salomon.
He agreed to do so on two conditions: first, to be considered in all appointments
and treatments as only a botanist; secondly, to be in complete control of the
situation. M. Magon consented to these conditions.

The very small plateau of Môle soon appeared to Sieur Aublet to be good for
only garden-style cultivation. He separated the Germans from the Acadians, and
he established a kind of town which he called Bompardopolis. Two other groups
of people[101] were sent to Platforme and Henne Bay.

I spent three weeks during last October in these dependencies of Môle.
During this time I lived as much like the new colonists as possible. . . .

The slow work of the Acadians, constantly interrupted by illness and apathy,
which affects all new arrivals in Saint-Domingue, began, nevertheless, to show a
collection of houses constructed along the lines of a general plan. . . .

The bad health of Sieur Aublet, the horror of an honest artist who only
knows plants, seeing himself insulted by people who are always bickering, resulted in a request that he be allowed to return to France. I have agreed to that.
The conduct of affairs at Môle cannot be entrusted to him any longer. M. Du-
portal[102] agrees that I give command of Môle to M. Polchet, a royal engineer and
an excellent officer, trained by M. Bourcel. Polchet is the only man available who
can take a commission as dangerous as this is made by the unhealthy climate and
the many obstacles which he will have to overcome. It was Polchet who brought
to light the activities of Sieur Hanson, and has today rendered them profitable.
Thus, all the residents [of Môle] are conveniently housed in buildings belonging
to the king.

Sieur Aublet, who brings you the report I prepared today, can, under the
careful eye of M. de Bombarde, give the insight to a culture which, in my opinion,

will be hardly sufficient to assure a subsistence level for the residents. I have
sought in vain for the transport of livestock from Pointe de Maisi. . . .[103]

With sadness, sir, I can only foresee for Môle a constant state of want. Only
constraint keeps the residents there. An unhealthy place, because it is newly
established, without any primary agriculture or other source of income, it would
soon find itself abandoned. The expenditure of manpower there has already been
immense. It is to be feared that all the houses, built at great cost, will soon be
abandoned. No one must be allowed to envision this colony, so different from
the others[104] inasmuch as the farm laborers at Môle are white, as anything other
than an expensive military establishment. If you order a battalion stationed
there, sir, in a short time it will attract a market for the residents who in turn
will invest in agriculture. The troops selected for this duty, however, are to be
pitied, and they will be discontented.

The Acadians and Germans of Môle, Bombardopolis, and Platforme will
be eligible for a kind of military service different from that which you have
ordered for the rest of the colony. I have no doubt that those whom you have
deigned to charge with the editing of this ordinance will prescribe that which
will be the most useful for the defense and good order of this portion of the
colony which in composition differs so much from the others. . . .[105]

The letters of Polchet, royal engineer, whom d'Estaing put in charge of the
work at Môle in place of Aublet, form the continuation of Saltoris' reports.
Everything concerning the Acadians will be extracted.[106]

First of all, concerning this dispersion: in an undated letter, apparently
written in August 1765, Claude Fève, age 50, of Blainville, near Granville in Normandy, sick, married to Marguerite David, an Acadian, and father of one child,
asked to leave the colony. On September 1, Louis Broussard, at Môle for a
year, asked to leave for Cap Français with his wife and daughter. On October 1
it was Jean Clicasson who asked to leave with his two motherless children after
they had spent 17 months at Môle.

Another request to leave tended to complicate matters. Marie Forest,
an Acadian married to Pezant, former surgeon at Bombardopolis, wanted to
leave with her husband and his [her?] sister (October 5, 1765).

There is no worse subject than Pezant . . . whom M. Aublet caused to marry
Mlle Forest. He treats her horribly, and she comes to me to escape from the
beatings of that fanatic. I have had to put him in chains twice [handcuffed
him].[107] Nothing seems to help him. He makes all sorts of insolent and sedi-
tious proposals to the Acadians. M. de La Chauvignerais, officer in the Quercy
regiment, can give you an account of all this. I believe that it will be necessary
for us to get rid of such a subject, in order to free the unhappy wife who has
already been ruined.

Indeed, Marie Forest was not as innocent as described above. It was to
avoid punishment and being driven out that she asked to leave. She had sent
to the governor a long and calumnious denunciation of Courneuve, the storekeeper, as well as a tirade against Polchet, following an episode the details of

which are not perfectly clear. She had abused Aublet's trust when she borrowed money from him to buy two cows from the royal herd. She had also been in charge of watching over the entire herd, the milk from which was reserved for those who were ill, but instead of distributing the milk, she sold it.[108] She did not stay long at Môle after Polchet's complaint.

Another matter seems to have been the result of a moment of tension. Marin LeBlanc, a master carpenter, employed by the government, was arrested, imprisoned, and sent to Cap Français [for further punishment] for having the nerve to demand his salary from the director [at Môle]. He was not the first nor would he be the last to complain on this score. Polchet, nevertheless, wanted to make an example of him. Overall, he

> is the most honest man and a good worker, but he must cure a certain republican spirit within himself, a spirit which he no doubt acquired during his long stay with the English. It is the type of thing you would punish yourself. It is more than a year that he has demonstrated this fault.[109]

On March 25, Polchet asked for his release, and the following day, perhaps inspired by the commandant, a petition from Anne Cormier, the wife of LeBlanc, and the other government workers was addressed to the governor: "We were the ones responsible for LeBlanc's complaints. . . . We are like sheep . . . who have lost their shepherd, whom you selected to guide the poor flock."[110]

April 8

> I have the honor, sir, to thank you for the kindness which you have shown to Sieur Marin LeBlanc. Your action has produced good results and has cured the English sickness.

Polchet had employed 36 masons to build the barracks, but were they Acadians? He always speaks of the apprentices, among whom were Acadians.

December 16, 1765

> My 12 apprentice masons are doing very well. . . . Five are especially good workers. I am going to select the best of this group and I will reward the other four with a bonus each.

Many of the Acadian children worked at making shingles.

Without having mentioned the mortality rate, Polchet did state at the beginning of February 1766 that it was not as bad as it had been, and he also was becoming a confirmed optimist: "The work progresses very well. We are not

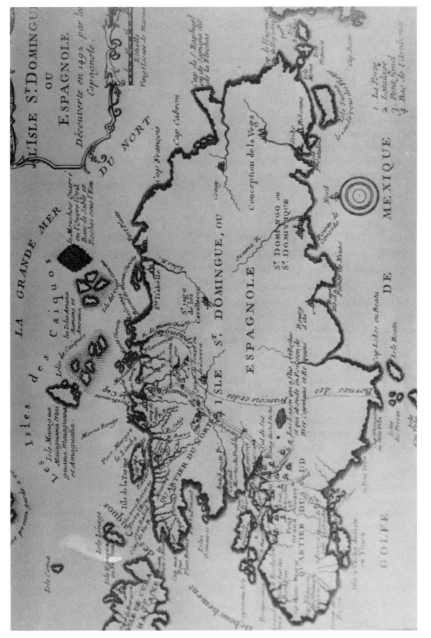

Saint-Domingue, 18th century

dying as much as we are being born." He reported on February 12 that a dozen marriages had taken place at Mole, 4 at Bombardopolis, and 2 at Plateforme.

The greatest problem was the lack of money. The government workers were being paid less and less on a more irregular basis.

March 5, 1766

I have some masons who will most certainly desert if M. Lescallier[111] does not find the money to pay them at the end of each month. Many workers have already abandoned what they had here to go in search of cash elsewhere. There is a carpenter who is owed six months of his pay, which he would rather lose and work on a plantation where he is earning cash. This case is well known among the others. All of this is talked about and spreads among them, and it makes me fearful that they will desert.

On July 16 Polchet noted, "The workers are deserting." On August 6 it was reported that 15 persons died of scurvy, dysentery and fever, but it is impossible to know how many were Acadians.

Count d'Estaing had suggested to Saltoris in 1764 to form a militia at Môle, and now Polchet took up the matter.

I have already thought about artillery and not knowing if we could obtain a detachment of artillerymen, I formed a brigade of cannoneers among our Acadians of good will. I had no doubt that one can put them to good profit, if it is possible to accord them some small advantages. I look forward to having the honor of advising you in this matter. I have already chosen an area where we can establish a school [for training the artillerymen]. Many of the Acadians have already handled artillery in the defense of their homeland. I can assure you, sir, that these are a very special breed of men. One does not always render to them proper justice. They are frequently misunderstood. Whenever one is given command of a people it is first necessary to know them, and to lead them properly it is necessary to know their mores and their character. The brutal and the ferocious are not led like the peaceful and mild. This is the exact difference between the German colonists and the Acadians. These Acadians are simple in their ways, peaceful in their society, and, above all, honest men, who want to be shown the way. It is only necessary to speak to them with affability....

We do not know when the church parish was created at Môle or how religious services were organized there. We have seen that the first colonists, those who arrived in February 1764, had asked for a priest. This first chaplain was a Capuchin, Father Maxime, who was then 70 years old. But he died in July. He was replaced by a secular priest, Abbé Bousquet, who, from his letters to Count d'Estaing, appears to have been the pastor of Môle. It seems, then, that the parish was created following the death of Father Maxime.

Bousquet did not hold the same sympathetic view of the Acadians as that held by Saltoris and Polchet.

April 9, 1765

You know well the Acadian character can be summed up as being always malcontent.

They have written against me—me who has sacrificed for them and who has relayed their complaints to you before your visit here—so that I risk being replaced.[112]

Ten or twelve of the most mutinous appear to have put action to their words—and this I've shown to the prefect[113]—by inserting at the top of two letters these words: *In the name of all inhabitants*, whom they certainly have not consulted. This has excited the colony against these ten or twelve inhabitants, and the result is a small war among the Acadians, a war which, indeed, is only verbal.

I can say that I am on good terms with the leaders and that about two-thirds of the Acadians are with me.

They want me to go on good to the cemetery to bury Pierre at 7 o'clock, Paul at 10, Philippe . . . ; they want me to carry the Holy Viaticum (which we do not keep here owing to the lack of a tabernacle) at all times and to administer it to some people for whom I have good reason not to do so. Then, they ask why I will not give it. There are also similar matters which are too involved to detail here.

These are the objectionable so-and-sos who, about two or two and one-half months ago, came and offered me money to write to the minister agianst M. Aublet, telling me to disguise my handwriting. I sent them away with a most serious reprimand. They have thus turned against me and calumniate me today.

And sensing that the growing complaints of the Acadians would cause his replacement, Bousquet sought to sidestep the inevitable by asking to be sent to Bombardopolis where he had a chapel.

What stands out most clearly from all this correspondence concerning the Acadians is that there was a wide divergence of opinion concerning them. "These people," the expression which Clugny used repeatedly cannot be considered brimming with praise. For the most part, Count d'Estaing never used warm phrases to describe the Acadians. One senses in his attitude a certain condescension which is somewhat scornful. The second in command writes in his letter of June 23, 1765, of "the laziness of the Acadians." how did Aublet judge them? He commanded them for six months, but his administrative inability produced difficulties, raising complaints to which his reaction was a complete lack of appreciation. On the other hand, in all of their letters, Saltoris and Polchet praise the Acadians, and come to their defense against the opinions of the officials and those of many other colonists. Thus, the Acadians are deprecated by those who see them from afar, but the view of those in close contact with the Acadians is usually quite favorable. But why the bad opinion of the Acadians?

First of all, there was a certain repugnance among the Acadians to go to Môle, a deserted place where everything had to start from scratch in order to survive. Moreover, when they were sent there, they were set to work clearing the land even though the majority of them were sailors or craftsmen. The government provided sufficiently for them, but in their eyes the government compensation was insufficient while in the eyes of the poor whites of Cap Français, where the Acadians had debarked and had been the main topic of conversation, it was a windfall, a privilege. The Acadian disenchantment in the face of immense tasks soon cast the impression that they were ingrates.

Moreover, they did not find at Môle what had been promised. Their housing was, for many long months, leaky tents always in a state of disrepair. Their food was comparable to that of soldiers on campaign; they lacked all bread. The first months they were forced to be content with saltmeat, a steady diet of which produced scurvy and diarrhea. They were most vociferous with their complaints and were therefore dubbed perpetual whiners, or were labeled as being lazy.

The bleakness of this area at the extremity of a peninsula which had no roads held them like prisoners. They saw themselves as being encircled, treated like children under the yoke of close surveillance. There was not permitted to them the slightest distraction, not even hunting. They appeared to be constantly unhappy with this apparent interdiction. Could they even fish in the sea?

This discontent with the situation, the absence of goodwill in reproaching their priest, the harshness with which Salomon and perhaps also Aublet had treated them, all of these things were at the bottom of their petitions. Count d'Estaing and Magon saw their complaints accumulate in their offices and concluded that the Acadians were not people of goodwill. This was a rather hasty judgement, but it was the same as that arrived at some years later by the intendancy of Poitiers with regard to the Acadians employed by the marquis de Perusse des Cars on his moors of Monthoiron and d'Archigny.[114] The thing which intensified criticism more than anything else was the considerable expenditures which their establishment at Môle had entailed, especially during a bad economic situation. The new arrivals had completely overwhelmed the resources of the colony; and yet, those who had been in the government employ to rechannel the river, to clear the site, to build the camp--masons, carpenters, and all other workers had not been paid in the beginning. Then, when they were paid, it was always late and far below the salaries received by similar craftsmen at Cap Français.

The carpenters were the most discontented. They had not been given work as naval carpenters. They worked with the others building a variety of houses of wood. This tended to depreciate the value of these men. They complained bitterly until they were put to work building some canoes.[115]

The reaction of a certain number of workers was to escape. The letters of the directors do not mention desertions during the first year when all the colonists were Acadians. In 1765, the lists which follow indicate the exact number, but the Germans had tripled the population of Môle. During the course of 4 months, January to April 1765, 45 Acadians and Germans left: 14 men, 4 women, 16 girls, 2 boys, 5 children, and 2 elderly persons. One can say that they were leaving by families.

In 1766 the Acadians are not frequently mentioned in the administrative correspondence and thereafter less and less. At Versailles, as at government headquarters at Cap Français, where the government had been located since the beginning of the Seven Years' War, interest in the Acadians waned. They are only spoken of in such a way as to indicate that they had not been forgotten.

D'Estaing to the Minister   March 11, 1766

I am prepared, sir, to bore you as much as you want with the story of Môle St-Nicolas. They make on the plains what nature has put on the heights of mountains, cheese from Brie, and La Prevalais butter, things which are most curious to Saint-Domingue. The women there give birth and fewer men are dying. The population was augmented by 12 men during the course of last February—which is more than one can say for the other districts.[116]

All the Acadians could produce for the governor and the intendant, however, were these "curious" things, for the Acadians who lived there did not have the means to establish a herd, nor could the colony support the expense. The officials even had the idea of addressing a circular letter to the richest planters of the colony in which they would propose that the planters would donate some animals. But the delegate Kerdisieu-Tremais found such an approach unworthy of the king's agents.

To the Minister   Cap Français, June 15, 1766

I can even report to you on M. de Trevell's project seeking means to procure for the Germans and Acadians of Môle a number of cows which will help to support them when the royal subsidy is curtailed, which will be fairly soon. . . . I am taking the liberty of attaching, together with the agreement of the Count d'Estaing, the model of the letter which the general[117] had projected be written to the principal farmers regarding this subject.[118]

Kerdisieu thought that the intendancy could support the expense of 30,000 *livres* necessary to buy the cattle. Asking that the animals be donated was asking for certain failure. Without doubt, he had sufficient experience to see that the appeal to the generosity of the planters would not result even in a serious echo.

Count d'Estaing left the government of Saint-Domingue on July 1, 1766. After his departure reports on the Acadians at Môle become rare. This is owing to the fact that the minister issued orders to cut off or to greatly reduce, whichever the case, the subsidy supplied by the king. The Acadians thus came to be overlooked by the administration, and, as a result, there is a dearth of information concerning them.

Once the government subsidy ended the Acadians were free to disperse— to establish themselves as small farmers. Few, however, seem to have left Môle, for many among them had permanent jobs: the barracks still had to be built, the warehouses, and the batteries had to be installed. And those who left Môle found little alternative to eking out a poor existence in some remote corner of the savannah.

Count d'Ennery, the governor, reported after a visit to Môle with the intendant in August 1771 that small plantations surrounded the town and that he was satisfied that the Acadians and Germans were well established and would no longer be an expense to the colony, inasmuch as they had cut out "for a long time and with reason the government ration."[119] But had the number of Acadians in Môle seriously diminished? When, in July 1771, Count d'Argout reported to the ministry on the fire at Môle which destroyed six and one-half town squares, including all of the more commercially important ones, he did not mention a word about the Acadians. Were they among the least active people of the small town? They had nothing more to say about these people when they were no longer under the protection of the government.[120]

There had been formed, in 1773, two companies of militia artillery comprised of 70 men each and a "division" of 25 dragoons. All were Acadians because they had not wanted to mix them with the Germans. It is true that there were a few Germans at Môle, whereas at Bombardopolis two companies had also been formed entirely of German militia. There was also a "division" of dragoons.[121]

III

The Acadians at Môle Saint-Nicolas,
1775-1788

Records of the Acadians at Môle begin with the 1775 entries in the registers of baptism, marriage and death. These registers are now deposited in the Overseas Section of the Archives Nationales.[122]

In the correspondence of Saltoris, Polchet, the Count d'Estaing, and Clugny, there are discussions of the difficult beginnings of this settlement which these administrators envisioned as being simultaneously military and agricultural in nature. The project was being created from nothing, and in time revealed itself as having no colonial future. But, in 1767, this was not yet apparent, and the administrators could still project that one day the garrison at Môle would be supported by the resources of the district. In the meantime, the chief means of income for the Acadians continued to be this government project. New colonists were still arriving, but many were also leaving. Sickness was decimating many families, but there remained at Môle a significant Acadian nucleus.

It is, therefore, an entirely different group of people found in the parish registers a dozen years after the settlement of Môle. By then, the Acadian families were more stabilized, but they were not intermingling with other peoples. There were as many Germans as previously encountered in the records, but now Genoese, Maltese, Irish, and Venetians had arrived. Immigrants from Ragusa, the Canary Islands, and Geneva augmented the number of foreigners. The Acadians now represented only about one-half of those residing "in the town" and in the district. Frenchmen and Creoles were widely scattered among this foreign population.

Complicating the process of locating the Acadians is the fact that less than half of them are designated as such. Many Acadians, therefore, have undoubtedly gone unrecognized. The *Dictionnaire des familles canadiennes*, compiled by Abbé Tanguay, is of little value in deciding the place of nativity of these people.

In 1775, when the registers of Môle begin, the Acadians had already been there eleven years. They no longer formed just an encampment, but now constituted a small, well-formed society. If the rate of their departure continued, however, they would never become very numerous. Môle was becoming a town: it had bakers, a notary, a candymaker; but, let us look at the Acadians there.

One cannot find in these records a great amount of detail regarding the origins of these Acadians. A majority of the acts merely state that they are "from Acadia." Thirty, however, are noted as being from La Pointe de Beausejour, eleven from Port Royal (renamed Annapolis-Royal in 1713), four from Mines, three from Saint Charles, one from Ile Royale [Cape Breton Island], one from Menoudie, one from Sainte-Croix, one from Grand Pré, one from Saint Jean, one from Saint Pierre, and one from the Southern colony. What is remarkable is the small number of persons listed as being from Louisbourg, only three, and only one from Beaubassin.

One discovers, despite the gaps in the years 1784 and 1787, that between the years 1775 and 1789 there were 225 births of children from marriages of two Acadian parents or from marriages where one parent was Acadian. During this same span of years 177 deaths occurred among Acadians. Of the 225 births, 161 were children born to unions where only one parent was Acadian and 64 were children of parents who were both Acadians. The 177 acts of burial involve Acadian children of mixed parentage. Of the fifty-one marriages occurring during these years, only thirteen were contracted between Acadians, of which the greatest number were young people. Indeed, few older people are found in these records. All of this, then, points to a high birth rate among Acadians and to a population composed mainly of young adults and teenagers. One might conclude, perhaps, that the Acadian aged and infirm had remained in New England.

The Acadian means of livelihood is often detailed, thereby affording some idea of the work each pursued. During the years for which there are records, it is interesting to note whether their livelihoods changed. A matter of great surprise is that not one of these people is listed as being a farm laborer. The records indicate that they were almost exclusively artisans; however, in reality, the number of farmers must have been great. Among these artisans the number of carpenters, master carpenters, masons, and master masons is outstanding. A few are listed as overseers and carpenter's helpers. Nearly all were in government employ, constructing wooden houses, warehouses, barracks, fortifications, a hospital, and a church. The records distinguish between carpenters, master carpenters, and ship carpenters, but these distinctions appear to be nothing more than self-generated labels, for some naval carpenters are later listed as master carpenters, and some master carpenters later appear simply as carpenters. Perhaps any carpenter was designated a naval carpenter if he happened to be working on a ship at the time. At any rate, only one sawyer is found in these records.

It is the sea which next occupies most Acadians, primarily the coastal trade, either toward Cap Français or toward Port-au-Prince. One finds listed many types of navigators, giving the impression that these livelihoods were somewhat different. Starting in 1779, however, the words "navigator," "sailor," and "coastal trader" (probably meaning buccaneer), were practically interchangeable. There were some sailmakers and coopers among them, including those in government employ. The category even included fishermen, but these were few in number. There were even two Acadian harbormasters.

By 1780 there appeared a Môle farrier–a blacksmith. By this time the records are a bit more precise, indicating sailor, carpenter, or fisherman "by profession." Does this, then, indicate that all the others were only part-time or seasonal workers? Might it also indicate that government work was occupying the Acadians far less than formerly?

At first–in the records of 1775–all coastal traders appear to have been Acadians. In time, however, they are replaced by Genoese. Acadian masons disappeared little by little as the years went by. Among them many overseers were the most numerous and directed the masons coming from France. No stonedresser or stonemarker is to be found among the Acadians. If the number of fishermen increased at the end of 1789 it is only because there was greater reliance upon fish to nourish an ever-growing population. In the end, an Acadian was named harbormaster, and another was named captain of the port. Claude Albert, who was married to Anne Sire, was first listed as a mason, then as a master mason engaged in government work, then, in 1780, as a singer, and finally as the schoolmaster.

After 1780 there appear some *marchands* and some *negociants*. But is there a distinction between these words? A baker is referred to as a *negociant*. What do these merchants sell, saltmeat, dried foods, tools, utensils? A tavern-keeper, however, cannot be found among the group.

Shortly after 1765, it would appear, the settlement at Môle began to attract foreigners, a great number of outsiders. There were, of course, the Germans who had arrived at Môle shortly after the Acadians. They were mainly natives of the Palatinate and Zweibrucken and were almost all Catholic. Joining them now were Genoese, Venetians, some Genevans, Ragusans, natives of Majorca and the Canary Islands. Except for the Germans, most of these newcomers were single men. Most of the French at Môle were natives of Bordeaux and the Béarn; there were few Creoles. One can rightfully ask, then, when were the Acadians eventually outnumbered by these other people? It would not appear that they attempted to establish and maintain a separate society. By 1775 the Acadians had long since begun intermarrying with the French and Germans, but, above all, with the Genoese who were mostly sailors. The number of marriages between Genoese and Acadians, as in the cases of Antoine Vinelli, Nicolai, Pittalugue, Assinelli, Capitanei, Joseph Carbon, Ambroise Bent, François Basileas, Bertolo Sasani, among others, increased until there were absolutely no ethnic sensibilities existing between Acadian and Genoese sailors. One discovers German and Genoese godparents of Acadian children, or finds them witnessing Acadian marriages and burials.

Later, in the 1770s, as many Acadian men were marrying German women as German men were marrying Acadian women. Joseph Giroir, who married twice, took German wives both times: Marie Hossein and Marie-Eve Hoffman. Jacques Charlier married Barbe Chiesman and J-B. Jourdan married Anne-Marie Verlingen. On the other hand, many more Acadian women married Genoese than Acadian men, for Genoese women were quite few in number, as noted above. It is interesting, furthermore, that among Acadian marriages, the women tended to marry non-Acadians far more frequently than did Acadian men.

The majority of Acadian women married artisans, but others found husbands who were economically better off. Anne Theriot, for example, married Jean-Francois Montamat, "owner of the royal bakery;" Marie Giroir married

Marcel Chatelier, "innkeeper and fisherman." Some Acadian women married merchants or royal clerks; for example, Marie-Madeleine LeBlanc married Joseph Feraud, an employee at the royal warehouse and a merchant. Marie Reignier married Michel Demory, the local administrative clerk. Marie Landry married Pierre Felgère, the local postmaster, who was succeeded by Jean-Louis Grosmidon, the husband of Josephine Bourgeois. Denis Pérost, a sea captain, married Marguerite Cormier, and Yves Travaille, the head surgeon, married Marie Doucet.

The military also enter into the picture, mainly former soldiers who retired and remained at Môle as workmen and artisans, such as the master tailor and shoemaker. Officers, such as Paul Meunier from Maçon, a sub-lieutenant in the Cambrésis Regiment, settled at Môle and married an Acadian.

It would appear that the Acadian women who had the best chance of improving their lot were those who married notaries or plantation owners. Such marriages were by no means the exception. Jeanne Giroir married Joseph Bonnafou of Bayonne, who was a notary. Marie-Louise Geneviève Paulet married Quentin Leroy, a notary from Petit-Goâve, a town on the southern peninsula. Elisabeth LeBlanc is listed as having been the wife of Courneuve Carabas who, before his death, was a notary at Môle. She remarried Achille Huet de La Chelle, Courneuve's successor. Marie-Madeleine Hugon married Jean-Baptiste Chaumette, also a notary at Môle. Their practices were not very large, but it is interesting to note that they owned a vegetable garden and a small plantation.

There were few planters at Môle, and marriages between the planter class and the Acadians were rare. Marie Hébert became the wife of François Guenever, a Breton. Marie Martin married Louis Faligaud, a planter on the Plaine d'Orange.

It is not, however, uncommon to find Acadians seeking godfathers for their children among the officers of the local garrison, among the militia captains, notaries, doctors, or even the planters of Jean-Rabel, the neighboring parish. They were obviously seeking protectors for their children. Such parental anxiety, however, is found everywhere, but here it seems to be far more apparent among the Acadians than among other ethnic groups.

There is another point which we must take a moment to examine. This is the time lapse which separates the date of birth from the date of baptism. An interval between the events is traditional, and few children are baptized on the day of their birth, even those whose parents live near the church. But here we find a different situation: five or six are listed as having been baptized the day after birth, three on the second day, one on the third day, four on the fourth day, one on the fifth day, and nine before the end of the first week. As the children grew older there were fewer baptisms; for example, only nineteen baptisms occur between the first and second months and twelve between the second and fourth months. After that there are but a few isolated cases of baptism. One can conclude, then, that, in general, Acadian children at Môle were baptized sooner, but occasionally Acadians, like other ethnic groups, would baptize two or even three brothers at the same time so as to have one grand celebration with the result that some children were christened at two or three years of age.

IV

The Dispersion Around Môle:
The Case of Jean-Rabel and Bombarde

The decline in baptisms, burials, and marriages among Acadians at Môle starting in 1780 naturally leads one to inquire about those who departed, and especially about those who had arrived in 1764 but were never noted again. After 1780 the records indicate only a single marriage of Acadians born in Acadia. Perhaps with the coming of the French participation in the American war [of Independence] work on the defenses slowed the planned dispersion of the Acadians to the countryside; but, to be frank, when the distribution of government rations ceased, the Acadians felt themselves free to quit the settlement. The development of Môle appeared to them to be nothing more than an administrator's dream. Polchet's reports indicate that the "desertions" had begun long before the government rations ceased.

The first Acadians to leave Môle appear to have gone to Jean-Rabel, the nearest parish seat toward the east, about thirty miles distant. Some coffee plantations had begun to develop there on soil which was considered little better than that around Môle. The registers of this parish, however, are extant only for the years 1778 to 1788, and this is really too late to get an accurate picture of the migration of the Acadians from Môle. It would appear, however, that few Acadians from Môle settled in Jean-Rabel.

With regard to Bombarde, a census of families in the Bombarde-Plateforme areas taken in 1769 fails to list a recognizable Acadian name. It should be noted, however, that the census is only of families receiving the royal subsidy, and any Acadian family which left Môle automatically lost the government ration. Some Acadians certainly must have gone with the Germans who settled this place about twelve miles south of Môle, but the registers of Bombarde are less complete than those of Jean-Rabel, existing only for the years 1784, 1785, 1787, and 1788.

V

The Acadians at Mirebalais

The parish registers of Mirebalais, complete between the years 1763 and 1789, are nearly the sole source of information on the Acadians who settled in this district. These registers present, then, a tenuous resumé of the Acadian stay in Mirebalais. This group was numerically smaller than that at Môle, but it was nevertheless an important group.

These Acadians arrived in Mirebalais in August 1764, having come to Saint-Domingue on two ships from "New England." Two reasons seem to explain their presence at Mirebalais, a district of rolling hills located about thirty miles to the northeast of Port-au-Prince. First, there were favorable reports on the area's climate which is steady and not too hot. Secondly, at Mirebalais were doctors, medicine, and even two small hospitals. For these newcomers, who had arrived in a deplorable state of health, ill with scurvy and perhaps even smallpox, this was a blessing. It was only natural that they dreamed of settling in a district which possessed such decided advantages.

They did not, however, migrate to Mirebalais on their own. They were directed there by the intendant. This broad region was envisioned by officials as being perfect for the development of coffee plantations. At the time, however, it was sparsely populated and constituted little more than a frontier area. The administrators, wanting to accelerate the settlement of the region, proposed to give the exiles enough land at first for small vegetable farms, then additional land for the development of small coffee plantations.

Influenced by a memoir originating in the Chamber of Agriculture of Port-au-Prince, which advertised the advantages of Mirebalais, M. d'Ennery decided to send the Acadians there. On October 26, 1764, he instructed M. Rolland, the civil engineer, to mark off on both sides of the Artibonite River the fifty paces belonging to the king,[123] beginning in the vicinity of Mirebalais, and then to establish 800-pace square plots which would be given to each Acadian family. This order gave rise to a great many rumors and much speculation among the planters of the area. Alarmed by this, the officials gave up the plan, and merely directed that the Acadians go to Mirebalais. They had scarcely arrived there when M. d'Estaing ordered a group of women to leave, for their husbands were dead and they had no means of support.[124]

One must not conclude from the Mirebalais experiment, which cost about 40,000 *livres*, that which has long been held; that is, that these people, overwhelmed by misfortune, were transported into a climate completely different from their own, and having endured a terrible voyage paid for through charity, continued to pay a cruel tribute everywhere and received only pity in exchange.[125]

Upon arriving in Mirebalais, the Acadians were housed in the town before being placed by family unit or groups of families on the plantations nearest the town. From the planters of the area officials requested draft animals to help haul the provisions, rice, hardtack, and cassava, for the Acadians at Croix-des-Bouquets. But there are some recalcitrants, and this raises the question whether these planters were unhappy with the new arrivals. Government officials reacted firmly, as seen from an order posted on the church door.

By Order of the General and the Intendant

M. de La Serre, a rich planter living in the district called Queue Espagnole,[126] having refused the orders of the syndic and the requests of the war commissary for three horses to be used for twenty-four hours in the service of his Majesty, to bring aid to 180 Acadians who have abandoned everything in order to return to their religion and their sovereign, the said refusal being made for the most illusory pretexts and indecent motives. Therefore, an officer of police has been sent to the plantation of the delinquent to report on the number of horses he finds there. The officer will then take three of the best horses, by order of the governor, to the pound in Port-au-Prince where they will be used on public projects for one month (August 18, 1764).

The first concern of the Mirebalais Acadians was to baptize their children who were born in New England. The majority of these had been conditionally baptized. All, however, were not baptized the same day, not even brothers. A child nine years old was even baptized. The first baptisms occurred at the end of August, only a short time after the refugees arrived at Mirebalais.

The baptisms really sum up the history of the Acadians at Mirebalais, for, with the exception of a few families, the Acadians appear to have remained there only briefly. After the forty-two baptisms in 1764, primarily of children born in New England, the group virtually disappeared. Even though there were thirty-seven burials in 1765, there were only two baptisms recorded for that year. In 1766, there were but two deaths and one baptism, and there is no question of vital statistics being omitted or overlooked. From 1766 to 1790 only fifteen deaths and thirty-eight baptisms are recorded, and between 1765 and 1790 only thirteen marriages took place, none occurring after 1779. The evidence, therefore, points to the fact that the Acadians were decimated by disease during the first months following their arrival at Mirebalais. Moreover, the sudden drop in births in 1765 and deaths in 1766 leads one to believe that the Acadians left Mirebalais--perhaps for Louisiana.

The priests of Mirebalais did not record the place of nativity of the Acadians. In only one case, that of Jean-Baptiste Poirier, who married Marie-Louise Baillif, is it noted that he was born at Port Royal. On the other hand, the priest of Croix-des-Bouquets, who, like those of Mirebalais, was a member of the Dominican order, never failed to supply this information in detail. Thus, we know that the Sollée family was from Louisbourg, as was Joseph Henry, Charles Decoux, and Marie-Madeleine Poissu. Hélène Landry, Marguerite Girouard, and Camille Pitre were from Sainte-Famille de Pesiguit.

The residence of parents and godparents, as well as the place of death, serve as an indication of the distribution of the Acadians around Mirebalais. It was in the town itself that the baptisms took place and where the new arrivals lived during 1764 and 1765. The first Acadians to die on nearby plantations [an indication that the exiles were fanning out from Mirebalais] were Marie Proard who died November 18, 1764, on the Falque plantation, and Jean Granger, fourteen years old, who died on the La Marillière plantation a year later. After that only the Driau dit Blondin, Cruble, Roussin, Chabaud, Deschamps, Levacher, and Pothenot Saint-Cyr plantations are mentioned. One can, then, only speak of their dispersion [from the original points of settlement in Saint-Domingue] after the Acadian departure from Mirebalais in 1765 and 1766, after the end of the government ration at Môle Saint-Nicolas, or after each family which remained received the land concessions promised it. Few children appear to have been born on a plantation; however, when the godfather was a planter, it appears that the mother of the child gave birth on the godfather's plantation.

The marriage registers indicate that those who lived at Mirebalais were to work on the coffee or indigo plantations where they would have constant employment. The first Acadian listed as a "planter," that is to say as a major landowner, is found in the records of 1773, nearly ten years after the Acadians arrived. This was Pierre Hébert, who was married to Anne Bourg, also an Acadian.

Some Acadians were settled at Boucan Carré, about ten miles from Mirebalais, north of the Artibonite River. Two Acadians were at the Capuchin canton, but the majority were to be found working at Montagne Terrible, near the canton of Pensez-y-Bien. The fact is, however, that there were far more Acadian plantation managers and workers than there were owners.

After the marriages recorded in 1764, there are only three unions contracted by Acadians out of a total of thirteen. Six Acadians married spouses from France, among whom were a tailor, a carpenter, a doctor, and a notary. This is certainly not the image of a closed society, but it is proof that the Acadians were not numerous in the area. The marriage of Marie Boudreau to M. Munoir de Saint-Prosper, a Port-au-Prince notary, leads one to believe that in 1774 her parents were people of means.

The Acadians found themselves in a religious situation at Mirebalais similar to that found in other parishes, and therefore the interval between births and baptisms was as long as that which occurred at Môle. Similarly, in the beginning, Acadians were not distinguished, and very little can be concluded from the records of those receiving the last sacraments. At Môle, for example, it would appear that few people died without receiving the last sacraments. At Mire-balais, on the other hand, staffed by Dominicans, those dying without the last sacraments appear to be more numerous. This is not to say that these religious did not work among the sick and the dying with a great deal of self-sacrifice, but it must be remembered that their parish was geographically immense.

This essay certainly does not represent a demographic study. Not only do gaps in the parish registers prevent this, but such a study is also precluded by the absence of a list of Acadians at the time of their arrival in Saint-Domingue. Moreover, we do not know the exact date of their arrival on the island; and of those who went to Louisiana only partial lists are extant. The confusion arising from the small number of surnames is a further source of difficulties.

The parish registers tell us very little of the Acadian life style in Saint-Domingue. These records fail to tell us which parts of the Môle or Mirebalais districts were preferred; they fail to tell us if these preferences were expressed, or if they were suppressed. One thing is certain: the point in time when Aca-dians began to intermarry with other ethnic groups and, after a few years, to what extent. Research into the registers of Cap Français, Port-au-Prince, St-Marc, Léogane, and Cayes du Fond provide the number of Acadians who re-mained in these towns following their arrival and whether those who went to Môle or Mirebalais ever returned. Except for those at Port-au-Prince, these registers possess considerable gaps, and an examination of them cannot result in definite conclusions.

It has often been said that a majority of the Acadians only passed through the island. This seems to be a gross exaggeration, especially in light of the fact that there are no records of their exact number, nor of their approximate pro-portion to the total population. After 1770 many Acadians were recorded in the towns, on the sugar or coffee plantations of Martinique, Guadeloupe, or Saint-Domingue. These familles considered themselves definitely settled. At the time of the French Revolution, however, their children were still there, married to individuals from France, or to Germans, or to Creoles; some were married to women of color. The events of the revolution in Saint-Domingue certainly scattered these families, but what became of those in Martinique or Guadeloupe? They may have gone to France or to the neighboring islands.

The essential point, however, is to know how those lived who remained in Saint-Domingue. Two pieces of evidence offer some suggestions. The first is that these people who remained were, above all else, workmen, artisans, and sailors. This is obvious in the case of Môle where most of the Acadians possessed a means of livelihood which permitted them to settle down.

On the other hand, few among them became farmers [or planters]. The government's attempt to establish the Acadians as yeoman farmers proved disappointing because the Acadian experience with agriculture was largely limited to the family garden. They tried, for example, to grow yams, cassava, potatoes, and bananas, but failed because they were completely ignorant of the culture of these tropical staples. Moreover, it was only after tremendous effort that the Acadian vegetable gardens began to provide for family needs; at no time, however, was production sufficient to provide for the local garrison. If plantations were subsequently established by Acadians, this was indeed exceptional. So long as the Acadians remained grouped at Môle, they did not have slaves, and those at Mirebalais possessed no slaves before 1770 and very few thereafter. In addition, the Acadians never had the finances necessary to undertake small sugar plantations. Such an enterprise was possible for them only after long years of experience as plantation managers. It is somewhat surprising, though, that they were so slow to enter into the coffee culture which requires far less investment than sugarcane. Acadians were to be found on coffee plantations, but only as workers. At no time did they ever attempt to form an agricultural cooperative, undoubtedly because of the competition from slavery, as well as the fact that they could not get financial backing owing to their inexperience in tropical agriculture.

At Môle circumstances surrounding their establishment and soil conditions did not aid the Acadians in becoming planters. *The Detailed List of Indemnities, Drawn Up by the Commission Charged with Indemnifying the Former Planters of Saint-Domingue, According to the Law of April 30, 1826*[127] is clear indication of who were planters in 1790. These planters, or their procurators presented demands for property losses [resulting from Toussaint L'Ouverture's revolution]. On the lists for Môle and Bombarde no Acadians appear other than the following owners of small houses or building sites: A. Theriot, Jacques Genton, Victoire Jourdain (wife of Poirier), Joseph Giroir, Michel Poirier, and Marie-Madeleine Poirier. However, the parish registers list François-Robert Vincent and Paul Boudrot, husband of Nathalie Giroir, as being "planters" living near Môle, and Hubert François Jouve as living in the canton of Mardi Gras. None of these people, however, appears on *The Detailed List*. The question arises: Did they possess only a partially improved concession which greatly limited the amount and variety of products which they sold prior to 1790? Another question comes to mind: Were they the people who joined their compatriots in France and later went to Louisiana in July 1785?[128]

At Jean-Rabel few Acadians appear to have become planters between 1778 and 1788. On April 19, 1778, Joseph Theriot and Rosalie Bourgeois were recorded as "planters" at Côtes de Fer. *The Detailed List* includes only one

Acadian, Joseph Bourg, who had established a small indigo plantation which the commission valued at 17,633 *francs*.

At Mirebalais where the registers are more or less complete, we recognize the names of at least twelve Acadian "planters": at Montagne Terrible (July 13, 1769), Marie Bourg; Pierre Hébert (August 29, 1778); Paul Hébert (November 28, 1778), who married Marie Repoussard, owned a small plantation which appeared to have come from his wife; Pierre Poirier (December 24, 1779) and Anne-Marie Lorrain who lived in the same canton; and Jean-Baptiste Hébert (January 18, 1779), husband of Marie-Louise Bailliff, a resident of Chemin Neuf canton.

In the Môle district an Acadian name stands out because of the person's marriage. This is Marie Pons, wife of Jean Perry, a merchant and militia captain, born in 1746. She married him in 1776, and they were owners of a coffee plantation, a vegetable garden, and a banana plantation located near the town.[129] After 1786 they lived at Plaine d'Orange in the canton of Bombarde. In 1789, they sent their son to Thouars College in Poitou.[130] Perry was the parish representative from Bombarde to the first colonial assembly, which was held in St-Marc. In the Year IX [French republican calendar] he was in exile in New York and then in Nantes, but it remains unknown whether his wife was with him or whether she had already died.

To a certain degree it appears that there was something of a contradiction between the Acadians and the agricultural pursuits of Saint-Domingue. The minute the Acadians moved out of the towns to the agricultural countryside, they felt out of place in the world of plantation agriculture. Perhaps this was because they had not come to the island seeking wealth, but rather seeking only to survive.

The arrival of the Acadians in Louisiana is not a simple story to recount. They left Saint-Domingue in groups, undoubtedly with the consent of the king and with the assistance of the administration. But why did the Acadians seek the banks of the Mississippi as the promised land? Did those who arrived in Louisiana before 1765 know that the colony had been ceded to Spain? Who was responsible for the propaganda which caused them to leave Saint-Domingue? The answers to these questions are beyond the scope of this essay. If answers to these questions are to be found, it must be the Acadians who supply them.

NOTES

1. Emile Lauvrière, *La Tragédie d'un peuple: Histoire du peuple acadien de ses origines à nos jours* (Paris, 1923).

2. Moreau de Saint-Méry, *Description topographique . . . de la partie française du Saint-Domingue*, 3 vols. (Paris, 1958), II, 724.

3. Brigitte Poussin, "L'Administration de Saint-Domingue sous le gouvernement de comte d'Estaing (29 décembre 1763-juillet 1766)," (Thèse de doctorat, Ecole des Chartres, 1953). This thesis forms the basis for the history of Môle presented here. Miss Poussin has carefully researched the D'Estaing collection at the Château de Ravel, something which the author was unable to do because of lack of time. The author is eternally grateful for the use of Miss Poussin's thesis.

4. A Dutch island east of Puerto Rico.

5. The name given by the English to Port Royal.

6. North of Guadeloupe.

7. This island is north of Antigua and was the first occupied by the French in the seventeenth century.

8. France. Archives Nationales, Archives des Colonies, Series C 8a, volume 61, folio 111; hereinafter cited as AC, C 8a, with volume and folio numbers.

9. Lauvrière (II, 178) does not cite his sources.

10. *Ibid.*, II, 173.

11. La Rochette to the Duke of Choiseul, London, December 12, 1763, Archives des Colonies, Series B, volume 116; hereinafter cited as AC, B, with volume and folio numbers.

12. France. Archives Nationales, Archives des Colonies, Series F 3, volume 145, folio 65; hereinafter cited as AC, F 3, with volume and folio numbers.

13. AC, B 118:112vo.

14. An island located south of Martinique and ceded to France by the Treaty of Paris (1763).

15. AC, B 118:91vo.

16. AC, B 118:267vo.

17. AC, B 118:186.

18. It is not precisely known when they arrived.

19. Being 11 HA 30.

20. Service dossier of Saltoris, naval sub-commissary, Archives des Colonies, Series E 80, dossier Bertrand de Saltoris.
"Memoir of the Chevalier de Montreuil Regarding the Establishment of Môle Saint-Nicolas," Cap Francais, January 24, 1764. AC, C 9a, 122:n.p. "Observations of the Chevalier de Montreuil on the Defenses of Saint-Domingue," undated, *ibid*. Montreuil to the Minister, February 1, 1764, *ibid*.

21. "Instructions to the Chevalier de Montreuil and M. de Clugny for the Establishment of Môle Saint-Nicolas," January 27, 1764. AC, C 9a, 122:n.p.; and AC, F 3, 176:28.

22. About twelve leagues (30 miles) east of Môle.

23. Saltoris' letters are to be found in AC, C 9a, 123, and in the D'Estaing papers at the Château de Ravel.

24. Montreuil sometimes speaks of 300 Acadians at Môle, sometimes of 400; Saltoris refers to 350 and sometimes to 400. Four hundred Acadians appears to be a more precise figure. Moreau de Saint-Méry (AC, F 3, 122:272) also speaks of 400 Acadians at Môle.

25. A district to the east of Jean-Rabel, about 100 kilometers from Môle.

26. The Chevalier de Rausanne commanded the Forez Regiment stationed at Môle.

27. Action taken probably by inference from the instructions to Montreuil which forbade arming the Acadians.

28. A cart or wagon drawn by two oxen or mules.

29. Chiconneau and Buisson were surveyors. Chiconneau was also assistant director of the Môle project.

30. Memoir for Saltoris, 1766, AC, E 30.

31. Buissons' plat is not to be found in the Archives des Colonies.

32. The request is not attached to the letter.

33. Apparently it was in reaction to news of the Môle project.

34. Saltoris, while providing reasons in April 1767 for his return to Saint-Domingue, states that a company had offered to reroute the river in order to bring water to the future village for a sum of 300,000 *livres*. He notes that he had accomplished the same task for 1,800 *livres*, thanks, of course, to the work of the Acadians. See Saltoris' dossier, AC, E 30.

35. The Chevalier de Montreuil who commanded the northern district before the arrival of the Count d'Estaing (governor-designate) assumed the functions of governor.

36. This was still below the average salary of a skilled worker, but this would be in addition to the government subsidy.

37. The travellers were correct in their assumption, for they had not travelled outside the colony.

38. 367 grams, 20 milligrams.

39. This produces an inclination of about 27 millimeters per meter.

40. 600 meters.

41. Martissan was assistant naval commissary at Cap Français.

42. After being placed on their farms, the Acadians would no longer receive the government subsidy.

43. That is to say, recorded in a church register after renewing their vows before a priest. Acadian marriages in the English colonies were performed not before a priest, but the marrying couple did have parental consent and exchanged vows before witnesses.

44. Carpenters were apparently numerous among the Acadians.

45. An animal native to Saint-Domingue.

46. A plateau southeast of Môle, the cliffs of which border the sea. Herding was done on the plateau.

47. It is curious that this form was directed to the intendant for approval and not the prefect apostolic who served at Môle. This is certainly an indication of the scornful attitude of the civil officials for the Capuchins and perhaps for the clergy in general. At the same time, the priest at Mirebalais, a Dominican, proceeded with the blessing of the marriages without referring the matter to the civil authorities.

48. *La Gazette de Saint-Domingue*, no. 9, March 28, 1764.

49. Wine was for the convalescents.

50. A pint measures 0 litre 43.

51. Without doubt, an administrative officer.

52. The clerk was undoubtedly Marchal, who served as Saltoris' secretary.

53. A little later there arrived a doctor by the name of Bell.

54. These medications were not sent with the Acadians but arrived in March as sickness spread.

55. AC, F 3, 176:101-104.

56. Henne Bay is east of Plateforme. It was the site of a small fishing village. The soil there was not fertile.

57. Moreau de Saint-Méry, *Loix et constitution de l'Amerique française sous le vent de 1550 à 1779*, 6 vols. (Paris, 1784-1790), IV, 825.

58. Aucoin is an Acadian name; Barbereau may also be of Acadian origin.

59. Clugny was preparing to leave the intendancy.

60. Luc Regnier du Tillet was military commissioner at Port-de-Paix (see AC, E 127).

61. A small port about half-way between Môle and Cap Français.

62. On the southern coast of the northern peninsula, about half way between Henne Bay and Gonaïve.

63. This list has been lost.

64. That is to say, they would furnish the garrison at Môle with fresh vegetables.

65. The Bahaman Canal lies between Cuba and the Bahamas.

66. The Windward Passage separates Cuba and Haiti. A *debouquement* refers to any sea passage from the Atlantic to the Caribbean Sea.

67. Therefore, Vaudois and Marie-Louise Dubois were Acadians.

68. A gold coin valued at about 66 colonial *livres*.

69. "Memoir for Saltoris . . . ," AC, E 30.

70. Archives of Ravel, 2 B 2, I.

71. AC, E 28.

72. AC, F 3, 259.

73. The nautical journal of Count d'Estaing, July 7-9, 1764. Archives Nationales, Archives de la Marine, Series B 4, volume 108. It will be necessary to closely investigate the correspondence of Berthelot and Courneuve which Miss Poussin worked with at the Ravel archives.

74. "Memoir for Saltoris . . . , 1766," AC, E 30.

75. AC, F 3, 132:50.

76. Archives of Ravel, 2 B 4, III.

77. AC, C 9b, July 21, 1764.

78. AC, B 119:173.

79. Copy of the agreement entered into by Magon and John Hanson, New York merchant. AC, C 9a, 129:n.p. List of the Houses for the Government and for Service in the Colony. AC, C 9a, 133:n.p.; AC, F 3, 176:269vo. Memoir for John Hanson. AC, F 3, 176:254-267. Presented here are the lists of Acadians coming from "New England" by various ships belonging to John Hanson. AC, F 3, 176:281. Note the difference between this list and the list of ships which entered Mole harbor in 1764 and 1765. AC, C 9a, 128:n.p.

80. "The List of English Vessels," mentioned in footnote 79, states that the *Recovery*, left New Boston, September 25.

81. The *Lady Anne Rachel* sailed October 1.

82. There is no discrepancy concerning this brigantine.

83. This schooner is recorded as having sailed January 26, 1765, with 13 Acadians on board.

84. This ship is not included on "The List of English Vellels."

85. "The List of English Vessels" indicates that the ship sailed October 30 with 40 Acadians on board.

84. This ship is not included on "The List of English Vessels."

85. "The List of English Vessels" indicates that this ship sailed October 30 with 40 Acadians on board.

86. According to "The List of English Vessels," this ship sailed form New York with 31 Acadian passengers.

87. "The List of English Vessels" states that this ship departed New England with 33 Acadians.

88. "The List of English Vessels" indicates that this ship left New York with 100 Acadian passengers.

89. "The List of English Vessels" refers to this ship as the *Little Robert* and states that it sailed on December 17.

90. AC, F 3, 176:279.

91. "Memoir for Sir John Hanson," undated, AC, F 3, 176.

92. Extract from the Hanson memoir, *ibid*.

93. Minister to Bourlamaqui and Paynier, Compagne, August 3, 1784. AC, B 119: 296vo.

94. Minister to D'Estaing, Versailles, AC, B 119:159.

95. "List of Expenses Incurred in the Establishment of Mole for the Years 1764, 1765, and the First Months of 1766." AC, F 3, 176:12. In 1764, 642,242 *livres* were spent on the Mole project.

96. "List of Germans Who Arrived in the Colony Between November 4, 1764, and 1765," Archives of Ravel, 2 B 4, III.

97. J-B. Fusee-Aublet (born Salon, 1723; died Paris, 1778), a pharmicist and the son of a pharmicist, studied at Montpellier where he was a friend of the famous Jussieu family of botanists. He served for a time as a military pharmicist, then, from 1752 to 1762, he was chief pharmicist for the Company of the Indies on Ile de France, where he constructed a botanical garden at Pemplemousse. He was in Guiana between 1762 and 1764, and in France until his death in 1778.

98. Aublet to the Duke of Choiseul, Port-au-Prince, September 11, 1764. AC, C 9a, 125:n.p.

99. Letter personally written by D'Estaing. AC, C 9a, 124:n.p.

100. In July, at the time of Saltoris' departure, he had seen him sick.

101. These groups were Germans.

102. Royal engineer.

103. Point Maisi is the easternmost extremity of Cuba, directly across the Windward Passage from Môle. This was a cattle-raising district. D'Estaing had hoped to see an active coastal trade spring up between Cuba and Mole, thus "opening a branch of commerce to the farmers" of Môle. But the Count de Ricla, the governor general of Havana, with whom D'Estaing had arranged this matter, had been replaced.

104. Different in the sense that other areas of the colony had been developed by slave labor.

105. AC, C 9a, 124:n.p.

106. All of the letters addressed to the Count d'Estaing are to be found in the papers of Ravel, see 2 B 2, II 1.

107. Practically speaking, he was handcuffed.

108. From the beginning it was the wife of Cormier, *pere*, who was responsible for distributing milk to the children, but there was never enough milk. See "Memoir for Saltoris ..., 1766." AC, E 30.

109. February 23, 1766.

110. It is difficult to determine to which leader reference is made.

111. Daniel Lescallier (born Lyon, 1745; died Paris, 1822), arrived in Saint-Domingue in 1764 in the company of the Count d'Estaing. He served as administrator of Môle at the end of 1764, and left the island with D'Estaing in 1766. He was naval commissary in Guiana from 1782 to 1788. In 1800 he served on the Council of State, and then served as naval prefect at Brest and then at Genoa. In 1810 he was named consul general to the United States.

112. It is not determined whether this letter was directed to the prefect apostolic, the intendant, or Aublet.

113. The prefect apostolic of the province of the North was at the same time superior of the Capuchin mission.

114. Ernest Martin, *Les Exilés acadiens en France au XVIIIe siècle et leur établissement en Poitou* (Paris, 1929).

115. Polchet to D'Estaing, September 25, 30, 1765, Ravel papers.

116. AC, C 9a, 129:n.p.

117. The term is presently comparable to "governor general."

118. AC, C 9a, 129:n.p.

119. AC, C 9a, 143:n.p., Môle, September 1, 1771.

120. AC, C 9a, 145:n.p., Port-au-Prince, August 7, 1777.

121. "Observations of M. de Nalivos on the Establishment of Môle Saint-Nicolas," March 27, 1773. AC, C 9a, 140:n.p.

122. The register for the years before 1775 is thought to be lost.

123. This was a strip of land along the seacoast which belonged to the crown.

124. The men referred to were the husbands of these women.

125. Moreau de St-Méry, p. 911.

126. Queue Espagnole was int he east in the Canton of Mirebalais.

127. Published in Paris by the royal printer between 1827 and 1833, 6 volumes.

128. Oscar William Winzerling, *Acadian Odyssey* (Baton Rouge, 1965), p. 224.

129. *Etat detaillé*, 1831.

130. Many children from the colonies were educated at this college.

THE ACADIANS:
THE SEARCH FOR THE PROMISED LAND

by Jacqueline K. Voorhies

Between 1764 and 1767 hundreds of Acadians immigrated to Louisiana. Arriving from Saint-Domingue, Maryland, and New York, these first Acadians were followed by scores of others. Their arrival in the colony marked the final stage of a tragic odyssey which had begun in Acadia and which lasted for nearly a decade. The long years of exile had neither broken their spirit nor undermined their ethnic unity. Anxious to protect their national integrity, they proceeded with characteristic tenacity to transform the virgin lands they were given in Louisiana into a *Nouvelle Acadie*. The circumstances of their early history had fashioned their character and their thinking, so that now in Louisiana they were determined to preserve and perpetuate their philosophy and their way of life.

Driven by the British from their native Acadia in 1755, thousands of Acadians were systematically and ruthlessly scattered throughout the English colonies, Great Britain, and France. Subsequently, several hundred were persuaded to go to the French West Indies. Despite hardships, sufferings, and losses, Acadian exiles exhibited stubborn determination and an uncommon aptitude for endurance. Similar qualities had been displayed by their French ancestors: the farmers, the fishermen, the craftsmen, and the adventurers who had arrived in Acadia at the beginning of the seventeenth century.

Led by Pierre du Gast, sieur de Monts, one hundred and twenty French *engagés* reached the Acadian shores in the spring of 1604.[1] Accompanying De Monts' expedition were Sieur de Poutrincourt, a comrade in arms; Samuel de Champlain, royal geographer; Dupont-Gravé, shipowner from Saint-Malo; Louis Hébert, an apothecary from Paris; and others. Together they explored the new territory, and Port-Royal, the first permanent settlement in Acadia, was established. In July 1606 a second group of French colonists, farmers and artisans, were brought to Acadia by Sieur de Poutrincourt.[2] Settling around Port-Royal, they cleared the land and planted the first crops which were harvested later that year.

Their pastoral pursuits, however, were short-lived, for in 1613 a British force under the leadership of Captain Samuel Argall attacked Port-Royal and destroyed the nearby settlements. From that time onward, Acadians faced the prospect of periodical English raids onto their territory. In addition, dissension among Acadian leaders, self-styled feudal lords, over carelessly awarded land grants brought continuous vexation and bloodshed among the colonists. Internal strife and almost incessant war with the English paralyzed the growth of the Acadian colony while its future was being determined by the fortunes of war.[3]

Port-Royal, continuous target for British attacks, was successively invaded in 1613, 1654, 1690, and 1710.[4] The two major Anglo-French wars of the era, King William's War (1689-1697) and Queen Anne's War (1702-1713) were followed by periods of precarious peace in Acadia.[5] Then, by the Treaty of Utrecht (1713), Acadia was definitively ceded to Great Britain; France retained Cape Breton (Ile Royale), Prince Edward Island (Ile Saint-Jean), and the southeastern part of present-day New Brunswick.[6] By the terms of the treaty, Acadians had the choice of remaining in Acadia or of leaving the province within a year. This time limit was later indefinitely extended. Allowed to sell their property and take their moveable goods, a small number of Acadians left for neighboring French territories. For the Acadians who chose to remain, Article 14 of the treaty guaranteed free exercise of religion and property rights.[7] Attached to their country, reluctant to leave their rich lands, the majority of the Acadians remained, and patiently waited for the turn of events which would restore Acadia to France.[8] At the same time Acadians obstinately opposed English demands to take an unconditional oath of allegiance to the British crown. Unwilling to bear arms against the French, yet fearing occasional Indian hostility, the Acadians requested a neutrality clause be inserted into the oath which would allow them to remain neutral in any Anglo-French conflict, but permit them to bear arms for protection from hostile Indians. "Essentially the Acadians' strategy was neutrality, for, in their view, neither France nor England could be guaranteed as the final victor."[9]

No decision regarding the oath was reached, however, until the arrival of Governor Richard Philipps in 1720. Anxious to settle the matter as expeditiously as possible, Philipps agreed to the Acadians' terms. However, unbeknown to the Acadians, the neutrality clause was never inserted into the oath. On April 30, 1730, Governor Philipps, writing to the council, stated that all inhabitants of the Acadian province, with the exception of seventeen families at Chignectou and nineteen families along the seacoast, had pledged their unqualified submission to the British crown. Thus, in the years which followed, prosperity and some measure of tranquility returned to the Acadian colony.[10]

This period of relative calm ended in 1744 when war erupted once again between England and France. Referred to in the colonies as King George's War (1744-1748), this conflict brought renewed turmoil to Acadia and its people. Although the great majority of Acadians abided by their neutrality status, a

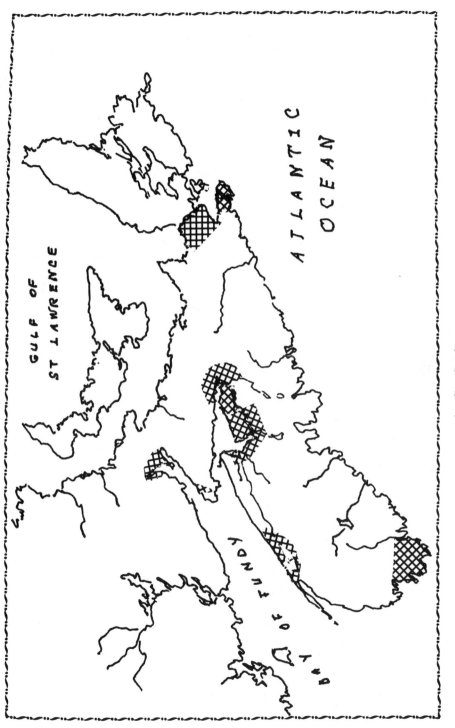

Acadian Settlements,
ca. 1755

few overtly defied the English.[11]   But, by 1748, important changes were taking place in Acadia.   To better protect the Acadian peninsula Lord Cornwallis, governor of Acadia, built the military citadel of Halifax on the Atlantic Coast. Over 2,500 Irish, German, Swiss, and French Calvinist emigrants were brought to Acadia to counteract the influence and undermine the morale of the French-Acadian population.[12]   Describing the status of the Acadians in 1748, a Canadian historian writes: "The Acadians considered themselves Acadian, the French considered them unreliable allies, and the English, unsatisfactory citizens."[13]   British efforts to assimilate the Acadian population met with very little success; therefore, a new, unconditional oath of allegiance to the English crown was imposed on the resisting Acadian population.   The result was an increased spirit of insubordination, mutual distrust and insidious hostility in the Acadian colony, contributing new irritants to the already tense Anglo-Acadian relations.   This hazardous state of affairs, complicated by the continuous struggle for North American supremacy between Great Britain and France, led to a new outbreak.

In 1753, shortly before the outbreak of war, Charles Lawrence became the new governor of Acadia.   His deep hatred of the Acadian people, whom he accused of obstinacy, trickery, and partiality toward France, culminated in a series of drastic measures which, for the English, settled once and for all time the vexing problem of the Acadians.[14]   Renewed efforts were made by the administration to force the Acadians to pledge their unconditional allegiance to the British crown.   Refusal to comply carried the penalty of confiscation of all property and deportation.   As expected and desired by Lawrence, the Acadains rejected the oath; the inevitable resulted: properties were confiscated, families were scattered, and the unhappy Acadians were loaded on ships destined for exile in the British colonies.[15]   Thus began the painful Acadian odyssey which historians refer to as the Grand Dérangement.   Dispersed indiscriminately throughout the English colonies, England, and France, the Acadians suffered destitution, disease, mental anguish, and loss of human dignity.[16]

Louis XV of France was successful in rescuing some from English captivity, and many of these were brought to France.   In an effort to relocate them, the French government granted the Acadians land in France, while others were coaxed into going to the French West Indies.   Unable to bear the tropical climate of the islands, generally dissatisfied with settlement conditions, they hurriedly left for Louisiana.   Some attempted to return to Acadia, but only a few reached their native land.   The ones remaining within British frontiers sought every opportunity to leave, especially after the Peace of Paris of 1763.   Using all of their meager savings to pay for their voyage, scores of Acadian exiles arrived in Louisiana determined to carve out of the wilderness a new Acadian homeland.[17]

The tragic historical events which culminated in the expulsion of the Acadians from their native province left a lasting imprint on the Acadian national character. However, to better understand the evolution of this national character, a closer examination must be undertaken of the progressive changes which occurred in the ethnic, social, and economic development of the Acadian people.

The long-standing conflict between England and France emerged as the crucial factor in the slow development of the colony of Acadia and in shaping the attitudes of its population. For almost a decade after M. de Poutrincourt's arrival at Port-Royal in 1606, relative peace reigned throughout the Acadian province. Attacked by the English in 1613, Acadia fell into British hands in 1628, but was restored to France in 1632. A number of people who had migrated to Acadia in 1629 chose to remain after the retrocession and became assimilated into the French-Acadian population. They were the Melançons, the Pitres, the Collesons and others.[18]

A meaningful colonization of Acadia, however, did not begin until 1632. Isaac de Razilly, dispatched by Cardinal Richelieu to take possession of the territory of Acadia, brought along three hundred handpicked, able-bodied men, well suited to colonial purposes. They were followed in 1636 by another contingent of colonists and *engagés* who arrived on the *Saint-Jehan*. Recruited in Champagne, Anjou, Brittany, the Basque country, Dijon, and La Rochelle, these newcomers were in many instances accompanied by their families. Although some immigrants eventually returned to France, many did remain on the Acadian peninsula. Three surnames, for example, appearing on the rolls of the *Saint-Jehan* are later found listed in the 1671 census of Acadia; Pierre Martin and Guillaume Trahan, both from Bourgueil; and Isaac Pesslin from Champagne The 1671 census ordered by M. de Grandfontaine, governor of Acadia, reveals an estimated population of three hundred to four hundred people.[19] Subsequent census records indicate that in 1714 the population had reached 2,500, and by 1755 had increased to 16,000.[20]

This steady population growth which in later years became a source of continuous irritation for the English administration, was due to the Acadian tradition of having large families. Bound by mutual devotion, these large family units played a significant part in the social and economic organization of Acadian life. Youths were encouraged to marry young and urged to settle around the paternal household. In time these family concentrations became villages bearing the name of the original settler. Kinship ties extending beyond the immediate family group led to clan mentality and created a sense of solidarity and belonging among people often descended from a common ancestor.[21] Genealogical studies reveal that eighty-six percent of the contemporary Nova Scotians are descended from seventy-six early Acadian colonists.[22] As a result, the number of Acadian surnames are relatively few. Intricately interrelated, the Acadians developed great concern for filiation and deep respect for their elders as well as the family in general.[23]

Family devotion was only rivaled by a profound attachment for the new land. Primarily farmers, the Acadians also engaged in herding, fishing, hunting, and lumbering. Their numerous children who started working at an early age constituted a practical and inexpensive work force inside and outside the home. The long winter months were devoted to cottage industries, such as tanning, spinning, weaving, candlemaking, and similar pursuits. Experienced hunters (although they preferred trapping), Acadians traded furs with the Indians with whom they generally maintained close and friendly contacts.

Frequent warfare and enemy incursions kept the Acadian population prepared for all contingencies. When their modestly furnished homes were destroyed by the enemy, they patiently rebuilt them and quickly resumed their daily activities. Except for a minority who had achieved some wealth, they lived well yet frugally, never envious of each other and content with the bare necessities. Although they were often resigned to their difficult lot in life, they were occasionally guilty of vanity, flippancy, and often exhibited the querulous Gallic temper of their forebears. By and large, however, they were a simple, happy people. They knew how to take things in stride: charitable and neighborly, they helped the widow and the orphan; fond of leisure, they had a decided predilection for beer, music, dancing, and the processions of the church; deeply devoted to their Catholic faith, they looked to their clergy for spiritual and judicial counsel; ignorant of world affairs, they sometimes turned to their priests for temporal guidance. As a result anti-British sentiments expressed by certain members of the clergy were reflected in the attitude of the Acadian population, leading, on occasion, to serious and unfortunate results.[24] It should be noted, however, that the political influence of the frequently understaffed Catholic clergy on the Acadian population has been exaggerated. Individual cases, such as that of Father Le Loutre, for example, have led to many generalizations which are still a matter of considerable debate among historians.[25]

Controversy, emotionalism, and the impact of Longfellow's *Evangeline* have contributed to many stereotyped and over-simplified characterizations of the Acadian people. They have often been described as innocent, simple, virtuous peasants when in fact "they were as complicated and as varied a group of humans as any other such society."[26] Isolated from Canada, neglected by France which failed to provide them with adequate leadership, consistent financial and military backing, the Acadians learned to deal with their problems and act swiftly and wisely in their best interest. By and large, answerable for their own administration and food supplies, they developed organizational resourcefulness and *esprit de corps*. Displaying genuine inventiveness, they developed necessary skills in order to survive in the semi-wilderness in which they lived. Under British rule, which was in the beginning improperly enforced for lack of adequate civil and military forces, the Acadians often resorted to a policy of stubborn resistance and over disobedience. Governor Philipps described them as "proud, lazy, obstinate and intractable," and one of their own French governors referred to them as "*demi-republicain*."[27] Quite capable of handling their affairs on a local level, they lacked the ability and the competency to deal with the ambiguous political situation which preceded their expulsion from Acadia. Ignorant of their rights, bewildered by events, they became the victims of ruthless and ambitious politicians.[28] Separated from their families, driven from their country, they endured the hardships of exile, sustained by their religious faith and the hope of being reunited again. Hoping for a better lot in Louisiana, several hundred Acadians arrived in the colony and, supplied with tools, weapons, ammunition and provisions, settled at Opelousas, the Attakapas (St. Martinville), and Cabanocey (St. James Parish).[29]

Although the first Acadians to reach Louisiana appeared satisfied with settlement conditions, the ones who followed voiced innumerable complaints. When ordered by Spanish Governor Antonio de Ulloa to settle around the royal fort of Saint Louis de Natchez, they made every effort to overturn the governor's decision in order that they might join relatives and friends at Cabanocey. Every conceivable excuse, therefore, from safety and poor land to ill health was shrewdly invoked. Their elected spokesman obstinately opposed the administration of the post commandant and his aides and went so far as to approach the governor himself. Governor Ulloa, commenting on their insubordination, depicted them as rebellious, ungrateful, and obstinate people.[30] Irritated by their disobedience and lack of gratitude, he issued strict orders forbidding Acadians and others from travelling throughout the province or sheltering non-residents without proper authorization. All infractions to the rule were punishable with immediate expulsion from the colony.[31] Yielding to the governor's threats, the Acadians reluctantly complied with the orders and proceeded to prepare the land and build their homes.

Spanish policy toward the Acadians was one of firmness tempered by justice, and great efforts were made to give them assistance. The Spanish, just as the French before them, clearly saw the positive contributions which the newcomers could make to the further development of Louisiana. For several decades the French had patiently, but unsuccessfully, attempted to attract new people to the colony. This sudden influx of people who had a reputation of being hardworking, experienced, industrious farmers could only benefit the shaky economy of the sparsely populated province.[32]

Strict instructions were issued regarding any new Acadian settlements. Post commandants were directed to prepare accurate rolls of all Acadian families under their jurisdiction, listing names, ages of all household members, as well as all subsequent statistics such as births, deaths, and marriages. Tracts of land, ranging from four to eight arpents mainly along the river, were granted to each family according to its size and need. But even bachelors who had no family responsibilities as yet were entitled to land grants. Employed on the post and compensated according to their skills, the Acadians earned the same wages as the Spaniards engaged in similar trades. In order for the Spaniards to justify expenditures made for their settlement, bachelors were urged to marry and establish families as soon as possible.[33] Census records of the period indicate that as a possible result many middle-aged widows with large families, unable to work the land, married men younger than themselves.[34]

Ordered to erect shelters, build levees, and start cultivation, the Acadians complied without delay. They worked the land with the help of their large families which often included young, orphaned relatives. Census records suggest that within a year many Acadians were beginning to be self-sufficient.[35] By 1770 they were producing above their needs. Directed by the administration to sell their excess crops to the government, they used a variety of excuses to conceal the fact that they were selling their grain to the British conveniently located across the Mississippi. Their long-time aversion for the British had somehow handily disappeared when advantages or profits were at stake.[36] Subject to government decisions regarding civil, political, and certain economic matters, the Acadians were continuously scrutinized by a punctilious Spanish administration, which minutely regulated their activities.

Unable to assume the proper defense of the colony with their own small military force, the Spanish organized civil militias. All able-bodied Louisiana colonists, including Acadians, between the ages of sixteen and fifty-five were enlisted in militia companies, led by a commandant, captain, and two lieutenants.[37] Responsible for the safety of the posts, operating as a police force, these militia units were often entrusted with community projects. Since most of the new settlements did not have places of worship and mass was often celebrated in a crowded home by a neighboring parish priest, the need for appropriate buildings became a matter of urgency.[36] For example, under the direction of their respective commandants, the militia units of Cabanocey and Lafourche de Chetimachas provided the money, the lumber, and the skill to build the chapel of St. James and the Church of the Ascension. Owing to ill-defined boundaries between these adjacent parishes, however, many Acadians were assessed twice for these buildings. Outraged by this injustice, and with characteristic stubbornness, the Acadians refused to pay their share. Endless quarrels and bitter dissension followed.[39]

The traumatic experience of the exile had neither broken their spirit nor taught them submission. Many Acadians joined the Creoles and German Coast

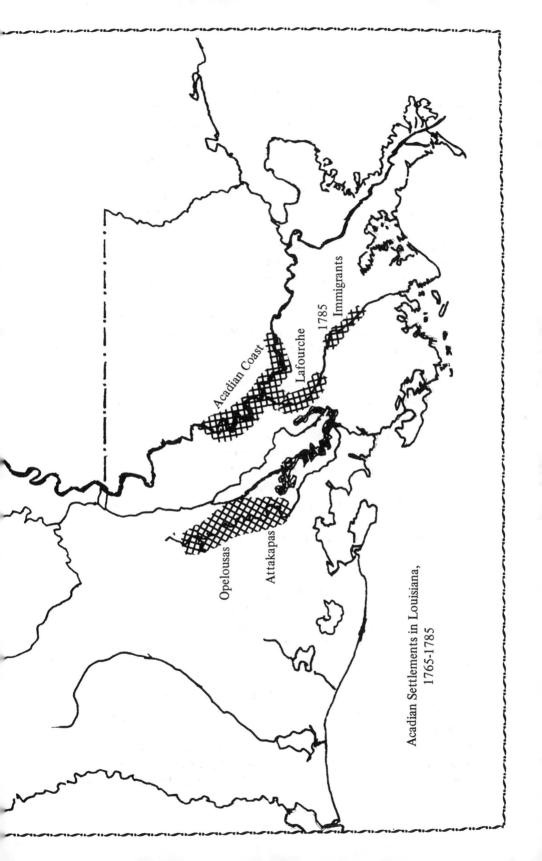

Acadian Settlements in Louisiana, 1765-1785

Opelousas

Attakapas

Acadian Coast

Lafourche

1785
Immigrants

population in the 1768 insurrection against Governor Ulloa who had clumsily imposed a series of commercial restrictions upon the colony. Led by Creoles, the Acadians proceeded to New Orleans to add their own grievances to the long list of complaints presented by the colonists to the Superior Council. The Acadians thus became involved in those events which eventually resulted in the hurried departure of Ulloa and his replacement by Governor O'Reilly. Upon arrival in the colony, O'Reilly had the insurgent leaders arrested and eventually punished with imprisonment and death.[40] Forced in the end to yield to Spanish rule, the Acadians turned to the more difficult problems of adjusting to their new life in Louisiana.

Despite the protective levees, rising water, caused by storms and hurricanes, destroyed crops and cattle, leaving the Acadians once more destitute and dependent on the king's charity.[41] Bad weather, but mostly disease, was one of the leading factors hampering the normal progression of their economic development. Not accustomed to the hot, humid climate of Louisiana, weakened by years of exile, they fell prey to flu and fevers endemic to the colony. Measures taken by colonial authorities to care for the sick proved inadequate. Royal surgeons attached to settlements and forts were literally overwhelmed by the increasing number of patients. Short medical supplies and empty warehouses compounded the problem. Primitive sanitary conditions were deplored by post commandants and physicians alike. Plans for better infirmaries were made and suggestions to upgrade medical care proposed. These proposals would have eliminated costly, lengthy (10 to 18 leagues) pirogue journeys undertaken daily by some of the surgeons to visit the ailing Acadians placed in their care.[42]

Residing in remote areas not readily accessible, the Acadians lived isolated from each other and with little contact with the outside world. Suspicious of strangers, they vigorously resisted all assimilation and continued to live according to their own customs and traditions. In 1785 they were joined by approximately 1,500 fellow-Acadians who had formerly resided in France, and who were brought to Louisiana through the combined efforts of the French and Spanish governments. Upon arrival in New Orleans, the new colonists were granted necessary assistance and quickly dispatched to the settlements of New Galvez, Cabanocey, Lafourche, Manchac, Baton Rouge, Bayou des Ecores, Attakapas, and Opelousas, where many were reunited with relatives and friends.[43]

When, at the beginning of the nineteenth century, a Frenchman travelling in Louisiana visited the Acadian settlements, he was struck by the similarity of traits and customs existing between these Acadians and the French peasants of Beauce and Brie provinces. Although they appeared to be capable farmers, they lacked initiative and zeal. Discouraged by a series of commercial restrictions which prevented them from selling their goods, the Acadians lapsed into indolence, producing only for their own consumption. Despite the fact that a few had become successful planters or well-to-do cattlemen, and owned slaves, most of the Acadians lived frugally in crudely built cabins, tilling the soil with the help fo their families. Except for some who engaged in hunting, trapping, moss picking, fishing, and lumbering, the Acadians were primarily farmers and ranchers. They raised cotton, corn and rice, and their large herds of cattle roamed the prairies unattended. Involved in domestic chores, the women milked the cows, spun and wove the cotton into a coarse muslin which was used for their garments. Seldom clean, these garments were of the greatest simplicity, the men wearing *carmagnole* jackets and women plain cotton dresses. Barefooted most of the time, they only wore shoes on special occasions. Their diet consisted of rice, corn, several kinds of beans, melon, pumpkin, salted pork and beef. Keenly aware of their rustic manners, their quaint seventeenth-century *patois* and their lack of education, they wisely avoided the company of the sophisticated upper classes with whom they thought they had little in common.

Reserved in appearance, they were a fun-loving people with an unusual fondness for music, dancing,and above all for their beloved balls. On horseback, on foot, and by pirogue, they traveled as much as ten to fifteen leagues to attend these dances. At the sound of a couple of fiddles, young and old alike danced to their heart's content, usually well into the night. Pungent spicy gumbos, weak tafia, gossip and pleasant conversation brought additional enjoyment to the festive event.[44] Just as popular as the balls, but by far more practical, was the widely practiced Acadian custom of the boucherie. Taking turns to provide the animal to be slaughtered, neighbors and friends gathered for the day to cut and prepare the meats which were later divided among the participants. Intended originally to furnish people who did not have refrigeration with a reasonable amount of meat for immediate consumption, the boucherie became, in time, a social occasion. It provided lonely people with an opportunity to visit, exchange news,and maintain contact.[45]

A closely knit people, their lives revolved around the family unit and the home. Families gathered during the evening *veillees* to review daily activities, discuss weather, crops,and especially to reminisce. Storytellers par excellence, typical of an illiterate society, the Acadians were well versed in their rich history and folklore. They related over and over again the tales of their beloved Acadia, keeping the past alive for their children and their grandchildren.[46]

As the eighteenth century was coming to a close, the Louisiana Acadians were slowly surrounded by an increasingly Protestant, Anglo-Saxon population and scores of newly arrived Spanish colonists. Although some Acadians were gradually achieving some measure of wealth, education, and status, the majority remained subsistence farmers (*petits habitants*), moss pickers, hunters, trappers, fishermen, and lived obscurely in the most humble circumstances. Largely underestimated by their fellow Louisianians, they were mocked for their rustic simplicity, their lack of education, and their Cajun dialect. The loneliness generated by prolonged solitary rural living, the sense of inferiority caused by their inability to compete socially and linguistically increased their tendency toward isolation and hampered their progress and their development. They emerged into the nineteenth century as an independent, strong-willed, unsophisticated agrarian society. Resistant to change, suspicious of foreign influences, these early Louisiana Acadians jealously guarded their religious and ethnic inheritance and left an indelible cultural pattern for many generations to come.

NOTES

1. Bona Arsenault, *Histoire des Acadiens* (Quebec, 1966), p. 15. Sieur de Monts was granted by Henry IV of France the title of «vice-roy et capitaine-général . . . du pays de Cadie, du Canada et autres terres de la Nouvelle-France, du 40ième degré au 46ième degré, Tadoussac, rivière du Canada (fleuve Saint-Laurent) tant d'un coté que de l'autre, avec mission de peupler, cultiver et fortifier lesdites terres et en conventir les indigenes, avec droits exclusifs pendant dix ans de trafiquer avec les sauvages desdites terres.» M. de Monts' expedition was financed with his own money and moneys contributed by the merchants of Saint-Malo, Rouen, La Rochelle, and Saint-Jean-de-Luz.

2. *Ibid.*, pp. 15-17.

3. E. Rameau de Saint-Père, *La France aux colonies; études sur le développement de la race française hors de l'Europe* (Paris, 1859), Part I, pp. 20-28.

4. Oscar William Winzerling, *Acadian Odyssey* (Baton Rouge, 1955), pp. 7-8.

5. King William's War and Queen Anne's War were also respectively known in Europe as the War of the League of Augsburg and the War of the Spanish Succession.

6. Arsenault, *Histoire*, pp. 100-101. Article 12 of the Treaty of Utrecht reads as follows:

Le Roi Très Chrétien [Louis XIV] devra livrer à la Reine de Grande-Bretagne [Anne] la Nouvelle-Ecosse, ou Acadie toute entière, comprises en ses anciennes limites, et aussi la cité de Port-Royal, maintenant Annapolis-Royal, ainsi que tout ce qui dépend desdites terres et îles de ce pays.

Since the boundaries of the Acadian territory could not be clearly determined, a commission was entrusted with settling the problem and endless controversies ensued.

7. Thomas B. Akins, ed., *Acadia and Nova Scotia, Documents Relating to the Acadian French and the First British Colonization of the Province, 1714-1758* (Cottonport, La., 1972), see note p. 264. Article 14 of the Treaty of Utrecht stipulates the following:

The subjects of the said King may have Liberty to remove themselves within a Year to any other Place with all their movable effects. But those who are willing to remain and to be subject to the Kingdom of Great Britain, are to enjoy the free exercise of their religion according to the usages of the Church of Rome, as far as the laws of Great Britain do allow the same.

Queen Anne's letter to General Nicholson of June 23, 1713, reads as follows:

To permit such of them [the subjects of the French king] as have any lands or tenements in the places under your government in Acadia and Newfoundland, that have been or are to be yielded to us by virtue of the late treaty of peace, and are willing to continue our subjects, to retain and enjoy their said lands and tenements without any molestation, as fully and freely as other of our subjects do or may possess their lands and estates, or sell the same if they shall rather choose to move elsewhere.

There was no mention, however, of a qualified oath of allegiance.

8. Antoine Bernard, *L'Acadie vivante: Histoire du peuple acadien de ses origines à nos jours* (Montréal, 1945), pp. 62-63. While French authorities were continuously exhorting the Acadians to leave Nova Scotia for neighboring Cape Breton, the British administration made every effort to retain the Acadian population. Unwilling to lose an industrious population who kept the English forts supplied, the British secretly opposed the Acadians' departure.

9. Naomi Griffiths, *The Acadians: Creation of a People* (Toronto, 1973), p. 23.

10. Akins, ed., *Acadia and Nova Scotia*, p. 267, note. Until 1730, no oath had been taken by the people of Acadia except by a few inhabitants of Fort Annapolis. Promised a neutrality clause, which was, however, never introduced into the written oath, they pledged their allegiance. The Acadians who became known as French Neutrals firmly believed that their right not to bear arms was now guaranteed.

11. Bernard, *L'Acadie vivante*, p. 66. A group of young Acadians, led by Father Le Loutre, a fiery Breton missionary, fled to the isthmus of Chignecto (territory claimed by France) and there organized a *Nouvelle Acadie*. Several Acadian families joined them and continuous contact was maintained with the French fort at Louisbourg.

12. Bernard, *L'Acadie vivante*, p. 66. See also Emile Lauvrière, *La Tragedie d'un peuple: Histoire du peuple acadien de ses origines a nos jours*, 2 vols. (Paris, 1924), 1, 329-330.

13. Griffiths, *The Acadians*, p. 37.

14. Thomas B. Akins, ed., *Selections from the Public Documents of the Province of Nova Scotia* (Halifax, 1869), pp. 212-213. In a letter dated August 1, 1754, addressed to the Lords of Trade, Governor Charles Lawrence complains of the insubordination of the Acadian population continuously incited to rebellion by their priests. He also states:

As they possess the best and largest tracts of Land in the Province, it cannot be settled with any effect while they remain in this situation and tho' I would be very far from attempting such a step without your Lordships' approbation, yet

I cannot help being of opinion that it would be much better, if they refuse the Oaths, that they were away.

See also *ibid.*, pp. 235-237. In an extract of a letter dated October 29, 1754, written by the Lords of Trade to Governor Charles Lawrence, the Acadians' obstinate refusal is deplored, and their ambiguous situation examined. Governor Lawrence was directed, however, to withhold all measures «until His Majesty's Pleasure can be known» and consult with the «Chief Justice upon this Point, and take his Opinion, which may serve as a foundation for any future measure it may be thought advisable to pursue with regard to the Inhabitants in general.»

15. Winzerling, *Acadian Odyssey*, pp. 9-18. Governor Lawrence was determined that the Acadians would take the unconditional oath of allegiance. The Acadians, however, insisted that Article 14 of the Treaty of Utrecht guaranteed their religious freedom, neutrality in time of war and property rights. By refusing the oath, the Acadians placed themselves in an ambiguous situation. Although they were living on British territory, under the protection of the British crown, they wanted to remain loyal to the French king. When war was declared in 1754, the Acadians surrendered their arms and ammunition and reiterated their desire to remain neutral in the Franco-British conflict. In June 1755, however, after the fall of Beauséjour, two hundred Acadians, fully armed, were made prisoners by the British. This permitted Governor Lawrence to conclude that all Acadians were treacherous and that they should be forced to take the oath without further delay. Acadian delegates meeting with Governor Lawrence on July 3, 1755, presented a tactlessly worded memorandum asking to be allowed to keep their arms and conditional oath. More convinced than ever of Acadian treachery, Governor Lawrence remained adamant. Rumors of an impending French naval attack and fear that, if the Acadians were allowed to leave, they would join the French, forced Governor Lawrence to order the immediate expulsion of the Acadians. His decision, eventually upheld by the home government, resulted in the immediate deportation of the Acadians.

16. *Ibid.*, pp. 18-23. The total deported Acadian population was estimated to be between 8,200 and 10,000. Between the years 1755 and 1763, 2,000 Acadians were shipped to Boston, 700 to Connecticut, 250 to New York, 754 to Philadelphia, 2,000 to Maryland, 1,500 to South Carolina, 500 to North Carolina, 400 to Georgia, and 1,500 to Virginia. The Acadians sent to Virginia were refused entrance to the colony and shipped directly to England.

17. *Ibid.*, chaps. IV and V. See also, Abbadie to Choiseul-Stainville, April 6, 1764. Archives Nationales, Archives des Colonies, Series C 13a (Louisiana: Correspondance générale), volume 44, folios 37-38; hereinafter cited as AC, C 13a, with volume and folio numbers. Acadians of Miquelon to Sr. Perrault, September 16, 1764. Archives Nationales, Archives des Colonies, Series C 11d (Acadie: Correspondance générale), volume 8, folio 256. (?) to comte d'Estaing, September 19, 1764. Archives Nationales, Archives des Colonies, Series B (Correspondance envoyée), volume 119, folio 150. Dupla to comte d'Estaing, October 30, 1764. AC, B 119:172.

18. Bernard, *L'Acadie vivante*, p. 23.

19. Geneviève Massignon, *Les Parlers français d'Acadie: Enquêtes linguistiques*, 2 vols. (Paris, 1962), I, 32-34.

20. Winzerling, *Acadian Odyssey*, p. 168, notes 79-80.

21. Rameau de Saint-Père, *La France aux colonies*, Part I, 102; Félix Voorhies, *Acadian Reminiscences: The True Story of Evangeline* (New Orleans, 1907), pp. 27-28.

22. Massignon, *Les Parlers français*, I, 42-74.

23. *Collection de documents inédits sur le Canada et l'Amérique*, 3 vols. (Quebec, 1888-1890), pp. 165-167. It appears the Acadians who had received asylum in Belle-Isle-en-Mer when asked for specific information relating to their ancestry supplied accurate and detailed data about their families.

24. E. Rameau de Saint-Père, *Une Colonie féodale en Amérique, l'Acadie (1604-1881)*, 2 vols. (Paris, 1889), I, 150-153, 226-235.

25. Griffiths, *The Acadians*, pp. 46-47.

26. *Ibid.*, pp. 21-22.

27. Governor Philips to Board of Trade, August 3, 1738, in Akins, ed., *Selection*, p. 102. See also, Rameau de Saint-Père, *Une Colonie féodale*, I, 232.

28. Winzerling, *Acadian Odyssey*, pp. 11-14.

29. Aubry and Foucault to (?), April 30, 1765. AC, C 13a, 45:21-24.

30. Don Antonio de Ulloa, «Observations on the manifesto presented by the people of Louisiana to the Superior Council,» 1769. AC, C 13a, 47:64-222. Ulloa stated that despite the fact that the Acadians had been generously supplied with all the necessities, they were demanding cloth for garments and home furnishings. Ulloa further comments that they must have exhibited the same annoying traits while in Santo Domingo and that the governor of the island must have been quite happy to see them leave. For the facts relating to the settlement of the Acadians at Fort Saint-Louis de Natchez and their objections to settling there, see also, Nicolas Verret to Ulloa, March 26, 1768. Seville, Archivo General de Indias, Papeles Procedentes de Cuba, legajo 2357; hereinafter cited as PPC, with legajo number. Pierre Joseph Piernas, «Reasons given by the Acadians for not settling at Natchez and replies concerning their ill-founded reasons,» March 27, 1768, PPC, 2357:non-paginated.

31. Memorandum from Don Antonio de Ulloa to Fusilier de la Claire and Jacques Patin, commandants at Opelousas; René Trahan and Jean-Baptiste Broussard, commandants at the Attakapas; Duplesis, commandant at Pointe Coupée; Louis Judice and Verret, commandants at Kabahanossé; and D'Arensbourg, commandant at Côte des Allemands, April 4, 1768, PPC, 2357:non-paginated.

32. Aubry to Choiseul-Stainville, April 24, 1765. AC, C 13a, 45:45-52.

33. R. E. Chandler, ed. and trans., «End of an Odyssey: Acadians Arrive in St. Gabriel, Louisiana,» *Louisiana History*, XIV (1973), 74-79.

34. Jacqueline K. Voorhies, comp., *Some Late Eighteenth-Century Louisianians: Census Records of the Colony, 1758-1796* (Lafayette, La., 1973), pp. 421-528.

35. Corn production in the parishes of Iberville, Pointe Coupée, Fausse Rivière, Ascension, for the year 1770, PPC, 188-2:non-paginated.

36. Governor to Judice, August 11 and August 30, 1770, PPC, 188-1:non-paginated. See also, Judice to O'Reilly, August 27, 1770, 188-1:non-paginated.

37. Chandler, «End of an Odyssey,» 77-78.

38. Louis Judice to Ulloa, Novamber 18, 1767, PPC, 187-A-1 non-paginated. See also, Judice to Ulloa, July 2, 1768, *ibid.*

39. Louis Judice to Unzaga, March 28, 1770, PPC, 188-1:non-paginated. Louis Judice to Unzaga, August 18, 1770, *ibid.* Louis Judice to Unzaga, August 27, 1770, *ibid.* Louis Judice to Unzaga, September 2, 1770, *ibid.* General to Judice, September 13, 1770, *ibid.*

40. David Ker Texada, *Alexandro O'Reilly and the New Orleans Rebels* (Lafayette, La., 1970), pp. 70-94. See also Aubry to duc de Praslin, March 8, 1769. AC, C 13a, 49:9-12. Alexandro O'Reilly to marquis de Grimaldi, October 20-26, 1769. AC, C 13a, 49:210-309.

41. Voorhies, *Some Late Eighteenth-Century Louisianians*, pp. 524-528.

42. Louis Judice to Ulloa, June 10, 1766, PPC, 187-A-1:non-paginated. Leduc, royal surgeon at St. Gabriel to Ulloa, September 30, 1767, *ibid.* Duplessis, commandant at Pointe Coupée, to Ulloa, October 21, 1768, *ibid.* Delavillebeuvre, commandant at St. Louis, to Ulloa, September 18, 1768, *ibid.* Jacques Leduc, royal surgeon at St. Gabriel, to Ulloa, February 14, 1768, *ibid.*

43. Voorhies, *Some Late Eighteenth-Century Louisianians*, pp. 489-523.

44. C. C. Robin, *Voyage to Louisiana, 1803-1805*, trans. and annot. by Stuart O. Landry, Jr. (New Orleans, 1966), chaps. XLVIII and LXII.

45. Steven L. Del Sesto, «Traditional Social Institutions in Southwest Louisiana: A Sociological Note on the Study of Culture,» *Attakapas Gazette*, X (1974), 72-76.

46. Jay K. Ditchy, *Les Acadians louisianais et leur parler* (Paris, 1911), pp. 227-270.

IN AND OUT THE MAINSTREAM:
THE ACADIANS IN ANTEBELLUM LOUISIANA

by Vaughan B. Baker

In this age of increasingly bland cultural homogenization, Southwest Louisiana's Cajuns have continued to attract widespread popular and scholarly attention.[1] The Cajuns, descendants of the Acadians exiled from Nova Scotia in 1755, have maintained an enduringly vital and distinct way of life against all onslaughts of the twentieth century. Despite persistent pressures to merge into the broad classification of "American," Cajuns remain Cajuns. Folk traditions remain strong, Cajun music is a dynamic expression of individuality. and Cajun cuisine is nationally celebrated.

Fascination with folkways, however, has perpetuated interpretations which distort the realities of the Cajun experience. Contrary to the prevailing myopic perception, not all Cajuns–not even all Acadians–rejected the seductions of the mainstream. Indeed, almost as soon as it was transplanted to Louisiana, the Acadian culture, which had evolved in Nova Scotia, Acadie of memories and myth, began to yield to the diffusional pressures of the new environment. Although the Acadian majority, it is true, remained rather more out than in the mainstream until the middle of the twentieth century, the Cajuns nevertheless adopted and adapted new directions almost from the moment they settled in Louisiana.

The conventional stereotype depicts a happy savage living in a moss-draped bayou paradise, fishing and trapping for sustenance. Expressing a simple devotion to Catholic ritual and a naive, not to say stupid, response to the modern world, he speaks an unintelligible French patois or perhaps thickly accented English to a large brood of barefoot children and spends every Saturday night at the *fais do-do*. The nineteenth-century evidence sharply contradicts this comic-book simplification. Even a cursory glance at the political record shows active Acadian participation in the highest levels of government from the earliest years of Louisiana statehood. Acadians fought the British during the American War of Independence, supported Andrew Jackson's forces in 1815, lent vital leadership to the antebellum political development of the state and contributed noteworthy leaders in the troubled time of secession and rebellion. Two Acadians served as governor and one as lieutenant governor between 1840 and 1860. It is difficult if not impossible to reconcile such a record of military and political prominence with the popular caricature.

95

Further contradictions in the historical evidence abound. St. Martin Parish's Felix Voorhies remembers hearing stories of his centenarian Acadian grandmother, a survivor of the deportation and years of exile, lament to her grandchildren in the 1840s ". . . the Acadians are losing, by degrees, the remembrance of the traditions and customs of the mother country; the love of gold has implanted itself in their hearts, and this will bring no happiness to them."[2] Change in Acadian culture--its creeping contamination by the material values of the broader American culture--is apparent in her complaint. Yet the popular view of an Acadian population fiercely resistant to acculturation is not without foundation. William Henry Perrin recorded in 1895 that the Acadians were still as primitive as when they left Nova Scotia, and Louisiana author Lyle Saxon noted in the 1930s that "many still live in rude shacks, weave their own cloth, continue to cling to a chronic aversion to wearing shoes."[3]

Certainly no one will deny that some--indeed, numerous--Acadians resisted acculturation until well after World War II, when improved transportation and communications brought mainstream America to the darkest reaches of the swamp, now conspicuously emblazoned with Clorox bottles and Budweiser cans. But to accept the view that few Acadians submitted to the mainstream culture until the latter half of the twentieth century, as is commonly done, is to reduce to an absurdity the diversity and complexity of the Acadian heritage. Great damage has been done to the understanding of Louisiana's social, political, and economic development by overlooking the cultural contributions of the Acadian population. Although no purely Acadian political movement ever existed, Acadian influence on the emerging state was significant at a time when Louisiana was developing its southern character. An examination of some actualities of the Cajun experience in the early part of the nineteenth century clearly reveals that Cajun acculturation to the white Southern sub-culture did indeed occur.

Of the Acadians who migrated to Louisiana, the largest numbers settled in the Bayou Lafourche, St. James-Ascension, and Attakapas areas. By 1810, the Attakapas district held the largest Acadian population--that area which now comprises Lafayette, Vermilion, St. Martin, St. Mary, and Iberia parishes and is popularly called Acadiana. Officials of the Spanish government granted Acadian immigrants land holdings measuring four to eight arpents with a usual depth of forty arpents, forming long narrow farms between the bayous and the unclaimed lands beyond. The land grants firmly established an enduring pattern of small, independent farms which effectively retarded the wholesale development of the large plantation.[5] Although many Acadians rapidly began to consolidate larger holdings, the Acadian parishes remained strongholds of independent small farmers. Cattle grazing became the principal agricultural industry in the Attakapas, with much of the region occupied by thriving Acadian *vacheries*.[6] One traveller noted that, with few exceptions, Acadian homes were spread widely apart and that large Acadian communities were rare.[7]

In some locations ethnic heterogeneity prevailed; the Acadians in these areas mingled with diverse ethnic elements, including a significant number of Creoles, native Louisianians of Spanish and French descent, who attempted to retain political and social supremacy in the rapidly changing state. After statehood, ethnic diversity was compounded as waves of new immigrants moved in—Germans, Spaniards, Irish, French, refugees from other areas of the United States and the West Indies and Anglo-Americans in large numbers. The black population also steadily increased.

These new immigrants brought with them cultural baggage that inevitably influenced the Acadian population. The 1830s were a boom time in Louisiana, with the state experiencing the benefits of an expanding economy and a rapid population growth, largely in the southern sections.[8] The thriving Acadians were not immune to the imperatives of the dominating American culture, and economic and social upward mobility tended to establish a distinctive form of class stratification within the Acadian ethnic group, which by 1840 represented a minority of the population in their bayou parishes.[9] Adapting rapidly to clutural innovations, many Acadians abandoned the older cultural patterns and began to pursue the system which placed them squarely within the planter-dominated regional sub-culture.

Historians generally accept that the Cajuns in nineteenth-century Louisiana owned few or no slaves[10] and remained outside the dominant Southern slave economy. While it is true that few Cajuns became owners of large-scale plantations of the type prevalent in other sections of the state and of the South, the belief that Cajuns rejected the institution of slavery does not bear scrutiny. The public records of Lafayette Parish, one of the most heavily Acadian-populated parishes in the state, reveal that acceptance of slavery was widespread within the Cajun populace.

The police jury minutes for the early decades of the nineteenth century show an almost obsessive concern with the protection of slaveowners and the regulation of potentially unruly slaves. Patrols comprised of local citizens with a captain appointed as "chefs de patrole" insured obedience to both local regulations and the Louisiana Code Noir. All free white parish residents between the ages of sixteen and forty-five were subject to patrol duty. As early as 1826 the parish had nine captains of patrol, eight of whom were Acadians.[11] The patrols, armed with guns and pistols, searched the parish every fifteen days, punishing severely any violation of the slavery regulations. Any slave found off his owner's plantation without permission was arrested and the master heavily fined. The slave suffered a severe beating—fifteen stripes for the first offense, twenty-five stripes for each repeated offense. The patrols had wide-ranging

Ile Copal, home of Acadian planter Alexandre Mouton

Nineteenth-century Acadian cottage

powers to enter slave quarters without notice and to arrest any whites or free persons of color who contributed "to the disorderly conduct of slaves by admitting them into their [sic] society."[12] Cajun police jurors dominated the juries which established these regulations--in 1823 and 1824, of eight jurors, five were Acadian.[13]

Although patterns of slave ownership in the South varied considerably, general norms have been established. Over seventy percent of Louisiana families owned no slaves. In the South as a whole, membership in the "planter class" required the ownership of twenty or more slaves. The typical southern slave owner could not be thus categorized, as eighty-eight percent of Southerners owned fewer than twenty slaves and seventy-two percent fewer than ten. Almost fifty percent of Southern slave owners held fewer than five slaves.[14] An examination of the Seventh Census of the United States (1850)[15] indicates that the patterns of slave ownership among Lafayette Parish Acadians correlate closely with the averages for the South.

Of the 374 slave owners in Lafayette Parish in 1850, 269--a startling sixty-eight percent--were Acadian. Twenty-one percent of the Cajun slave owners owned only one slave, fitting the conventionally accepted pattern of the small, independent farmer considered representative of the entire Cajun population. Of the Cajun slave owners, thirty percent owned between two and five slaves and twenty-three percent owned between six and ten. Thus, 74.8 percent of the Cajun slave owners held fewer than ten slaves, a percentage slightly higher than the Southern norm.

Of the 36.2 percent of Cajun slave owners who owned above ten slaves, 10.15 percent owned between eleven and fifteen slaves and 5.4 percent owned between sixteen and twenty. Only 8.56 percent of the Cajun slave owners can be classified as members of the planter class, owning over twenty slaves. Thus, 91.4 percent of the Acadian slave owners held fewer than twenty slaves. Of the larger Cajun slaveholdings, 7.8 percent of the owners held between twenty-one and fifty slaves, and 1.5 percent (four Acadians) owned over fifty slaves, being placed thus in the ranks of the large slaveholders in the state. By 1860 the number of large slaveholding Acadians in the parish had increased to ten of the twelve large slaveholders to be found in the parish.[16]

A survey of the evidence in only one of Louisiana's Acadian parishes is an insufficient base from which to challenge strongly the orthodox interpretation of the Cajuns as a non-slaveholding population. The data obtained in Lafayette Parish does, however, give rise to serious questions about the accuracy of any such description of the Cajuns as a whole. The sample attests, however, that the Cajuns were not invulnerable to the imperatives of Southern plantation culture.

Parish records yield further evidence of the acculturation to the dominant Anglo-American model. By 1854, many of the formerly dominant French

customs had begun to weaken. After statehood, most legal documents were
written in English, the dollar became the preferred currency (although many
Cajuns still refer to it as the *piastre*) and the acre as a standard of land measure-
ment was more frequently used. Literacy among the Acadians increased. Despite the still fierce ethnic competition, amicable commercial exchanges between
Anglo-Americans and Acadians were common and intermarriage not unusual.[17]

In essence, acculturation to the broader American cultural pattern proceeded apace among the Acadians living near the town and in the prime locations
along the waterways. The dynamic interplay between Creole French, American
sugar planters, and the surging Cajun population, created an Acadian upper
class which rapidly divested itself of some of the primary aspects of its Cajun
culture and affiliated socially and politically with the Creole elements in the
ethnic controversy which dominated Louisiana's political picture in the antebellum years.

Aware that the Creoles looked down upon the Acadians as peasants,[18] the
upwardly mobile members of the Acadian population sought to model themselves upon the Creole pattern. Manners, dress, home decor and social exchanges were determined by Creole mores. Local tradition insists that the
town of St. Martinville, once the obscure *Poste des Attakapas*, became *Le
Petit Paris*, where Creole families from all over the state mingled with the Acadian upper class at parties, balls, and productions of the New Orleans Opera
Company.[19] Successful Acadians, benefitting from increasing prosperity and a
developing social sophistication, assumed an aristocratic demeanor based on
their economic ascendency which apparently became fundamentally indistin-
guishable from the Creole landowners.

Individual examples of this process are myriad. Bannon G. Thibodaux, a
wealthy sugar planter in Terrebonne Parish, studied law in Hagerstown, Maryland, and became a prominent Louisiana Whig.[20] On the other side of the
political fence, Alexandre Mouton, son of an Acadian immigrant, became the
first Democratic governor of the state. He pursued classical studies at Georgetown University and married first the Creole Zelia Rousseau and secondly the
American Emma Gardiner.[21] His interests were so completely identified with
the planter aristocracy that he was elected president of the state's secession
convention in 1861.

Upper-class Acadians were politically inconsistent. In the early decades of
the century they aligned with other French-speaking elements seeking to retain
French supremacy. Their votes for such Creole gubernatorial candidates as
Jacques Villeré, Jacques Dupré, André Bienvenu Roman, Pierre Derbigny, and
Bernard Marigny, unquestionably served to maintain the state's enduring ethnic
division and the almost impregnable political position of the French Creole
population.[22] In general, the Acadian parishes were traditional Whig strong-

holds,[23] which suggests a relatively high degree of prosperity. Democratic doctrines nevertheless attracted many adherents and an analysis of voting patterns in these parishes indicates little political consensus.[24]

Jacksonian doctrines attacking aristocracy and privilege appealed to the fundamentally equalitarian Acadians and to the more ambitious among them-- even to such successfully acculturated Acadian planters as Alexandre Mouton, whose political attitudes exhibit a paradoxical (but not uncommon) blend of Whig sympathy but Democratic affiliation. Wealthy and unquestionably a member of the privileged elites, in his gubernatorial inaugural address in 1843 he clearly revealed commitment to Jacksonian principles in sentiments consistent with his Acadian origins. He declared,

> I am opposed to the creation of any corporation or monopoly which may give exclusive or undue advantage to a portion of the community over the mass of the people, holding such legislation unjust and oppressive, as taking rights and privileges from the many to be conferred upon the few who are thus favored.[25]

On the local level, political concerns within the Acadian parishes mirrored the vital interests of the rest of the state. The minutes of the police jury in Lafayette Parish, with its predominately Acadian jurors, indicate an almost total absorption with the regulation of slavery and with building and repairing bridges and roads, clearing the waterways, and other internal improvements--matters more appropriate to the interests of an agri-business community than to a simple, ignorant people satisfied with their lowly status.[26]

The ability of the more pretigious Acadians to continue to ascend socially and politically was dependent upon their ability to maintain close ties with both the Cajun planter minority and with the prosperous Cajun yeoman farmer class. Utilizing these affiliations, enculturated Acadians assumed a position of social and political importances in alliance with the Creole elements with whom their interests coalesced. In the decades between 1810 and 1860 the upper strata of Cajun society continually broadened. At the maximum, however, the elite remained a small percentage of the total Acadian population.

And what, if anything, can be said of the other Acadians, those less prestigious, far more typical ones who constituted the majority? First of all, it is they who gave rise to the Cajun stereotype. The popular nineteenth-century conception, in the Longfellow tradition, pictured the Acadians living in Elysium, their land the "abode of contented and perhaps wise ignorance."[27] The cold eye of reality, however, dissipates the romantic delusion of a pastoral paradise. Joseph Tregle in "Louisiana in the Age of Jackson" presents a more valid view. Their homes were crude, built of posts packed with mud and moss, sometimes, though not always, whitewashed, and surrounded by barns, pigpens and hen houses. The appearance of the people suggested a hard existence.[28] William Darby, who travelled the state between 1811 and 1815, described them as simple and independent, living in rough but solid buildings.[29] They were, as tradition tells, characterized by a legendary *joie de vivre*, with a vigorous cultural tradition preserved from their homeland of Nova Scotia. Francis Parkman described the fundamental orientation of Acadian society before the dispersion, "a phenomenon of a primitive little democracy, hatched under the wing of an absolute monarchy," a social equality so unceremonious that they never addressed anyone as *monsieur*.[30] These equalitarian attitudes were preserved in Louisiana, along with the values inherited from the past which lent security to their lives. Religion, family, and the land remained dominant in their value system, serving as tightly integrating factors in the small communities.[31]

The indifference of the majority of the Acadians to politics created an enormous sense of frustration in those who sought to improve the material condition of their lives. Supreme Court Justice Edward Simon of St. Martin Parish, condemning the failure of the majority of the residents to vote in the 1826 election, remarked, "The inhabitants attend very little to their interests," and lamented, "*Ils sont perdu.*" (They are lost.) He urged their newly elected representative to the state legislature to endeavor to educate them in the political processes and not just to represent them.[32]

The geographical realities of Louisiana in the first decades of the nineteenth century determined, in part, Acadian cultural development. Many Cajuns remained isolated subsistence farmers or fishermen, almost totally removed from contact with the centers of commercial activity. Despite the sophistication of urban New Orleans, Louisiana in this period was still a frontier state. Thomas W. McQueen, travelling to Texas in 1834, was attacked just forty miles west of New Orleans by a band of Indians and died several weeks later of his wounds. He survived long enough to write that, should he recover, he never wanted to be as much as a hundred yards west of the Mississippi.[33] Much of Southwest Louisiana was isolated beyond the almost impenetrable barrier of the Atchafalaya Swamp. A journey through it was unpleasant, even frightening, as the missionary Sister Philippine Duchesne attested when describing her trip from New Orleans to found a convent in the Opelousas district in 1821. "One can have no idea of what this section of the country is like unless one actually sees it, . . ." she wrote, ". . . access to the place is most difficult, there being only one route through swampy woods and number of bayous and pools." She told of a harrowing trip over "black and evil smelling water," through "the most dismal forests."[34]

Within these dismal forests isolated Acadians found economic opportunities which permitted them to sustain a relatively comfortable existence independent of the outside world. The wildlife in the swamp provided an abundant food

Traveller's impression of a nineteenth-century Acadian cottage

supply for swamp dwellers, who augmented their fishing and trapping with farming on the peninsular strips of fertile land along the edges of the waterways and
in the marshes. Further subsistence needs were met by cutting and marketing
swamp cypress and Spanish moss. The swamp became a retreat for those excluded from the more prosperous agricultural economy. It was a world accessible only by boat, however, and generally only by the round-bottomed pirogue
which successfully traversed the shallow waters of the swamp.[35]

The Acadians living in these hinterlands and in the more isolated rural
areas had little part in the emerging cultural pattern loosely termed "American."
They preserved instead their own version of the lives they lived in Nova Scotia.
Inhabiting their remote corner of the world, they clung to their own traditions
scarcely touched by the dominant American cultural mode. Since their lives
were essentially unmarred by the broader social or economic patterns and processes, they developed no higher loyalty than to their own community and in
many cases the ultimate loyalty remained to the family.

But while they were isolated from cultural contact, they were not entirely
removed from outside society. In the penumbra the Acadians mingled with
civilization's outcasts in an unstable mix of Spanish, black, Indian, American,
and perhaps Caribbean elements. Travel accounts yield clues that diverse ethnic
elements lived together in a comparative harmony in the fringe areas of Louisiana. On their journey through the swamp, the intrepid Philippine Duchesne and
her sister-travellers encountered "a canoe filled with Indians, Negroes and

whites, mostly naked except for loincloths, the most frightful looking men, yelling and whistling."[36] But despite the total democracy of the Cajun frontier, where all were economically and socially equal, and where all the evidence attests to cultural and genetic inbreeding, the strength of the Acadian tradition of independence within a tight system of communal integration maintained Cajun ethnic integrity. The Cajun cultural pattern remained dominant and tended to accept outside influences only to absorb them in Cajun folkways.[37]

Present-day Cajuns recognize the ability of their culture to attract the affiliation of others and are contemptuous of those who try to change their fundamental outlook. One proudly unregenerate Cajun expressed the common Cajun attitude when he told journalist Lawrence Wright, in characteristic Cajun English,

> The trouble wit' most Anglo-Saxon people in America is that they want aver'body to t'ink lak' they do. But if only they would come down here, see the way we live, they see our way of life is superior. Lots of people try to change us, but six mont's after they come they're Cajuns too.[38]

The tendency to absorb other ethnic groups into the Cajun way of life was infinitely stronger in the nineteenth century than it is today. One can find, for example, in many areas in the Cajun parishes, families of German descent who have adapted completely to the Cajun culture, speaking only French. Even their names became gallicized.

The Acadians in the outlying areas comprised a distinctive and well-delineated sub-group, clearly differentiated from the acculturated Acadians in the more highly developed areas. Living on the periphery--beyond the pale, as it were--unexposed to the dominant cultural modes of antebellum Louisiana, they nurtured and preserved their culture well into our own day. In this age when ethnic minorities are often termed hyphenated-Americans, the term Acadian-American is a legitimate description, valid at least for those who failed in whole or in part to submit to assimilation into the American mainstream.

The Cajun heritage of equalitarianism remained far stronger among the isolated than among the acculturated Acadians who achieved positions of prestige; indeed, evidence suggests that status was jealously guarded. The research of Dr. T. F. Thurmond of the Heritable Disease Center at Louisiana State University Medical School gives interesting corroboration to the importance of status in the Cajun community. Thurmond and his co-workers noted a startlingly high incidence of recessive genetic disease in heavily Acadian St. Martin Parish. Such high incidence is directly related to genetic inbreeding, and his investigation of the family histories of his clinic patients reveals that the practice of the deliberate family intermarriage was an accepted custom in Acadian communities. He argues that inheritance laws in the early nineteenth century encouraged status- and property-conscious Acadians to seek partners within their own family group as a method of protecting hard-earned gains, employing the concept of "focal consanguinity" to describe the Acadian practice of marrying a relative--generally a first or second cousin--of equal rank and status from the same ethnic group in a nearby community.[39] His work suggests extensive stratification within Cajun society.

An awareness of the extent of class differential and social stratification in the Acadian population resolves the difficulties in the historical evidence. It explains why the Acadians could contribute both capable and articulate politicians to state government and at the same time merit the disgust of an ex-Confederate soldier who exclaimed, "They don't know no more'n a dead alligator."[40] The realization that Cajun society throughout the nineteenth century was infinitely more complex than is generally recognized is the necessary first step to liberation from the simplistic interpretations of the Cajun influence which presently prevail. This means that an examination of the wider influence of the Acadian tradition on Louisiana's development is long past due. As economic and social developments within the state increasingly broadened the upper ranks of the Acadian population, the hardy Acadian cultural pattern inevitably affected the dynamics of change in Louisiana. The Acadian contribution to the growth of Louisiana in the eighteenth century is well understood and properly applauded; the formative role Acadian culture played in molding the emerging character of the young state in the nineteenth century has yet to be defined.

NOTES

1. See, for example, Mathé Allain and Barry Jean Ancelet, "*Feu de Savane*: A Literary Renaissance in French Louisiana," *Southern Exposure*, IX (Summer, 1981), 4-10; William Faulkner Rushton, *The Cajuns: From Acadia to Louisiana* (New York, 1979); Bern Keating, "Cajunland, Louisiana's French Speaking Coast," *National Geographic*, CXXIX (1966), 353-391; Naomi Griffiths, *The Acadians: Creation of a People* (New York, 1973).

2. Félix Voorhies, *Acadian Reminiscences: The True Story of Evangeline* (1907; reprint ed., Lafayette, La., 1977), p. 31.

3. William Henry Perrin, ed., *Southwest Louisiana Biographical and Historical* (New Orleans, 1891), p. 198; Lyle Saxon, *Gumbo Ya-Ya* (New York, 1945), p. 182.

4. Approximately 200 Acadian heads of families, easily distinguished by family surname, are listed in the Attakapas district, equaling 47.8 percent of the total population. The legible entries in the census show 70 Acadian families in Lafourche Parish (25.6 percent of the population) and 96 in Ascension Parish (46.2 percent of the population). Most

of the Acadians in the Attakapas district were settled along Bayous Teche, Carencro and Vermilion. U. S. Bureau of the Census, Third Census of the United States, 1810.

5. Plat maps, nos. 119 to 173 (1840-1865), Southwestern Archives, University of Southwestern Louisiana; Lyle G. Williams, "Some Effects of Acadian Settlement on the Pattern of Land Occupancy in Lafayette Parish," *Attakapas Gazette*, VI (1971), 19-29.

6. Alfred Duperier stated that "the entire Opelousas Country, including Lafayette, was used for grazing purposes." Somewhat confused in his geography, since Lafayette was never part of the Opelousas district, his narrative nonetheless states clearly that the principal industry in the region was grazing large herds of cattle. Alfred Duperier, "A Narrative of Events Connected with the Early Settlement of New Iberia," *New Iberia Enterprise*, March 25 and April 1, 1899. See also Thomas J. Arceneaux, "Vacheries Acadiennes," *Attakapas Gazette*, IV (1969), 75-79; Keith P. Fontenot, "Livestock of Old Southwest Louisiana," *Attakapas Gazette*, VII (1972), 78-92; Lauren C. Post, "The Old Cattle Industry of Southwest Louisiana," *McNeese Review*, IX (1957), 43.

7. Charles Dudley Warner, "The Acadian Land," *Harper's New Monthly Magazine*, LXXIV (1889), 158-160.

8. Merl Reed, "Boom or Bust—Louisiana's Economy During the 1830's," *Louisiana History*, IV (1963), 35-53. Forty percent of the state's population resided in South Louisiana, including the bayou parishes.

9. By 1840, legible entries in the Lafayette Parish census, with still the largest Acadian population, show 481 non-Acadian heads of families of Anglo-American and other, chiefly French, origin. The census lists 385 Acadian heads of families giving the parish 44.5 percent Acadian to 55.5 percent Anglo-American and other population. U. S. Bureau of the Census, Sixth Census of the United States, 1840.

10. Clement Eaton, *The Growth of Southern Civilization, 1790-1860* (New York, 1963), p. 143; Joe Gray Taylor, *Negro Slavery in Louisiana* (Baton Rouge, 1963), p. 79.

11. Police Jury Proceedings, 1824-1870, Lafayette Parish Courthouse, September 14, 1826.

12. *Ibid.*, June 3, 1823.

13. *Ibid.*, June 1823 and June 1824.

14. Kenneth Stampp, *The Peculiar Institution* (New York, 1956), p. 30.

15. United States Bureau of the Census, Slave Schedules of the Seventh Census of the United States, 1850.

16. Joseph Karl Menn, *The Large Slaveholders of Louisiana, 1860* (New Orleans, 1964), p. 260.

17. Louisiana. Lafayette Parish, Notarial Acts, 1853-1855, *passim*.

18. Eaton, *The Growth of Southern Civilization*, p. 128.

19. Perrin, *Southwest Louisiana Biographical and Historical*, p. 71. I have been unable to verify this tradition in any primary materials.

20. *Biographical Dictionary of the American Congress, 1774-1949* (Washington, 1950), p. 1606.

21. Alexandre Mouton Papers, Southwestern Archives, University of Southwestern Louisiana.

22. Joseph G. Tregle, "Political Reinforcement of Ethnic Dominance in Louisiana, 1812-1845," in Lucius F. Ellsworth, ed., *The Americanization of the Gulf Coast, 1803-1850* (Pensacola, Fla., 1972), p. 79. In the 1824 gubernatorial election in Lafayette Parish French candidates Jacques Villeré and Bernard Marigny received respectively 27 and 203 votes, while Anglo-American candidate Henry Johnson received 80. *Louisiana Senate Journal*, First Session, Seventh Legislature, November 17, 1824. In 1828, in St. Martin Parish, Pierre Derbigny received 140 votes, Bernard Marigny 123, and Thomas Butler 5. Isaac Butler to Alexandre Mouton, July 9, 1828, Alexandre Mouton Papers, Southwestern Archives, University of Southwestern Louisiana.   In 1839 in Lafayette Parish, André Roman received 119 votes, Denis Prieur 366, Henry Johnson 0. In St. Martin Parish as well, Johnson failed to draw a single vote, while Roman drew 206 and Prieur 163. *Louisiana Senate Journal*, First Session, Fourteenth Legislature, January 7, 1839.

23. William H. Adams, *The Whig Party of Louisiana* (Lafayette, La., 1973), p. 190.

24. Perry Howard, *Political Tendencies in Louisiana, 1812-1952* (Baton Rouge, 1957), pp. 30, 47.   Unfortunately, no thorough analysis of Acadian voting patterns in the first half of the nineteenth century exists.

25. *Louisiana Senate Journal,* First Session, Sixteenth Legislature, January 30, 1843. Mouton had a high personal regard for Jackson, but his attraction to the Democratic party seems to be based on more than simple admiration for its leaders. He was drawn to Jackson, at least in part, because of the general's defeat of the British in 1815. On the anniversary of the Battle of New Orleans in 1830 he attended a mass where a *Te Deum* was sung in celebration of the victory. "It awoke in me very lively sentiments of gratitude toward the Divine Providence who saved us from the hands of so barbarous and tyrannical an enemy as the British," he wrote to his wife. "Those who defended the state on that occasion from the most unhappy of dangers should be recognized in the country and history for centuries to come." Mouton's anti-British sentiments are those of the true Acadian. Alexandre Mouton to Zelia Mouton, January 8, 1830, Alexandre Mouton Papers, Southwestern Archives, University of Southwestern Louisiana.

26. Minutes of the Police Jury, 1824-1870, Lafayette Parish Courthouse, *passim.*

27. "A Trip to the Attakapas in Olden Times," New Iberia *Louisiana Sugar Bowl,* April 15, 1880, reprinted in the *Attakapas Gazette*, VIII (1973), 21-25; Warner, "The Acadian Land," 334.

28. Joseph G. Tregle, "Louisiana in the Age of Jackson: A Study in Ego-Politics," (Ph. D. dissertation, University of Pennsylvania, 1954).

29. William Darby, *A Geographical Description of the State of Louisiana* (Philadelphia, 1816), p. 61.

30. Francis Parkman, *A Half-Century of Conflict* (Boston, 1892), pp. 360-368.

31. Harlan W. Gilmore, "Family-Capitalism in a Community of Rural Louisiana," *Social Forces*, XV (1936), 72.

32. Judge Edward Simon to Alexandre Mouton, July 6, 1826, Alexandre Mouton Papers, Southwestern Archives, University of Southwestern Louisiana.

33. *Attakapas Gazette and St. Martin, St. Mary and Lafayette Advertiser*, May 10, 1834.

34. Philippine Duchesne to Madeleine Sophie Barat, September 8, 1821, in Louise Callan, *Philippine Duchesne: Frontier Missionary of the Sacred Heart* (Westminster, Md., 1957), pp. 361, 363.

35. Harlan W. Gilmore, "Social Isolation of the French-Speaking People of Rural Louisiana," *Social Forces*, XII (1933), 79-80.

36. Philippine Duchesne to Madeline Sophie Barat, September 8, 1821, in Callan, *Philippine Duchesne*, p. 364.

37. T. Lynn Smith and Vernon J. Parenton, "Acculturation Among the Louisiana French," *American Journal of Sociology*, XLIV (1938).

38. Lawrence Wright, "In Quest of the Unreconstructed Cajun," *Southern Voices*, I (1974), 34.

39. Dr. T. F. Thurmond, interview July 17, 1974; Theodore F. Thurmond and Ellen B. DeFraites, "Genetical Studies of the French Acadians of Louisiana," (Unpublished report, The Heritable Disease Center, Louisiana State University School of Medicine, 1974). Dr. Thurmond's studies show a high degree of deliberate family intermarriage in the Acadian population in the 1820s in St. Martin, Lafourche, and Terrebonne parishes. Recessive genetic disease is found in remarkably high incidence in these parishes. As examples: the Acadiana area supplies one-third of the state's population but between two-thirds and three-fourths of the total cases in Louisiana of phenylketonuria (PKU), the state total is ten times higher than any other state per capita. There is also a very high incidence of cystic fibrosis. Ehler's Danlos syndrome, a rare skin condition, occurs at a rate of about one case in 500,000 in the general population. Dr. Thurmond has isolated six cases in Acadiana, where the total population does not exceed 469,000. Twenty cases of Hunter's Syndrome, with a similar incidence in the general population, have been found. One Acadian family has the largest number of cases of premature aging in the entire world.

40. Warner, "The Acadian Land," 160.

LOUISIANA'S ACADIANS:
THE ENVIRONMENTAL IMPACT

by Malcolm Comeaux

The environment in which a people live can greatly influence them. It cannot determine how they live, but it will offer certain opportunities which can be either accepted or rejected. It does present some limitations on any life style.[1] This is certainly true in the case of the Acadians in Canada and later in Louisiana.

As compared with Louisiana, the environment of Canada is cold and harsh, but Acadians adjusted to the Canadian environment quickly, for it is not too different from that of northwestern France. There were, moreover, few fundamental changes in the mode of living. Louisiana, on the other hand, has a hot, humid, subtropical environment. Thus, much of the Acadian experience in Acadia was useless in Louisiana. Nevertheless, they entered an alien environment which resulted in many adjustments in their culture. They had to learn to grow new crops, eat new foods, cope with new diseases and insects, build new types of houses, and so forth. The resulting cultural change was so complete as to establish a new culture, the "Cajun," which, within the second generation after the Acadians' arrival, was different from that held by their cousins who remained in Canada.

There are four distinct environments in South Louisiana, and through time Cajuns learned to inhabit and exploit each. These environments are: 1) the levee lands, as along the Mississippi River and Bayous Lafourche and Teche, 2) the prairie of Southwest Louisiana, 3) the swamps, as in the Lafourche and Atchafalaya basins, and 4) the marsh along the coast. Cajuns have exhibited different life styles and occupations in each, and in the process four unique Cajun subcultures have developed.

The Canadian Experience

The French began their active interest in Acadia in the early seventeenth century. They were particularly attracted to the furs and fish produced in that area; but, by the mid-1600s, there was a resident population in Acadia which was sedentary and agricultural and from which a large proportion of the Acadians have descended.

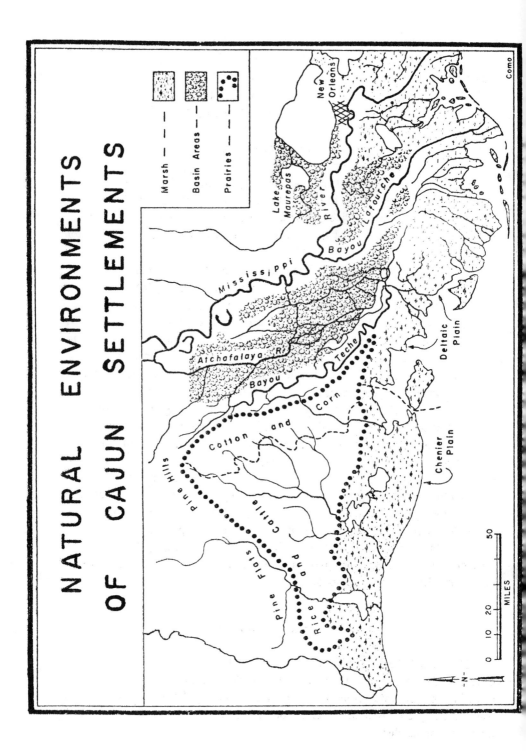

NATURAL ENVIRONMENTS OF CAJUN SETTLEMENTS

Marsh ---
Basin Areas ---
Prairies ---

New Orleans
Lake Maurepas
Bayou River
Lafourche
Mississippi
Atchafalaya R.
Teche
Bayou
Deltaic Plain
Corn
Cotton and
Pine Hills
Cattle and
Chenier Plain
Rice
Pine Flats

Como

MILES
0 10 20   50

N

Most Acadians in Canada were agriculturists.[2]   Almost all of their farms were on marshlands protected from flooding by extensive dykes. The building of dykes in Europe was developed in the Low Countries, and the idea spread to northwest France where settlers going to Acadia either learned it or saw enough of it to understand it. The major crops grown on these fertile marshland soils were fodder crops and grains, with wheat exceeding the combined acreages of oats, rye, and barley.[3]   Flax and hemp were grown for home use. The Acadians also had many garden crops, such as cabbages and beans. The uplands surrounding the marshes had poor soils, and about the only use of this land was for apple orchards. Livestock were also important in the economy of the Acadians, particularly cattle. These animals provided meat, milk, butter, and hides, and were the major draft animals. Also important were swine and sheep, along with some poultry and horses.

Occupations other than farming were also practiced by the Acadians. Fishing for home consumption provided an important source of food, fish being taken mostly in streams during the spring spawning runs. Many of the Acadians were also employed as extra hands aboard New England or French vessels fishing the Grand Banks. The gathering of forest products was yet another important occupation. The Acadians were very dependent on wood for fuel, building material, tools, and the like, and some wood was gathered for export. Although furs were a valuable export of Acadia, most of the Acadians were farmers who left the trapping to the Indians or to a few Frenchmen who lived among them, and Acadians acted only as middlemen in this trade.

The Acadians had thus become well adapted to this harsh environment. They were basically intensive agriculturists farming small areas of drained marshland, and using the surrounding woodlands for orchards, forest products, and some grazing. These people were certainly not completely self-sufficient, and needed to trade for iron goods and luxury items. To pay for these imports, Acadians sold farm goods, such as grain and livestock, and forest products, or they earned wages on fishing vessels.

The expulsion of the Acadians from Nova Scotia (the *Grand Derangement*) occurred in 1755, and they were to be wandering exiles for at least ten years before arriving in Louisiana. Those who made their way to Louisiana found a completely alien environment.

Levee Land Environment

The levee land of South Louisiana is the land along the major rivers and bayous, particularly along the Mississippi River and Bayous Teche and Lafourche (Figure 1). These lands, considered well elevated by South Louisiana standards, and very rich, were built by the rivers as they overflowed their banks. The coarser material settled out first and formed the highest, best drained, and richest land, while the finer sediments settled out farther back from the stream, near the swamp, and formed heavy clay-like soils that were poorly drained, hard to work, and susceptible to flooding.

When the Acadians began arriving in Louisiana in 1765 with little more than the clothes they wore and a determination to survive as a culture, they settled this levee land along the Mississippi River above the "German Coast," and along the upper portions of Bayou Lafourche. Some Acadians also settled to the west, along the natural levee of Bayou Teche, in the area of the present-day town of St. Martinville. Land for these farmers was subdivided into long, narrow strips, usually 40 arpents deep and 5 wide. The early Acadians invariably settled on the high, easily worked lands near the river and avoided the heavy soils to the rear.

THE LEVEE-LAND ENVIRONMENT

Note how the houses face the bayou and are on the highest land. To the rear of the houses the terrain slowly lowers, and the swamp begins at the tree line seen to the right rear.

This was a completely new environment, however, and they must have experienced a difficult period of adjustment. None of the crops grown in

Canada would grow in Louisiana, and this brought about many changes in their life style. For example, apple trees will not produce in South Louisiana, so the Acadians could no longer make hard cider and had to accept another "national" drink, beer.

The Acadians also began to accept new house styles. The homes they occupied in Canada were designed to withstand extreme cold, not Louisiana's wet, sub-tropical climate. The house design which they accepted has a very complex origin, but was certainly in Louisiana long before their arrival, and it is usually called a "Creole" house.[4] This house was made of heavy timber construction with mud-and-moss nogging between the posts. Other basic features were a wide porch across the front of the house, raised above the ground on pilings, and a steep roof extending over the porch. This home, with modifications, is now considered the traditional "Cajun" house.

The Acadians in Louisiana initially became small independent farmers (*petits habitants*) producing enough for subsistence and very little for export. The major subsistence crops were rice and corn, and their major cash crop was cotton. Vegetables were also grown, but they learned to grow many new ones, such as okra, an African crop. Cattle were also important and provided most of the protein in the diet. The Acadians probably did very little experimenting with crops, but were told what to grow, and how, by government officials or by the already experienced Germans living along the German Coast a few miles below the Acadian settlements. Things went along very smoothly until the Louisiana Purchase in 1803.

Soon after the Louisiana Purchase the second major migration of the Acadians began. This one, unlike the first, was to go largely undocumented and would result from many wealthy Americans moving onto the levee lands, thereby displacing Acadians. Areas once densely settled by white yeoman farmers were soon transformed into plantations occupied by a few wealthy *Americains* with many black slaves. This displacement process was particularly swift along the Mississippi and Bayou Lafourche. In 1802, for example, the major crop along Bayou Lafourche was cotton, but by 1828 a plantation economy based on sugarcane was dominant in most of the area.[5] Of course, not all Acadians fled before the surging plantation system. Some remained to become wage laborers.[6] A few remained as yeoman farmers. As late as 1873 a traveller found a thickly settled community of small farmers two miles above Bayou Lafourche along the Mississippi, but along Bayou Lafourche there was only a continuation of the "tier of magnificent plantations."[7] Seventy years earlier the traveller would have found the area inhabited only by small independent farmers.

The Americans coming into Louisiana first settled the poorer unoccupied back lands, but soon began buying the better lands owned by Acadians. There are several reasons for the French-speakers selling to the Americans. First, they could not afford to build or maintain the levees and roads along the rivers as required by law for all front holders. Second, they feared debt, and once in debt would sell their land.[8] Third, these poor independent farmers were considered a bad influence on the slaves, as slaves could see them leading an easy life as small independent landholders. Planters thus often bought the land just to force the Acadians to move away.[9] And fourth, this front land was quite desirable for agriculture, and so brought a good price. The displacement of these people, as early as 1814, is reflected in a contemporary statement: "Lands have risen here in price, since they have grown in demand for sugar plantations, and many of the *petits habitants* bought out."[10] The displaced Cajuns either moved west to the Teche and prairie country or retreated to some little ridge of high land in the nearby swamp. In 1881, a writer described the resulting situation.

> In the rear of the plantations . . . are found dry bayous having high lands on each banks [sic]: these ridges are mostly occupied by small proprietors, who cultivate cane, corn, cotton, and rice, and such other crops as contribute to the comfort of their homes and the support of their families.[11]

Several early authors mention the migration by Cajuns away from the good lands along Bayou Lafourche and the Mississippi River. One of the better descriptions of this migration is given by W. H. Sparks:

> At irregular distances between these Acadian settlements, large sugar plantations are found. These have been extending for years, and increasing, absorbing the habitats of these primitive and innocent people, who retire to some little ridge of land deeper in the swamp, a few inches higher than the plane of the swamp, where they surround their little mud-houses with an acre or so of open land, from the products of which, and the trophies of the gun and fishing line and hook, and an occasional frog, and the abundance of crawfish, they continue to eke out a miserable livelihood. . . .[12]

There was probably much resentment toward these wealthy English-speakers, for it was the second time Acadians had been displaced by them. They seemed to have been cowed by the aggressive Americans who, in the eyes of the Cajun, always appeared to have the law on their side. This reaction is understandable, when one considers that most Cajuns had a very narrow experience, no understanding of the political situation, a limited education, and probably considered themselves as second-class citizens in this ever-changing English-speaking country. The Cajuns who fled attempted to maintain the old culture by establishing a social barrier and physical distance between themselves and the aggressive Anglo-Americans. Those who remained apparently could not maintain their cultural traits and were soon swallowed up in the American life style.

As one writer commented in 1880, those who remained were "rapidly becoming Americanized."[13]   Thus a viable Cajun culture was largely submerged in the area along the Mississippi River and Bayou Lafourche, but it did survive hidden and tucked away in the backswamp on many small ridges of land. Here, Cajuns maintained their culture and continued to eke out a livelihood as subsistence farmers. Some were still living this way, almost untouched by modern civilization, as late as 1937.[14]

It was almost the same situation along Bayou Teche, only it took longer to develop because it was farther removed from the mainstream of nineteenth-century life along the Mississippi. As an Anglo population moved in, however, prices for land increased dramatically along the Teche by the 1840s, and remained high until the Civil War. Some Cajuns sold their land and moved westward to the prairies, while others remained as small farmers producing small quantities of cane as their cash crop. A few persons of Gallic origin in the area entered the plantation economy and became wealthy. Most of these, however, were not Cajuns, but a more affluent group which migrated from France. A strong French culture thus survives, particularly around St. Martinville, with much of the leadership coming from these latter-day arrivals. The lower Teche was not considered Cajun country in the early 1800s. The area (St. Mary Parish) was initially settled by Anglo-Americans interested in establishing a plantation economy. They have dominated the area into the twentieth century, though many Cajuns have since migrated into the region.

The Swamp Environment

A second major environment exploited by Cajuns is the swamp.[15]   There are three extensive swamps in South Louisiana, the Atchafalaya Swamp, the Lafourche Basin, and the area around Lake Maurepas. These swamps are quite different in that only the Atchafalaya receives a large annual flood due to its connections with the Mississippi River. The Atchafalaya Swamp is thus much more productive of wildlife, and in this environment a true "Cajun swamp culture" evolved.

The first Cajuns to live in the swamp were those who migrated to small ridges of land called *brulés* that are really old natural levees. These are found particularly on the eastern side of the Atchafalaya Swamp. Cajuns attempted to live there as they had on the high natural levees of the Mississippi and Bayou Lafourche.[16]   Most of the swampland, however, had been surveyed in the American township system.[17]   Cajuns, ignorant of laws which might give them title to the land, such as homesteading laws, had no money to buy the land, and just about all became squatters. Most of this land is today owned by large lumber companies, and many Cajuns lease the land on which they live.

There was a slow cultural change throughout the 1800s as Cajun agriculturists became swamp dwellers. Most were eventually forced to accept the
swamper's way of life because of the increasing severity of floods throughout the
mid-1800s.[18] This changing life style brought many changes to the lives of
these people. Agricultural crops, even gardens, were abandoned. The traditional
home could not withstand the flooding, so the owners gave up building this
type of house and constructed only crude structures. In the late 1800s, the
houseboat was introduced from the upper Mississippi River system, and many
Cajun swamp dwellers began to build these and live on them. There next occurred a dispersal of these farmers turned fishermen as they moved throughout the
swamp to be near their fishing grounds. The houseboat allowed them to live
anywhere. Now, Cajuns had to learn fishing techniques all over again. The
Canadian experience served them little as it was three to four generations earlier
and in a different environment. Actually, all of the major fishing techniques
and fishing boats used by Cajuns were introduced into the Atchafalaya Swamp
by commercial fishermen drifting into the area from the upper Mississippi River
system.

THE SWAMP ENVIRONMENT

A typical swamp scene during the spring flood. At other times of
the year, as in late summer, this could be dry land.

These swamp dwellers soon began selling products of the swamp in surrounding communities. The sale of game, particularly ducks, began first in the
area around New Orleans.[19] Large-scale movement of swamp goods started in
1873 when boats began going into the Atchafalaya Swamp to buy fish.[20] This
era also marked the beginning of the modern period of commercial exploitation, and ever afterwards the swamp dwellers were to be a part of the national
economy and dependent upon it. Swamp dwellers thus began selling fish, but
eventually other swamp products moved to the market, such as frogs, crayfish,
Spanish moss, turtles, crabs, and the like. With the money thus earned, they
bought vegetables, fish hooks, twine, cloth, iron goods, and other necessities
and luxuries.

These Cajuns had thus changed from farmers who once cursed floods to
fishermen who welcomed them. The floods increased the fish supply and only
caused minor inconvenience to houseboat dwellers. Although this way of life
was quite similar to fishing cultures throughout the Mississippi River system,
Cajuns exhibited a different culture from Anglo fishermen further north in
that they were French-speaking, Catholic, and exploited the environment
much more fully, for example, by gathering Spanish moss and eating frogs and
crayfish.

The U. S. Corps of Engineers has recently brought many changes to this
physical environment, as levees have been built and the floods confined to a
narrow "floodway." This activity has brought many changes to the people and
their culture. Today most swamp dwellers live outside the floodway in small
communities, and commute to their fishing grounds in boats with outboard
motors. They are still, however, a unique Cajun sub-culture, with a store of
knowledge and techniques very different from the levee farmer.

The Prairie Environment

The prairie of Southwest Louisiana was an open, relatively flat area when
the Acadians first arrived. It was not one unbroken grassy area, but many
grassland areas separated by strips of woods which skirted the bayous of the
region. Each of these open areas, called a prairie or cove, had a name, but together they formed one distinct region.

Early Spanish and French administrators divided the prairie region into
two districts and named them after the local Indians: Opelousas to the north,
above Bayou Carencro; and the Attakapas to the south. The administrative
centers for these were Poste des Attakapas (St. Martinville) and Poste des Opel-
lousas (Opelousas). It was from these two centers that expansion onto the
prairies would originate.

When the Cajuns settled the prairie they tried to maintain their culture unchanged, but the environment was different, and inevitably change occurred.[21] The settler began to survey the land as they always had, in long narrow strips that fronted on a river.[22] Soon all of the land along the streams was taken, and the open land went unclaimed. The Cajuns thus lived around the prairies and near the woods. They lived near the forest because of the availability of wood and water, both scarce on the open prairie. As Cajuns moved onto the prairie, however, they planted groves of trees, such as catalpa or chinaberry, for use as firewood or fenceposts. Water for livestock came from small circular ponds (*platins*) that were once very common. It is generally believed that these ponds were made by cattle as they tended to stand in puddles and track out a considerable amount of mud each time they left.[23] Drinking water came from small wells dug with an augur, about 20 feet deep, lined with wooden casings. On the prairie the Cajuns built the typical Cajun house. Such a house was well adapted to the prairie; thousands were built, and many still survive. One interesting aspect of house building was that houses were often built along the edge of the forest where cypress and Spanish moss were available, and then they were hauled to where they were to be used.

The prairie can be divided into two cultural zones, the corn-and-cotton section and the rice-and-cattle section.[24] The corn-and-cotton country was to the east, on the richest and most productive lands of the prairie. A farmer had about 40 percent of his land in cotton and 40 percent in corn, and the two were rotated the following year. The other 20 percent was used for pasturage, a garden, and for farm buildings and animal pens. Sweet potatoes were another important crop, particularly on the northern edge of the prairie. These potatoes were usually stored in a small hill (*butte*) in the yard and covered with straw and dirt. The garden crops were okra, melons, beans, and the like. Cattle and mules were important: the cattle for their meat, hides, milk and butter, and the mules as draft animals. This was an area of small, mostly subsistence farmers (many farms about 40 acres), who either owned their land or were sharecroppers. This was a densely settled area, and Cajun culture was dominant.

The situation in the rice-and-cattle country to the west was quite different. The soils there were not so rich, and a hard claypan lay beneath the topsoil. The area was only thinly settled by Cajuns, who lived scattered along the edges of the woods, raising cattle and planting small gardens. Most of the area was largely uninhabited, but in the 1880s there occurred a great flood of immigration. Most of the immigrants were Midwesterners who had been induced by the railroad to settle the prairies and grow rice as they had once grown wheat. This immigration resulted in still another displacement of Cajuns. Some traded rice-producing land on the prairie for cotton-and-corn land to the east, while others simply became landless.[25]

THE PRAIRIE ENVIRONMENT

This was open, flat grassland environment when the Cajuns arrived, and the trees were found only along the stream courses. In this picture, a pump house for irrigating rice is in the foreground, and rice fields extend toward the horizon.

The first Acadian occupation on the prairie was cattle raising, but Cajuns were not the first cattle raisers there. Indians had horses and were selling them as early as 1733, having acquired these animals from Mexico by way of Texas.[26] The first cattle were rangy beasts related to the longhorn and were also from Mexico.[27] By 1769, just a few years after the first Acadians arrived, there were nearly 4,000 head of cattle on the prairie.[28] At the time, the Spanish government considered the cattle industry important and required stock fencing and branding. A grantee of land had to have at least 100 head of cattle.[29] Cajun ranching techniques on the prairie were thus greatly influenced by the Spanish, whether from Mexico or from New Orleans.[30]

Prairie Cajuns became cattlemen living on the grants of land along the woods and grazing large herds on the unowned prairie. There was annual branding and sorting of cattle to be sold, and sales were made to plantation owners along the levee lands or in New Orleans. In the earliest days animals were waled to market, but later many were taken by steamboats when that mode of transportation finally came to the edge of the prairie. Large herds, for example, were shipped by steamboat from Washington. The development of rice farming greatly changed the cattle industry, for cattle could no longer be raised "at large." Today, cattle are still important in the rice country, and rice land is usually rotated with pasturage every second or third year. With fencing there occurred controlled breeding, and the quality of stock improved greatly.

The growing of rice is an old tradition in Louisiana. It was grown by subsistence farmers along the levee lands as early as 1719.[31] It was planted in the backswamp and given little attention. On the prairie, it was called "providence" rice as its success depended upon watering by Providence. Early settlers on the prairie planted this rice in *coulees* and ponds, and if it produced a crop, it was cut, threshed and hulled with primitive tools. The late nineteenth century, however, saw a revolution in rice production. The Midwesterners turned it into a highly mechanized operation, using pumps, harvesters, threshers, gangplows, and the like. Except for the fact that farmers were growing rice, it was literally an extension of the wheat belt into South Louisiana. Cajuns were soon raising rice, and it became, and still is, an important part of their diet.

Two Cajun life styles evolved on the prairie. To the east was a densely settled area of *petits habitants* that was definitely Cajun. These small largely self-sufficient farmers grew cotton as a cash crop and corn for themselves and their animals. In many ways their life resembled that found on isolated *brulés* in the swamp, except there was less hunting and more of a dependence on livestock. On the western end of the prairie a different life style developed. There Cajuns maintained large herds of cattle, and had little agriculture except for gardens. In time, however, this area developed into a very open environment, producing rice and cattle, with much of the land owned by Anglo-Americans. This entire prairie, however, was strongly Cajun in character, and many of the early Anglo immigrants were absorbed into Cajun culture. It was in this region that Cajun culture was strongest and where many of the folk ideas, such as music, have survived the longest.

The Marsh Environment

The marsh is the last major environment settled and exploited by Louisiana Cajuns. This region is flat, under water most of the year, and the natural vegetation is grass. This coastal marsh is usually divided into two physical regions, the Deltaic Plain to the east and the Chenier Plain to the west. The Deltaic Plain is made up of many small ridges of land, old natural levees, following streams that were once distributaries of the Mississippi River. These ribbons of high land extend in a north-south direction to the Gulf of Mexico, so offer to residents living on them an easy access to the Gulf and to the levee lands to the north. Much of the marsh in the Deltaic Plain is not firm, and is therefore called the "floating marsh" (*flotant*), and generally will not support cattle; whereas the marsh in the Chenier Plain is firm and does support cattle.[32] The Chenier Plain also has some high land. These are small sandy ridges called *cheniers* because of the oaks growing on them. They were former beaches, but are not isolated in the marsh. These ridges, in contrast to those in the Deltaic Plain, run east-west, and the only ease access to the Gulf or to land to the north is by water where major streams, the Calcasieu and Mermentau, cut the ridges. As might be expected, two Cajun life styles developed in these contrasting environments.

Occupation of the Chenier Plain came late. Cajuns first avoided this area because the sandy ridges were small and isolated, and the mosquitos were attrocious. Exploitation of this environment began when cattlemen on the prairie began to use the marsh for winter grazing. By the 1880s there were ranchers permanently living on *cheniers*. Many were Cajuns, but Texans had also expanded into this region. Eventually cattle ranching, hunting, and trapping all developed as important occupations, but settlement remained sparse in this area.

Many cultural traits, such as food, language, and religion, survived in this marsh. One aspect of the culture which did not survive was the Cajun house. Instead, sawed lumber was barged to the ridges, and large frame houses were built. Cattle ranching meanwhile did not change, and many aspects of this industry survive exactly as they were on the prairies in the 1850s. For example, very poor quality cattle are raised, and very little attention given to them, even when they are dying during a hard winter. A writer in the early 1800s mentions this.[33] Later, in 1877, the Abbeville newspaper stated: "Cattle are commencing to perish from the inclemency of the weather and lack of forage, and if the winter continues as severe as it is now, the grim skeletons which will dot the surface of the prairies by spring will be legion."[34] The same condition existed in the marshes in 1973 when cattle died by the hundreds and ranchers did nothing. Urban dwellers were aghast, but it was simply an old Cajun custom.[35]

Occupation of the Deltaic Plain came early in comparison to the Chenier Plain. Cajuns began moving here, as they did also to the *brulés* in the swamp, soon after displacement from the better levee lands in the early 1800s. These people continued as subsistence farmers, growing the traditional crops. Hunting also became important very early, especially in those areas nearest New Orleans, where game could be sold. Since the bayous gave access to the Gulf and many inland bays and inlets, fishing and shellfishing also became important. Trapping also evolved into a major occupation.

THE MARSH ENVIRONMENT

These cattle are seen standing on a *chenier* covered with oaks (for
which they were named). To the rear the marsh extends outward to
a line of trees that mark the presence of another chenier.

Two life styles therefore developed among Cajuns in the Louisiana marsh.
Trapping is found in both marshes, but there the similarity ends. Fishing was
very important in the Deltaic Plain, whereas the Chenier Plain has only one fishing village, Cameron. Farming and gardening are still important in the eastern
marsh, whereas in the west, cattle raising remains a significant industry. Population on the ridges in the Deltaic Plain is fairly dense, probably because of
rich soil and access to market, and folk houses still remain, both of which are
untrue for the Chenier Plain.

Conclusions

Cajuns have inhabited four environments, and, as a result, have exhibited
four distinct life styles. There are many differences between these four Cajun
sub-cultures. Think of the different technical skills and knowledge a person
from the western prairie would have to learn if he were to become a fisherman in

the Atchafalaya Swamp, a shrimper, oysterman or trapper in the Deltaic Plain, or a *petit habitant* on the levee land. Exploitation of each of these environments requires specialized knowledge and skills that have taken years for the local inhabitants to acquire. There is little mixing or communication among peoples in different environments, and each group has developed independently. This writer has spoken to several farmers whose agricultural land abuts a swamp, but those farmers have never really gone into the swamp, an environment too alien for a farmer.

The Acadians were a conservative group and suffered much in Canada because they would not change. Upon their arrival in Louisiana they were still conservative and tried not to change, and in some ways they have been successful. They have maintained their religion. Their language was retained, though many words of English, Spanish, and African origin were added, and their music has been retained, though it too has evolved in Louisiana. Many other aspects of the culture, however, changed dramatically, such as cuisine, agriculture, housing, and the general methods and techniques of exploiting Louisiana environments. Within two generations the Acadians in Louisiana had become Cajuns, and exhibited a culture different from that of the Acadian area of Canada.

The degree of isolation seems to have been the determining factor in the success or failure of Cajuns in Louisiana at least until the twentieth century. Because of the good land and the availability of transportation along the levee lands, the area was desirable for plantations, and was soon acquired by aggressive Anglo-Americans. The Cajuns, at the time a downtrodden people experiencing culture shock, seemed to have no pride in themselves, their heritage, or their ability to compete, and considered the best defense a retreat.[36] Once isolated, however, as on *brulés* in the swamp, or on the prairie, Cajuns proved to be a very resilient and adaptable people, with a real determination to survive. They must be admired for their ability to inhabit and exploit sucessfully so many environments, and for their ability to retain so many aspects of their culture.

The four environments, marsh, swamp, prairie and levee land, still influence the lives of Cajuns as they have for 200 years. Many Cajuns still follow traditional occupations as firshermen, farmers, or cattlemen. With the twentieth century, however, this close relationship between the Cajun and his environment is changing. Most Cajuns are now educated and employed in industry, particularly the oil industry, and have accepted many modern American values. But as long as our American culture survives, many aspects of Cajun culture will remain, such as religion, cuisine, strong family ties, survey system, and so forth. Though Americanized, the Cajuns will remain a distinct group.

NOTES

1. This study of the relationship between man and his environment is an old theme in geography. Many American geographers in the early part of the twentieth century were unfortunately "environmental determinists," and believed that the environment determined the actions of a group. As an alternative, French geographers proposed the idea of "possibilism," the concept that the environment presents opportunities that a cultural group can accept or reject. For the most recent comment on this see Vincent Berdoulay, "French Possibilism ·as a Form of Neo-Kantian Philosophy," *Proceedings, Association of American Geographers*, VII (1976), 176-179.

2. The best study of the Acadian and his relationship to the environment is by Andrew H. Clark, *Acadia: The Geography of Early Nova Scotia to 1760* (Madison, Wis., 1968).

3. *Ibid.*, p. 242.

4. Much has been written on the Creole house. Examples are Jay Edwards, "Cultural Syncretism in the Louisiana Creole Cottage," (Unpublished manuscript, Louisiana State University, 1976); Fred B. Kniffen, "Louisiana House Types," *Annals, Association of American Geographers*, XXVI (1936), 179-193; William Knipmeyer, "Settlement Succession in Eastern French Louisiana," (Ph. D. dissertation, Louisiana State University, 1956); Milton B. Newton, Jr., "Louisiana House Types: A Field Guide," *Melanges*. No. 2 (Baton Rouge, 1971); Yvonne Phillips, "The Bousillage House," *Louisiana Studies*, III (1964), 155-158; and R. Warren Robison, "Louisiana Acadian Domestic Architecture," in Steven Del Sesto and Jon Gibson, eds., *The Culture of Acadiana: Tradition and Change in South Louisiana* (Lafayette, La., 1975), pp. 63-77.

5. Pierre-Louis Berquin-Duvallon, *Travels in Louisiana and the Floridas in the Year 1802*, trans. by John Davis (New York, 1806), p. 171; and J. Carlyle Sitterson, *Sugar Country: The Sugar Cane Industry in the South* (Lexington, Ky., 1953), p. 47.

6. In a detailed listing of inhabitants along the Mississippi and Lafourche, many persons with French surnames were listed, but they were not farmers, so we must assume that they were laborers; Adolph Henry and Victor Gerodies, *The Louisiana Coast Directory, of the Right and Left Banks of the Mississippi . . .* (New Orleans, 1857).

7. Samuel H. Lockett, *Louisiana As It Is: A Geographical and Topographical Description of the State*, ed. Lauren C. Post (Baton Rouge, 1969), p. 111.

8. For examples of this see W. H. Sparks, *The Memories of Fifty Years* (Philadelphia, 1882), p. 377; and Frederick Law Olmsted, *The Cotton Kingdom*, 2 vols. (New York, 1861), II, 46.

9. A good example of this is given by Frederick Law Olmsted, *A Journey in the Seaboard Slave States* (New York, 1856), pp. 673-674.

10. H. M. Brackenridge, *Views of Louisiana* (Pittsburg, 1814), p. 173.

11. William Herbert Harris, *Louisiana Products, Resources and Attractions, With a Sketch of the Parishes* (New Orleans, 1881), p. 105.

12. Sparks, *The Memories of Fifty Years*, p. 379. Another good account is given by Charles Lyell, *A Second Visit to the United States of America*, 2 vols. (New York, 1849), II, 123.

13. Anonymous, "The Acadians of Louisiana," *Scribner's Monthly*, XIX (January, 1880), 383.

14. Herman Joseph Jacobi, *The Catholic Family in Rural Louisiana* (Washington, D. C., 1937).

15. For the best study of life in a swamp, see Malcolm L. Comeaux, *Atchafalaya Swamp Life: Settlement and Folk Occupations* (Baton Rouge, 1972).

16. As an example, the Labadie Brulé in 1857 had 46 individuals growing cotton for a living, and all but two or three had French surnames. Henry and Gerodies, *The Louisiana Coast Directory*, pp. 41, 43.

17. The American government did survey some land in the French system of "long lots." This was the only time the American government ever deviated from the American township system once it had been accepted.

18. These floods were caused by the removal of a large raft on the upper Atchafalaya River; see Malcolm L. Comeaux, "The Atchafalaya River Raft," *Louisiana Studies*, IX (1970), 217-227.

19. Anonymous, "The Acadians of Louisiana," 391.

20. Barton Warren Evermann, "Report on the Investigations by the United States Fish Commission in Mississippi, Louisiana and Texas in 1897," *U. S. Commission on Fish and Fisheries, Report of the Commissioner for 1898* (Washington, D. C., 1899), Part 24, p. 299; C. H. Townsend, "Statistics of the Fisheries of the Gulf States," *U. S. Commission on Fish and Fisheries, Report of the Commissioner* (Washington, D. C., 1900), Part 25, p. 159.

21. The best works on man-land relationships in the prairie are Lauren C. Post, "Cultural Geography of the Prairies of Southwest Louisiana," (Ph. D. dissertation, University of California, Berkeley, 1936); and James W. Taylor, "The Agricultural Settlement Succession in the Prairies of Southwest Louisiana," (Ph. D. dissertation, Louisiana State University, 1956).

22. Much of the surveying was done during the Spanish period, but they continued the French system. There were some very large Spanish land grants for cattle raising, but most of the open prairie was surveyed according to the American rectangular survey system. The best study of surveying in Louisiana is John Whitling Hall, "Louisiana Survey Systems: Their Antecedents, Distribution and Character," (Ph. D. dissertation, Louisiana State University, 1970).

23. See, for example, Lauren C. Post, *Cajun Sketches* (Baton Rouge, 1962), pp. 22-23. Recent research indicates they were formed for other reasons, see Warren E. Landry, "The Distribution of Platins: Circular Depressions on the Prairie of Southwest Louisiana," (MA thesis, University of Southwestern Louisiana, 1973).

24. Post, *Cajun Sketches*, pp. 70-82, with end maps.

25. According to Post, the Cajuns considered themselves as getting the better deal. Post, "Cultural Geography," 191. A good, though very unsympathetic view of the dis-

placed Cajuns on the prairie was given by the Franklin *Planters' Banner*, September 23, 1847.

26. Dunbar Rowland and A. G. Sanders, trans. and eds., *Mississippi Provincial Archives, 1729-1743*, 3 vols. (Jackson, 1927), I, 204.

27. Post, *Cajun Sketches*, pp. 39-42.

28. David Bjork, ed., "Documents Relating to Alejandro O'Reilly," *Louisiana Historical Quarterly*, VII (1924), 35, 38.

29. Benjamin F. French, ed., *Historical Collections of Louisiana*, 5 vols. (New York, 1876), V, 290.

30. Fred B. Kniffen, "Material Culture in the Geographic Interpretation of the Landscape," in Miles Richardson, ed., *The Human Mirror* (Baton Rouge, 1974), pp. 258-280.

31. Chan Lee, "A Cultural History of Rice with Special Reference to Louisiana," (Ph. D. dissertation, Louisiana State University, 1960). This is by far the best overall study of the history of rice in Louisiana.

32. Richard Joel Russell, "Flotant," *Geographical Review*, XXXII (1942), 74-98; Richard Joel Russell and H. V. Howe, "Cheniers of Southwest Louisiana," *Geographical Review*, XXV (1935), 449-481.

33. C. C. Robin, *Voyages dans l'intérieur de la Louisiane, de la Floride occidentale, et dans les isles de la Martinique et de Saint-Domingue, pendant les années 1802, 1803, 1804, 1805, et 1806*, 3 vols. (Paris, 1807), III, 29-30.

34. Abbeville *Vermilion Banner*, January 13, 1877. See also Philip C. Tucker, "Le Loup Blanc of Bolivar's Peninsula," in J. Frank Dobie, ed., *Follow de Drinkin Gou'd*, Texas Folklore Society Series, No. 7 (Austin, 1928), pp. 62-68.

35. George Fawcett, "Cattle Said Starving to Death," Lafayette *Sunday Advertiser*, June 3, 1973.

36. It is very distressing for a modern Cajun to read accounts of his ancestors in the nineteenth century. Very few of these accounts are complimentary, and most characterize the Cajuns as lazy, sickly, backward, and extremely poor. Most of these accounts were written by Anglos, but they report the situtation as they saw it. The picture they paint is not a pretty one, but given the conditions as presented in this paper, the attitude and the plight of the Cajuns are understandable.

THE ACADIAN FAITH ODYSSEY:
IMPRESSIONS OF AN ACADIAN PARISH PRIEST

by Alexander O. Sigur

Europe in the sixteenth century was a continent in ferment, and France was not spared. Nations and kings had shared the bond of Catholicism for centuries, but now the Protestant Reformation created divisions and religious tensions which affected every segment of society from courtiers to fishermen, both of whom would play a role in the founding of Acadia.

Fishermen were particularly prominent in the period of initial European contact with the region which would become Acadia. Fishing expeditions across the Atlantic were numerous at a time when, with 150 days of abstinence a year, fish was in great demand for European tables. Sailors from Brittany, Normandy, and the La Rochelle area developed French commerce and enriched the royal treasury, but exploration and missions were slow in coming. Explorations were undertaken by more visionary citizens and business entrepreneurs rather than by royal initiative. Missionaries are scarcely mentioned in the records until efforts were made to colonize the New World. But as soon as colonization was begun, missionaries accompanied the settlers.

In the earliest effort to colonize Acadia (1604), Pierre de Monts, a Huguenot, brought along a Protestant minister and a Catholic priest. In 1607, the king revoked De Monts' letters patent in favor of the Baron de Poutrincourt and indicated his intention of sending two Jesuits to Acadia. In 1610, nevertheless, Poutrincourt was accompanied to Acadia by a secular (diocesan) priest, Abbé Jesse Fleché, whose intemperate zeal led him to baptize local Indians within three weeks of arrival, even though they had inadequate religious instruction. Two Jesuits, Frs. Biard and Masse, did take part in the colonization expedition of 1611, perhaps to set matters in order.

Missionaries to Acadia generally divided their time between Indian conversions and ministering to the spiritual needs of the French colonists. The people who settled in Acadia came from regions of France where traditional religious practices shaped much of the culture. Bishops and priests, monasteries and convents had strong influence in local communities, and family life largely organized itself around the liturgical calendar. In small villages the church was a focal point of social activity as well as religious life. This was the pattern the colonists, predominantly Catholic, carried into the New World.

Motives for immigration were as varied among the Acadians as they were among many other European emigrants and included land hunger, desire to escape religious strife, enthusiastic recruitment by agents like Vincent Landry, and encouragement from the crown and religious leaders. The 1604-1605 winter had been disastrous, but later, colonization was given a strong impulse by Cardinal Richelieu, who appointed his kinsman, Isaac de Razilly, governor of the colony. Razilly's first charge was to retrieve Acadian possessions that the Kirke brothers had captured for England in the 1620s.

On July 4, 1632, Razilly sailed from Auray in Brittany with 300 men, among them soldiers, gentlemen, and three Capuchin priests. The expedition landed on September 8, 1632. These were, as historian William Ganong has noted, the true ancestors of the Acadian people, for they established the first permanent settlement in Acadia. Razilly brought new colonists yearly until his death in 1635. In 1636, Charles d'Aulnay moved the settlement and founded Port Royal. The earlier settlement, Capuchin Fathers Leonard and Joseph, in a letter of April 15, 1633, had called *Portus Sanctae Mariae*, Port St. Mary.

The Capuchins preached the gospel and provided a rudimentary education for Acadian children, sometimes in open air or at homes. They praised Razilly for trying to establish a priory of St. John of Jerusalem, Order of Malta, even though he was ultimately unsuccessful, and claimed that he had banished vice and fostered charity in a colony which could become an asylum for poor Frenchmen.

Yet, the direct influence of the church was limited, for priests were few and often distant on the Acadian frontier. The immigrants, however, knew how to conduct prayer services and how to baptize infants in an emergency. They knew that they could enter into marital contracts and then have the union solemnized or "blessed" in the sacrament of matrimony when their abbé or curé, their itinerant minister, came to call. The sacrament of confirmation was administered by the prefect apostolic, the ecclesiastical superintendent of the area, and later, when Quebec became a diocese, by the bishop. They continued the domestic practices learned in the homeland: They displayed the crucifix in their homes, said the Rosary, and recited their prayers. The settlers showed particular devotion to Mary who had been declared "Patroness of the Kingdom" by the king on August 15, 1638, feast day of the Assumption of the Blessed Virgin Mary.

The Acadian religious community also retained strong French ties through the labors of the colonial clergy who always came from the mother country. Chaplains and missionaries were supplied by the ruling authority with the assent of the church. There never were enough priests--one area remained without a resident pastor for forty-three years, but elders led prayer services and children were taught at home, often by catechists called *montreuses de cate-*

chisme. Chapels and churches were erected near the forts and settlements, centers where later the English would read the exile proclamation. The colonists had left France before Jansenist austerity dampened the traditional Gallic *joie-de vivre*, and thus the Acadians felt warmer affection toward their priest than did most eighteenth-century French peasants.

The attachment between pastors and parishioners reinforced the settlers' faith. The Acadians tended to look to the clergy for spiritual and often temporal guidance, though the scarcity of priests reduced the supposed political impact of the church. Accustomed in Acadia to the church services, the liturgy, the celebration of feasts and seasons, the Acadians drew comfort from their religious practices during the sufferings of the deportation.

The Acadian diaspora or *grand dérangement*, called for all the strength of spirit one could muster. As early as 1754, some Acadians began voluntarily a trickling migration which with expulsion would soon become a steady stream. In that year five Acadian families arrived in Louisiana. The next year, disaster struck. As Roger Baudier points out:

> In 1755, the British with wanton cruelty had destroyed the villages of the peaceful Acadians and had perpetrated that almost unbelievable crime of deporting the whole populace with a savagery and ruthlessness that almost defies belief. Many of the Acadians, who were devout Catholics, remembering the French settlements in Louisiana, turned their weary steps towards the lower Mississippi Valley....

The Acadian exiles wended their way to Louisiana through many, often circuitous, routes. Some were dumped at Eastern Seaboard ports; others were imprisoned in England, then transferred to France; some arrived later in the Antilles, particularly Saint-Domingue. Eventually, about four thousand Acadians found their way to Louisiana. Only a few would later return to Acadia. During the traumatic displacement and years of wandering that followed, these hardy people preserved their faith and religious practices despite the lack of priests and the sporadic administration of the sacraments.

Many of the Louisiana arrivals settled in St. James Parish, the first permanent Acadian parish in what would become known as the Acadian Coast. In 1765, Fr. Jean-Francois founded St. Martin of Tours Church to serve the Acadians settled at the Poste des Attakapas (St. Martinville).

In Louisiana, the Acadians found themselves again in a rural setting where they engaged in farming and trapping. They were little affected by the French religious and secular institutions available in more densely settled areas near New Orleans and thereby retained their own customs and practices, as well as their langauge, already transformed by 150 years in colonial Acadia.

The Acadians found themselves even more isolated in the Attakapas

St. Martin de Tours Catholic Church
St. Martinville, Louisiana

country, far from New Orleans. Schools and teachers were scarce in the triangle pointed by the Lafourche area, present-day Lafayette, and Alexandria; commerce was scant; transportation by water restricted communication; priests came to settlements only periodically for mass, baptisms, marriages, instructions, encouragement.

Yet, family life flourished and seasonal practices of the traditional faith were observed at home, with occasional distortions caused by a lack of instruction. Moreover, as folklorists have noted, there occurred an accretion of dubious practices, learned in contact with cultism both in the Caribbean and in Louisiana. Nevertheless, their religious tenacity is remarkable, because, as in Acadia, the Acadians produced no native clergy and remained dependent on French and Spanish missionaries. When Spain took control of Louisiana in 1769, the French Capuchins remained.   In a 1770 report the French superior, Fr. Dagobert, had indicated a need for eighteen priests, twelve for the predominately Acadian outposts beyond New Orleans. As a consequence, in 1772, Spanish Capuchins began to arrive.

The exiles' dependence upon a missionary clergy would continue after April 25, 1793, when New Orleans and the two Floridas became a diocese, the third in America after Quebec and Baltimore. No clamor arose among the Acadians "for our own priests" as they had neither the tradition nor the culture to produce a native clergy. This problem survived until the early part of the twentieth century. The Acadian reluctance to provide the community with priests was reinforced by French priests who felt the native sons were "not yet ready," an attitude that persisted even into the '30s and '40s of this century. One priest of Acadian descent recalls that when, as a young man, he expressed his desire to enter the seminary, he was told "It is not time yet for the Cajuns." It would take two centuries from *grand dérangement* to foster enough vocations to supply local needs. As late as 1960, even though a major seminary, Notre-Dame, had been founded in New Orleans in 1923, two-thirds of the priests in the Lafayette diocese were still "missionaries" from New England, Canada, Holland, France, and Italy. In the 1980s, the proportion reversed; ninety percent of diocesan priests (i. e., permanently attached) are natives, mostly Cajuns.

The growth of a native clergy reflects the fact that this dislocated people had retained its religious identity despite exposure to many dissenters. In France, they had been exposed to Huguenots; in Acadia to Anglicanism and Presbyterianism; in the United States they encountered many varieties of religious difference. Until recently, however, they remained unaffected. Reasons for their steadfastness are many: Catholicism had been an integral part of their life in Acadia; religion was associated with language and culture; cultural clash with the British emphasized their cultural and linguistic differences.

As Cajuns entered the mainstream of American civilization, however, their sense of distinctiveness eroded, affecting their religious integrity as much as their linguistic survival. In the past, to mention a Cajun name was to name a Catholic. Today, however, with intermarriage and proselytism by Protestant groups, many Cajuns have been drawn from their traditional religious allegiance. While the Catholic population continues to grow (58 percent of the total population of so-called Acadiana), old French names are seen among congregations and ministers of other denominations.   Moreover, Cajunism is not monolithic: the Cajun lifestyle of Barataria is not that of Opelousas, Vacherie, or Abbeville. In the main, however, Acadians have remained faithful.

ACADIAN EDUCATION:
FROM CULTURAL ISOLATION
TO MAINSTREAM AMERICA

by Carl A. Brasseaux

From the time of the Louisiana Purchase to approximately mid-twentieth century, Louisiana Acadians were the focal point for a continuing barrage of vilification by many of their Anglo-American neighbors. The cause of this unrelenting attack was Cajun reluctance to accept, or, in some cases to reject outright, the concepts of a formal educational system as had developed in the Western World during the nineteenth century. In particular, however, South Louisiana Cajuns became the target of constant pressure by Anglo-Americans to accept an educational system made in their own image and the values which had produced that system.

Greatly outnumbered in statewide democratic processes, lacking any control over the legal or governmental apparatus of the state, Cajuns could do little more, over the years, than employ delaying tactics to preserve some semblance of their cultural values. As they unconsciously pursued this policy, they automatically received a host of labels familiar to most contemporary Louisianians— epithets such as "ignorant," "stupid," and "hardheaded." Now, in the dust-settling aftermath of the ultimately successful Anglo-American campaign, certain questions arise: Were the Cajuns really "ignorant," or were such terms really only hasty excuses, taking on the form of simplistic reasoning, to describe the complete lack of understanding by Anglo-Americans for Cajun values? This question transposed as statement thus forms the hypothesis of this essay.

During the second half of the eighteenth century, successive waves of Acadian immigrants established these people along the Mississippi River and Bayous Lafourche, Teche, and Vermilion. There, in South Louisiana, the Acadian exiles, for the most part farmers and herdsmen, sought to perpetuate a way of life revolving around a trilogy of values: God, the family, and the land. These values, typical of an agrarian society, would, however, soon come into contact, and conflict, with those of the Anglo-American merchants, artisans, and professionals who were fanning out across Louisiana with the dawn of the nineteenth century.

Following the Battle of New Orleans, Anglo-American settlers streamed into Louisiana and came to represent, especially in Acadiana, a significant urban commercial-industrial class. Seeking to have their sons follow them as agents of Eastern America's industrial revolution, Anglo-American fathers easily recognized the need for formal education. Being shrewd businessmen, however, they also recognized that private formal education was expensive and not always readily available. There is no reason to wonder, then, why this commercial-industrial class so eagerly accepted Horace Mann's concepts of publicly supported education. According to Mann's theories, the agrarian majority (which at the time saw little need for formal education to pursue its life style) was capable of making a sizable contribution to public education. Acadian farmers, possessing a far different set of cultural values, viewed formal education as having no practical value for their sons' pursuit of the good life.

Anglo-Americans viewed this negative attitude toward education as a manifestation of ignorance and thereby gave rise to the myth of the addle-pated Cajun. Of course, this ethnocentric view of Acadians was a gross distortion of the truth. Though frequently illiterate, the Acadians were hardly simple-minded; living in an area blessed with great natural abundance, they found no need for educational tools to survive. More importantly, however, they lacked a conceptual basis for secular education.

Unlike their predominantly Protestant Anglo-American neighbors, the staunchly Catholic Acadians traditionally viewed education as a function of the Catholic church—not the state. The roots of this attitude can be traced to the development of education in France, where the Catholic church had served as the wellspring of fundamental learning from the Middle Ages well into the nineteenth century. Acadian ignorance of public education was further supplemented by experiences in Acadia, where the educational system had been also closely tied to the Catholic church. Priests and nuns acted not only as spiritual and political leaders, but also as "teachers of the Acadian children." For example, in 1701, Sister Chausson of the Congregation of the Cross opened a school at Port Royal, but it was another two years before the "first regular school . . . was started in Port Royal . . . by Father Patrice René. Later, one was built at Saint-Charles des Mines (Grand Pré) by Father Louis Geoffroy."[1] These "schools," however, were not educational facilities in the modern sense of the term, for the instructors offered the Acadian children little more than verbal religious instruction. Nevertheless, over the years, Acadians began to associate this form of learning, the only one which they had known, as being the total educational experience.

These institutions of religious instruction were supplemented by a form of bureaucratic apprenticeship. A few notaries public "contributed their share towards the education of the most brilliant Acadian youths."[2] These children were undoubtedly taught to be notaries in much the same manner that lawyers and physicians were admitted to the practice of their profession by apprenticing one of their kind--a practice carried on even as recently as the early twentieth century. Furthermore, scions of the most prosperous families were occasionally sent to France to study, but the overwhelming majority of Acadian children received their education at home, where the thread of cultural continuity was spun by the elders who transmitted their ethnic folklore, customs, and history to their progeny. Children therefore received from their parents an education based on practical need (just as the Anglo-American parent sought formal education as a practical need.) For generation upon generation Acadian fathers taught their sons basic farming and herding skills; Acadian mothers instructed their daughters in the domestic arts.

Following expulsion from Acadia and their subsequent arrival in Louisiana, Acadian exiles easily reestablished their informal educational system in the *Nouvelle Acadie*, and by the early nineteenth century, it was once again contributing to their cultural heritage.[3] Louisiana Acadian, or Cajun, attitudes toward formal education are reflected in the registers of Franklin College of Opelousas, St. Charles College, and Scared Heart Academy of Grand Coteau, antebellum Acadiana's leading educational institutions.[4] In 1838, for example, St. Charles College, a Jesuit school whose religious instruction and accessibility should have made it the educational center of Southwest Louisiana, boasted only fifteen Acadian students, less than twenty percent of the total enrollment.[5]

The colleges' collective failure to attract substantial numbers of Acadian youths may be attributed to the Acadians' disinterest in a "classical" education in the Anglo-American sense of the term. They viewed such education as being unnecessary, as nothing more than an expensive luxury. If, in the unlikely event, an Acadian farmer or herdsman considered a formal education for his children, he soon harbored second thoughts when he discovered the fees involved. For example, in 1844, annual tuition rates, boarding expenses, and incidental costs at Franklin College exceeded $160, an astronomical sum for subsistence farmers or herdsmen.[6] Moreover, the practical Acadian farmer realized that the educational system would deprive him of an invaluable labor source--his sons.

It is thus hardly surprising that the establishment of a statewide, public school system in 1845 elicited an unenthusiastic response from Louisiana's Acadian population. This is seen in the fact that in 1850 only 27.9 percent of all educable children in Lafayette Parish attended school.[7] This figure, representing mostly the children of the predominantly Anglo-American merchant, artisan, and professional classes, remained substantially unaltered at the outset of the Civil War.

Between the adoption of the state constitution of 1879 and the dawn of the twentieth century, Acadiana's public school system languished as the state's government devoted its efforts primarily to restoration of order and economic prosperity following fifteen years of civil war, natural disasters, and Reconstruction. Appalled by the deterioration of Louisiana's school system, Anglo-Americans throughout the state began clamoring by the early 1880s for increased educational activity. Reacting to political and economic pressure exerted by this interest group and persuaded that the salvation of Louisiana schools lay in improving training facilities for teachers, the general assembly established Louisiana Normal School (present-day Northwestern Louisiana State University) in 1884, the Industrial Institute and College of Louisiana (present-day Louisiana Tech University) in 1894, and Southwestern Louisiana Industrial Institute (present-day University of Southwestern Louisiana) in 1898.[8]

In crusading for a structured educational system during the 1890s, Anglos in Acadiana naturally continued to pursue their own interests, not those of the Cajun farmers and herdsmen who formed the bulk of the region's population. On the other hand, the Acadians, while paying taxes to support public schools, nevertheless continued to rely upon the informal educational system established by their ancestors, a system which they recognized as working to their benefit. Their genuine lack of interest in formal education was further reinforced by the dearth of jobs in Anglo-American commerce and industry available to the few Cajuns who broke with tradition and attended school.[9] Thus, as in the past, their practical secular education continued to be supplemented only by religious instruction.[10]

Just as these educational practices persisted with undiminishing vigor throughout the nineteenth and early twentieth centuries, so did the Anglo-American propensity for equating Acadian apathy toward public education with ignorance.[11] This predilection was reinforced by the Progressive movement, a reformist crusade espousing Anglo-American middle-class values, which swept through Louisiana during the second decade of the twentieth century. In 1916, motivated by this spirit of reform, which was simply a manifestation of Anglo-American ethnocentricity, the state legislature approved, and Governor Ruffin G. Pleasant subsequently signed, Act 27 which required mandatory attendance of all educable children at public schools.[12]

Although the mandatory school attendance act was a blatant form of cultural imperialism, the measure met with remarkably little opposition from the Acadians. Their tractability was produced by initial lax enforcement of the law, the widespread use of Americanized upper-class Acadian teachers, a severe postwar agricultural slump, and, paradoxically, concomitant growth of the commercial and industrial segment of the region's economy, making these pursuits, which required educational tools, increasingly attractive to Acadian youths.[13] Moreover, during the late 1920s and early 1930s, the construction of a modern road system linking Acadiana with the remainder of the state foreshadowed the introduction of the technological revolution into the region. Full em-

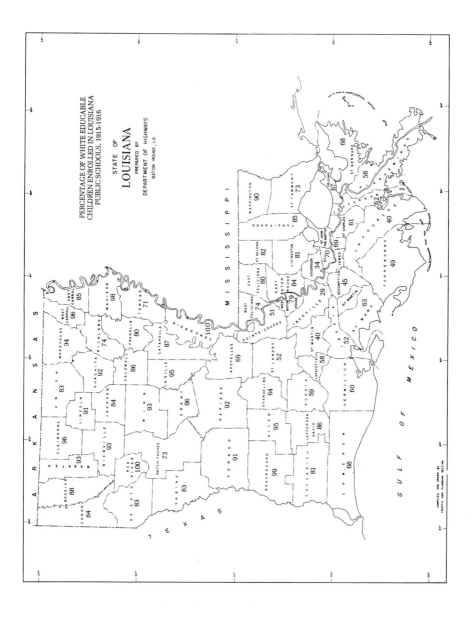

PERCENTAGE OF WHITE EDUCABLE
CHILDREN ENROLLED IN LOUISIANA
PUBLIC SCHOOLS, 1915-1916

STATE OF
LOUISIANA
PREPARED BY
DEPARTMENT OF HIGHWAYS
BATON ROUGE, LA.

joyment of the fruits of American industry was contingent upon both fluency in English and participation in the Anglo-American market economy.

The introduction of the automobile, radio, motion pictures, and other technological advancements of the early twentieth century drastically altered Cajun values and life styles. Suddenly propelled into the twentieth century by the communications revolution, most Acadian parents realized that their children's economic survival depended upon a formal education. As a consequence, with each passing year, increasing numbers of Cajuns encouraged their children to attend school, detaining them only during the harvest.[14] Moreover, realizing that, for the first time, large numbers of non-farming jobs, especially in the booming oil industry, were available, Cajun youths displayed increasing interest in education. Acadiana's school system consequently experienced unprecedented growth during the 1920s. In 1935, Dr. Edwin L. Stephens, president of Southwestern Louisiana Institute, formerly Southwestern Louisiana Industrial Institute, described this phenomenon.

> Where there were not a dozen high schools in all of southwestern Louisiana in 1900, there were more than 125 in 1930. Where there were less than 50 high school graduates in this territory in 1900, there were more than 1,000 for the year 1930. The Southwestern Louisiana Institute, which opened in 1901, had become a full-fledged college in 1921.[15]

Despite the unpredecented growth of Acadiana's school system, the Cajun plunge into the course of mainstream America was subdued by economic distress brought on by the Great Depression and the material shortages during and immediately after World War II. By 1950, however, these artificial impediments to cultural assimilation had been removed, and a plethora of now-perfected technological advancements, like the reservoir behind a bursting dam, swept over Acadiana, carrying the heretofore rigid cultural barriers before them.

South Louisiana merchants found a ready market for their new products; among the most voracious consumers were returning Acadian servicemen. These veterans, many of whom had been removed from their South Louisiana environment for the first time, had come into contact with the creature comforts of the materialistic Anglo-American world while serving in the armed services. Therefore, upon returning home, they seized the first opportunity to buy cars, and install electricity and telephones for their homes.

Acadians' military experiences also demonstrated that advancement in the Anglo-American business world was contingent upon literacy and mastery of the English language. Upon returning to Acadiana, veterans discovered that their homeland was being transformed by the recent oil boom into a quasi-industrial center--in short, an extension of the Anglo-American world. Realizing that they could reap the economic benefits of the burgeoning oil industry only through

Acadian High Schools Then (Napoleonville, 1899)
and Now (Lafayette, 1977)

(Courtesy Ellen Zink)

refinement of their meager educational skills, thousands of Cajun veterans availed themselves of the benefits provided by the so-called "GI Bill." These federal educational subsidies enabled literally thousands of ex-servicemen in South Louisiana to attend college, formerly regarded as a luxury beyond the means or desires of most Acadians.

The Acadian response to the "GI Bill" created significant problems for the state's system of higher education. Faced with surging enrollment at South Louisiana's institutions of higher learning, the state government established Francis T. Nicholls Junior College at Thibodaux and expanded John McNeese Junior College in Lake Charles as a four-year institution. Attendance at these colleges--now known respectively as McNeese State University and Nicholls State University--and the University of Southwestern Louisiana (formerly Southwestern Louisiana Institute), which have traditionally served as Acadiana's educational centers, has continued to expand into the 1980s.

The remarkable growth of Acadiana's institutions of higher learning has been matched by the rapid expansion of the region's vocational-technical school system. Increasing emphasis upon vocational education by the state school system, greater emphasis upon technical training by oil-related companies, and rapidly rising salary scales for technical positions in South Louisiana's oil industry interacted to draw ever greater numbers of young Cajuns into Acadiana's vo-tech schools during the 1970s. The growing popularity of these institutions is best reflected in the enrollment figures for the Gulf Area Vocational-Technical School of Abbeville, which rose from 836 in 1971 to 1,309 in 1979 (a 57 percent increase). Indeed, increasing demand for vocational-technical education precipitated a 58 percent increase in the number of Acadiana trade schools during the 1970s.[16]

The continued expansion of Acadiana's technical schools and colleges can be attributed to the Cajun's persistent drift toward acceptance of Anglo-American educational values. Their conversion has been produced in large measure by the demise of subsistence farming in Acadiana and the concomitant migration of Cajun farmers to South Louisiana cities, where many acquired blue-collar jobs, such as electricians, carpenters, and plumbers. In adapting to an urban, industrial, and, most importantly, a materialistic environment, the Cajun ex-farmer quickly realized that education was a springboard to economic success.

Like their counterparts throughout the United States, Cajun parents now view a college or technical-school diploma as a key to their children's future economic security. Moreover, cognizant that admission to an institution of higher learning hinges upon a successful grade school career, many Cajuns now take great pains to instill in their children a favorable attitude towards education. Unfortunately for their heritage, but in order to insure their children's success in the local school system, the overwhelming majority of Acadian

The University of Southwestern Louisiana
("Université des Acadiens"), Lafayette

parents, most of whom are proficient in the language of their ancestors, teach their children only English, frequently inculcating pride in this alien language by ridiculing those who continue to speak their ancient tongue. Since 1968, however, regional interest in preserving the unique French dialect has been renewed by the Council for the Development of French in Louisiana. This state agency has contributed greatly to the restoration of a sense of ethnic pride among Louisiana's Cajuns. Moreover, under CODOFIL's guidance, French, banned in Louisiana schools since 1913,[17] is once again taught as a second language in many public school districts. Growing Acadian and Anglo-American support for this second-language program is a manifestation of a distinctly Louisiana current in the now ethnic-conscious mainstream of American educational values.

NOTES

1. Bona Arsenault, *History of the Acadians* (Quebec, 1966), pp. 60-61. The failure of the clergy to teach their pupils to read and write is vividly illustrated by the Acadian leaders' inability to sign their names to a contract shortly after arriving in New Orleans in 1765. Grover Rees, *A Narrative History of Breaux Bridge, Once Called "La Pointe"* (Lafayette, La., 1976), p. 44.

2. Arsenault, *History of the Acadians*, p. 61.

3. Felix Voorhies, *Acadian Reminiscences: The True Story of Evangeline* (New Orleans, 1907), pp. 15-21, 28, 104-108.

4. Franklin College was chartered by the general assembly on March 5, 1831. This institution, however, did not receive students until April 1837. Anticipating a large enrollment, the state legislature had subsidized construction of at least five classroom and dormitory buildings; nevertheless, attendance was disappointingly light, reaching a maximum enrollment of sixty-five in 1841. Four years later, the subsidies which the school had received since 1831 were terminated by the new state constitution and the college was forced to close. Alcée Fortier, ed., *Louisiana: Comprising Sketches of Counties, Towns, Events, Institutions, and Persons, Arranged in Cyclopedic Form*, 2 vols. (Atlanta, 1909), II, 464-465.
   The cornerstone of St. Charles College was laid by Bishop Antoine Blanc on July 31, 1837. The school formally opened during the following January. This institution continued to serve as a "college" until 1922, when it became a Jesuit novitiate. Roger Baudier, *The Catholic Church in Louisiana*, 2nd ed. (Baton Rouge, 1972), pp. 328-330.
   The Academy of the Sacred Heart has served continuously as a primary and secondary school for girls since 1821. Odeide Mouton, "The Academy of the Sacred Heart," *Attakapas Gazette*, IX (1974), 190-195.

5. Register, St. Charles College, Grand Coteau, La., non-paginated. Microfilm copy on deposit in the Jefferson Caffery Louisiana Room, Dupré Library, University of Southwestern Louisiana.

6. Opelousas *St. Landry Whig*, November 7, 1844.

7. Carl A. Brasseaux, "Prosperity and the Free Population of Lafayette Parish, 1850-1860: A Demographic Overview," *Attakapas Gazette*, XII (1977), 105-108.

8. Edwin L. Stephens, "Education in Louisiana in the Closing Decades of the Nineteenth Century," *Louisiana Historical Quarterly*, XVI (1933), 39-48. Edwin W. Fay, *The History of Education in Louisiana* (Washington, 1898), pp. 101-102.

9. *Biennial Report of the State Superintendent of Public Education to the General Assembly, 1884-1885* (Baton Rouge, 1886), p. 96; hereinafter cited as *Biennial Report*, with date and place of publication. *Biennial Report*, 1890-1891 (New Orleans, 1892), p. 132; *ibid.*, 1891-1899 (Baton Rouge, 1900), pp. 34-35; *ibid.*, 1902-1903 (Baton Rouge, 1904), pp. 52-53. Interview with Cleobule LeJeune, June 19, 1973.

10. Cleobule LeJeune.

11. In an address before the Louisiana Historical Society in 1935, E. L. Stephens, president of Southwestern Louisiana Institute, succinctly described this attitude: "We are accustomed to think of the simplicity of English, and the stupidity of other people's not learning it. . . ." Edwin L. Stephens, "The Story of Acadian Education in Louisiana," *Louisiana Historical Quarterly*, XVHI (1935), 399.

12. The author of the compulsory education bill, Representative Ambrose Mayre Smith, was a Tennessean of Anglo-Saxon descent and the former superintendent of Vermilion Parish's public school system. *Acts Passed by the General Assembly of the State of Louisiana at the Regular Session . . . 1916* (Baton Rouge, 1916), pp. 59-60. Henry E. Chambers, *A History of Louisiana: Wilderness Colony, Province, Territory, State, People*, 3 vols. (Chicago, 1925), III, 306.
At the time Smith's bill was approved by the general assembly only 2,108 of the 5,253 educable children in predominantly Acadian St. Martin Parish attended school; on the other hand, 4,972 of the 5,314 school-aged children in predominantly Anglo Sabine Parish were enrolled in public schools. *A Brief Summary and Thirty-One Maps Showing the Public School Situation of Louisiana in a Few Essential Respects, Session of 1916-1917* (Baton Rouge, 1917), p. 29.

13. Interview with Robert E. Chaplin, June 17, 1976.

14. Vernon J. Parenton, "Notes on the Social Organization of a French Village in South Louisiana," *Social Forces*, XVII (1938), 79.

15. Stephens, "The Story of Acadian Education in Louisiana," 309.

16. Louisiana Department of Education, *Louisisna School Directory, 1971-1972* (Baton Rouge, 1972), p. 119; *ibid., 1980-1981* (Baton Rouge, 1981), pp. 197-198.

17. Like its 1879 counterpart, the 1898 constitution provided "that the French language may be taught in those parishes or localities where the French language predominates, if no additional expense is incurred thereby"; however, as the Progressive movement gained momentum during the first decade of the twentieth century, Anglo reformers, who, like their middle-class contemporaries throughout America, espoused the principles of ethnic superiority, quickly undermined Louisiana's French educational system. In July 1912, following the election of Progressive Luther E. Hall, the state legislature approved

"An Act in Relation to Free Public Schools and to Regulate Public Education in the State of Louisiana . . . " which created the State Board of Education and empowered it to select curricula and textbooks for all public schools in the Pelican State. During the following year, the Board adopted new courses of study stressing "English Classics," composition and English grammar for the state school system. *A Brief Summary*, pp. 19-20; Francis Newton Thorpe, ed., *The Federal and State Constitutions* . . . , 6 vols. (Washington, D. C., 1909), III, 1509, 1576; Minns Sledge Robertson, *Public Education in Louisiana after 1898* (Baton Rouge, 1952), p. 93.

THE SPOKEN FRENCH
OF LOUISIANA

by Hosea Phillips

French is spoken in daily life throughout the Acadian parishes of Louisiana, or Acadiana, a region consisting of twenty-two parishes from Avoyelles in the north to the Gulf of Mexico in the south, from Calcasieu Parish on the west to the Mississippi River on the east.[1] Here French has survived almost exclusively through oral transmission after three centuries of linguistic separation from the mother tongue, a testimony to the vitality of the language and culture of a group which seeks to keep its heritage alive.

Some say that as many as a million and a half Louisianians speak French as their first or second language, and, even though the exact number is uncertain, there is no doubt that a large number of Louisianians do speak French. Some of them, unfortunately, still make excuses for their French, saying that they do not speak "good French," that they speak only Acadian or "Cajun" French, *le 'cadien* /ka-Zè/. This modesty, this self-deprecation, is understandable. Over a long period of time, certain professionals, especially teachers, told Cajuns that their language was not "good French," but "Cajun French," the very term "Cajun" thereby taking on a negative connotation. The most rabid denunciations of Cajun French sometimes came from teachers who were of Acadian background. Elsewhere, Acadian children found their Anglophone schoolmates mocking them for speaking "an inferior language," one that existed only as the oral language of an uneducated people. Moreover, for a long time, students were forbidden to speak French at school, even during recess and the lunch hour and before and after the school day. Students guilty of disobeying this rule were punished, often paddled and sent home to write two hundred times, "I must not speak French on the school grounds." Thus arose the paradoxical situation where a child who could speak nothing else was forbidden to use French at school. After, he did not speak "good French;" he spoke only Acadian French.

There are three kinds of French spoken in Louisiana. One kind, quite similar to Standard French, we shall call Standard Louisiana French. It has, however, incorporated a number of structures and vocabulary items from

145

Acadian French. It is spoken by older persons who were educated in French private schools. These people also received their religious instruction in that language from French priests and nuns, using catechisms published in France or in Quebec. While most of these Louisianians still write French easily, they seldom do so except in addressing such groups as the *Athénée Louisianais* in New Orleans and *France-Amérique de la Louisiane Acadienne* in Lafayette, or to prepare a formal introduction for the French-speaking dignitaries who visit Louisiana.

Their children and grandchildren speak French, but less frequently than their elders. In the home or with friends, neighbors, servants, tradesmen and workmen, they speak Acadian French. As Gayle Calais states:

> There is some Standard French spoken in Louisiana or something approaching Standard French. There is less than claimed by some people who speak what they call 'good French' and who decry 'Cajun French' as being spoken only by the uneducated, the ignorant, the country folk, or the urban poor.[2]

Louisianians who speak Acadian French, the most widespread variety of French in Louisiana, can easily understand one another, despite the differences which could be expected among people living in geographically isolated regions. Louisiana Acadians speak a *langue commune*, a common language, which, according to Ferdinand Brunot[3] was developed by French colonists who spoke different *patois* and were obliged to resort to French as a common tongue. In Louisiana, the French spoken by the majority is Acadian French so that speakers of Louisiana French will often use Acadian French in speaking with family, servants, and tradesmen in informal situations.

A much smaller group, unfortunately growing smaller as time goes by, uses a language in which the phonetic, syntactical and grammatical systems have seen simplified. It is often called Negro French or "gumbo French," but we prefer to call it Creole French.

The three kinds of French in Louisiana--Louisiana French, Acadian French, and Creole French--are almost exclusively spoken languages. Louisiana French is the only one which is written, and not often at that, as already noted.

The three French languages of Louisiana have maintained certain archaic French forms: *s'assir* for *s'asseoir* (sit, seat oneself); *balier* for *balayer* (sweep); *bébel* for *jouet* (toy, plaything); *berce* (rocking chair); *faire le lavage* for *faire la lessive* (wash clothes, do the washing). Louisianians have kept the old pronunciation of /a-u/ for *août* /û/ (August) and *boëte* for *boîte* (box). They also pronounce the final consonant in the plural forms where modern French has dropped it in words such as: *un boeuf, des boeufs; un oeuf, des oeufs; un os, des os.* In Louisiana the word *poison* has kept the feminine gender which it had in

France until the seventeenth century. Masculine words with an initial vowel, such as *argent, enterrement, été, orage, ouvrage*, have also remained feminine as they were in France until the seventeenth century.

The three varieties of French in Louisiana also use regional French words, terms which are found in France in areas quite remote from one another. Louisianians use *canique* for *bille* (marble, a plaything), a word found in Brittany and Normandy in the north and Gascony and the Béarn in the south. They also say *se jouquer* for *se jucher* (roost, in speaking of chickens, turkeys, etc.) as people do in the north, south and west of France. The *-que* of these two words, which corresponds to the French *-che* is not "French," but it is difficult to say whether it is of Provençal or Normanno-Picard origin, although the latter seems more likely. Certain other words generally employed in Louisiana, such as *couverture* for *toit* (roof) or *placard* for *tache* (spot) can be found in regions of France as widely separated as Normandy in the north and Limousin in the south. These pronunciation and vocabulary items do not help us to identify the place of origin of the French who settled in Louisiana.

(Standard) Louisiana French

The syntax, grammar, and vocabulary of Louisiana French are very close to those of the language spoken in metropolitan France, but Louisiana pronunciation has fewer subtleties. For example, Louisiana French does not always make a clear distinction between the pairs of open and closed vowels: /a-â/, /è-é/, /ò-o/, /eù-eu/, and the "r" is a dental trill, not the dorsal "r" of standard Parisian French. A Frenchman hearing a Louisianian knows that the latter is not a Parisian, and probably will think him to be from a village in northern or western France, in the area of Amiens, Angers, or La Rochelle.

Acadian French

Acadian French is not a dialect. It is something of a common language which has assimilated certain dialectal elements, but, on the whole, resembles the French spoken in the villages and rural areas of northern and western France. It does not vary greatly from one Louisiana parish to another. Acadians can understand one another throughout South Louisiana. Areas have, of course, some characteristics such as the /wò/ often /wó/ of *moi, toi, roi* and the é̃ of *pain, faim, bien*, in Vermilion Parish; the /h/ of Lafourche Parish for the /ź/ of *jamais, deja*, etc. It is interesting to note that the /é̃/ of *pain*, is found in the French spoken in Morocco and Quebec, and that the /h/ of *jamais*, etc., is found in the French of the Poitou region.

Acadian French has kept some archaic forms of pronunciation, such as *août, boëte (boite)* as noted above. It has suffered phonetic accidents: 1) metathesis: *fourmi* became *froumi* or *fromi* (ant); *fermer, frémer* (close); *fourbir, frobir* (scrub); 2) assimilation; *cimetière* became *cimitiere* (cemetery); *labourer, rabourer* (plow); 3) dissimilation: *calculer, carculer* (calculate); *imaginer, émaginer* (imagine); 4) agglutination: *le hoquet, le l'hoquet* (hiccups); *l'endroit, le l'endroit* (right side); *l'envers, le l'envers* (wrong side, of material). Phonetic accidents are an important element of the pronunciation in a language which has not had for a long time a standard spoken or literary language to help maintain the "correct" form.

Acadian French has borrowed vocabulary items from other languages: 1) English: *back le char* instead of *mettre la voiture en march arriere* (back the car); *truck* instead of *camion*; 2) African: *name-name* for *manger* (eat, food); *ouanga* for *sort, envoutement* (spell, hex); 3) Indian: *bayou* for *ruisseau, rivière; chaoui* for *raton laveur* (racoon); 4) Spanish: *bossal* from *bozal* for *licol* (halter); *brème* from *berenja* for *aubergine* (eggplant).

In Acadian French, the possessive *lor* as in *lor maison--leur maison* (their house), has kept the old French form. The expression *cez-là* for *celles-là* (these, those) from middle French has been kept in Acadian. The expression *ce livre-ici* for *ce livre-ci* (this book) has kept the form recommended by Vaugelas in the seventeenth century.

Acadian grammar has been greatly simplified, as the verbs exemplify. A verb such as *donner* (give) has the form /dõn/ for all persons of the present tense (silent letters are bracketed).

Singular		Plural
1. Je donne	de l'argent aux pauv[r]es.	1. On donne[4]
2. Ti donnes	(I give money to the poor, etc.)	2. Vous donne
3. Il/Alle donne		3. Ça donne

The standard forms are sometimes used with *nous* and *vous: nous donnons, vous donnez aux pauvres*, usually by speakers who have had some formal French instruction or learned the forms from someone who has studied the language. The stressed form *nous-aut[r]es on donne* is frequently used for *we give* as is *vous-aut[r]es donne* for the plural *you give*. For the present progressive, "I am giving to the poor," an Acadian says, *"J[e] su[i]s après donner aux pauvres,"* instead of *"Je suis en train de donner aux pauvres."* In the imperative second persons singular, Acadians use the standard, *Donne de l'argent aux pauvres* (Give money to the poor). For the second person plural, they say *Donnez aux pauvres. Donnons aux pauvres* (Let's give to the poor), however,

is rarely, if ever, used for the first person plural; one usually hears instead
Allons donner aux pauvres. For the third person, one hears *qu'i[l] donne,*
qu'a[ll] e donne (Let him, her, give) in the singular, and in the plural, *que ça*
donne.

The same simplifying process occurs in verbs of the second and third con-
jugations. For *remplir* (to fill) the forms /rã-pli/ and *remplissez* are used as
/dõn/ and *donnez* for the first conjugation verb as are (sell) /vã/ and *vendez* for
vendre.

Auxiliary verbs are similarly simplified. The verb *avoir* (to have) has three
phonetic forms: *j'ai, t'as, il a/alle a/, on a, vous /a/, i[l] s ont*, the last being used
for both *ils ont* and *elles ont. Etre* (to be) also has three phonetic forms: *je*
suis /žsy/ or */šy/, ils sont* (for both *ils sont* and *elles sont*), and */é/* for the other
persons: *t'es, il est, alle est, on est, vous /é/.*

Aller (to go) also has three phonetic forms: va: *je vas, ti vas, il va/alle*
va, on va, vous /va/, ça va. Sometimes, *ils vont* is used for both *ils vont* and
elles vont. The other two forms *allez* and *allons* are used only in the imperative: *allez, allons là-bas.* As noted previously, *allons* is usually used with an
infinitive to form the exhortative: *Allons finir notre ouvrage,* for *Finissons*
notre ouvrage (Let's finish our work).

The other simple tenses are conjugated and used as in French, but with
reduction to a single phonetic form for each tense. For example, the *imparfait*
of *donner* (imperfect indicative) is reduced to the form */dõn-né/: Je donnais,*
tu donnais, i[l] donnait/a[ll] e donnait de l'argent aux pauvres. (I used to give
money to the poor.) In Vermilion and Evangeline parishes, by supercorrection,
there is a third person plural form, *i[l]s donniont,* under the influence, no
doubt, of *nous donnions.* This same pattern is used for the *imparfait* of the
other verbs: *je remplissais, tu remplissais, ca remplissait, i[l]s remplissiont;*
je vendais, j'avais, j'etais, j'allais, je venais, je voyais, je voulais. There is a third
person plural for *avoir: i[l]s avaient (i[l] s aviont)* and *etre: ils etaient, i[l]s*
etiont. There is no *passe simple* in Acadian.

To express the future, Acadian French generally uses *aller* plus the infinitive: *Demain, je vas donner de l'argent aux pauv[r] es. Toi, ti vas donner de*
l'argent aux pauv[r] es? However, in the negative, the future form is regularly
used. *Toi, tu donneras pas aux pauv[r] es? Non, je donnera pas aux pauv[r] es*
Will you give? No, I will not give to the poor). The future, when used, is
regularly formed with only one phonetic form (two at most) for each verb.
For *donner,* the form is *i[l] /dõn-ra/.* For the thrid person plural, they say,
i[l]s donneront pas or *ça donnera pas* (They will not give). The future form is
used in the positive form only for the verbs *avoir, être, pouvoir* (to be able) and
vouloir (to want): *Demain, j'auras, il aura de l'argent; je sera, i[l] sera content;*
je pourras, i[l] pourra acheter la maison; je voudras, i[l] voudra l'acheter tout de

suite. Here again, with the third person plural pronoun, we say: *ils auront, ils pourront, i[l] s voudront,* but *ça pourra* and *ça voudra* are also often used.

The Acadian conditional is formed as in continental French, but usually with only one phonetic form /dõn-ré/. In Vermilion Parish, however, it is *i[l] s donneriont*; in Evangeline, this form exists by supercorrection like *i[l] s donnont* in the present and *ils donniont* in the *imparfait.* In Acadian French, as in popular and regional continental French, the conditional is used in the if-clause and the result-clause: *Si j'aurais de l'argent, je t'en donnerais.* [If I had (would have) money, I would give you some.]

Compound tenses with *avoir* are formed as in French, but with a reduction in the number of phonetic forms. *Hier j'ai donné, t'as donné, il a donné/alle a donné, on a donné, vous /a/ donné* (plural, *vous aut[r]es /a/ donné), ils ont donné aux pauv[r]es* (Yesterday, I gave to the poor, etc.).

Intransitive verbs of motion or change, which are conjugated with *être* in Standard French, occasionally follow the same pattern in Acadian French. In Evangeline Parish, the verbs *venir* (to come), *revenir* (to come back) and *devenir*) to become) are conjugated with *être: Hier, je sus venu ici, t'es venu, il est venu/alle est venue, on est venu, vous /é/ venu (vous-aut'es /é/ venus), ils sont venus ici* (Yesterday, I came here, etc.). *Revenir* and *devenir* follow the same pattern: *Hier, Paul est revenu ici.* (Yesterday, Paul came back here.) *En 1977, M. Carter est devenu président des Etats-Unis* (In 1977, Mr. Carter became president of the United States.) *Naître* (to be born) and *mourir* (to die) are also conjugated with *être: M. Fontenot est né en 1910; il est mort en 1970* (Mr. Fontenot was born in 1910; he died in 1970.).

In Evangeline Parish, the other intransitive verbs of motion or change are conjugated with *avoir: Hier, il a resté longtemps ici. Là, il a sorti; il a rentré, il a parti, il a retourné là-bas* (Yesterday, he remained here for a long time.. Then he went out; he came in again; he returned over there.)

Those verbs in the other compound tenses are quite regular: *j'étais venu, t'étais venu; je seras venu, ti seras venu; je serais venu, ti serais venu.* The pattern applies for the verbs *revenir, devenir, naître,* and *mourir.* In certain regions of Acadiana, these intransitive verbs are conjugated with *avoir: j'avais venu; j'auras venu; j'aurais venu.*

In Evangeline Parish, reflexive verbs are conjugated with *etre: Hier tu t'es levé; il s'est levé; on s'est levé; vous /sé/ levé; ils se sont levés a huit heures* (Yesterday, you got up at eight o'clock.). However, we say, *Hier, je m/é/ levé à huit heures.* It is not clear whether it is an *est /é/* used by analogy with the forms used with *tu, il, on,* or whether it is using *avoir* as an auxiliary for a reflexive verb: *Hier, je m'ai levé à huit heures.* In Vermilion Parish and other regions, on the other hand, reflexive verbs are conjugated with *avoir: Hier, je m'ai levé, tu t'as levé, i[l] s'a levé, vous s'a levé, ils s'ont levés à huit heures.*

In general, in Acadian French, the other compound tenses of reflexive verbs follow the model of the Vermilion *passé composé: je m'avais levé, tu t'avais levé; je m'auras levé, tu t'auras levé; je m'aurais levé, tu t'aurais levé.* For verbs conjugated with *avoir,* the compound tenses are similar to those in continental French with phonetic simplification: *j'avais fini, t'avais fini; j'auras fini, t'auras fini; j'aurais fini, t'aurais fini.*

Creole French

Creole, like Acadian French, exists only as a spoken language and, like Acadian French, varies from one region to another. Even in a parish such as St. Martin where it is widely spoken, the St. Martinville Creole differs from that of Breaux Bridge and those two differ from the Cecilia dialect. St. Martinville Creole will be discussed here.

In Creole, as in Acadian French, pronunciation is simplified and has undergone various phonetic accidents. Creole has the same consonants as Acadian French. In both, we find palatalization of the consonant /d/ before /[j]/: *Dieu /Že/, un diable /ẽ Žab/;* the consonant /t/ before the semi-consonants /j/ and /y/ give /č/: *tiens /čě/ moitié, /mó-čé/, tuer /čwé/.* The /k/ before *eu, ui* shows the same change: *queue /čé/, cuire /čwir/.* As we can see in these examples, Creole French does not have rounded medial vowels: /eù, eú, y/. Phonetic accidents abound in Creole as in Acadian. ·Some examples are: 1) metathesis: *fermer* becomes *fremer; fourmi, froumi,* or *fromi*; 2) assimilation: *petit* gives *pitit; labourer, rabourer*; 3) agglutination: *un oiseau, in zozo* (a bird); *une oie, in zoie* (a goose).

Grammar and syntax are also simplified in Creole. The articles plus the noun, in the singular and in the plural, show various grammatical and phonetic elements of Creole French.

Definite Article (e. g., the man)			Indefinite Article (e. g., a man)	
Singular	French	Creole	French	Creole
man	l'homme	n'hõmme-là	un homme	in n'hõmme
woman	la femme	fõmme-là	une femme	in fõmme
dog	le chien	chien-là	un chien	in chien
cow	la vache	vacħe-là	une vache	in vache

Definite (e. g., the men)			Indefinite (e. g., some men)	
Plural	French	Creole	French	Creole
men	les hommes	n'hõmmes-yé	des hommes	des n'hõmmes
women	les femmes	fõmmes-yé	des femmes	des fõmmes
dogs	les chiens	chiens-yé	des chiens	des chiens
cows	les vaches	vaches-yé	des vaches	des vaches

The verbs had also been greatly simplified. The present of the verb *frapper*, for instance, becomes:

Singular: 1.) Mo frappe garçon-là, or Mo frappe li. Mo frapper.
2.) To frappes garçon-là, or To frappe li. To frapper.
3.) Li frappe garçon-là, or Li frappe li.   Li frapper.

Plural: 1.) Nous frappe garçons-là. Nous frappe-yé. Nous frapper.
2.) Vous frappe garçons-là. Vous frappe-yé. Vous frapper.
3.) Yé frappe garçons-là.   Yé frappe-yé.   Yé frapper.

The *imparfait*[5] (I beat, used to beat, the boy, him), is also reduced to one form:

Mo té frapper garçon-là.   Mo té frapper li.
Nous té frapper garçons-là.   Nous té frapper yé.

Other tenses are similarly simplified:

The future (I am going to beat, will beat, the boy.):

M'a frapper garçon-là.   M'aller frapper garçon-là.
M'a frapper li.   M'aller farpper li.
To aller frapper garçon-là.   To aller frapper li.
(The other persons of the future show the model with To, above.)

The conditional (I would beat the boy.):

Mo sé frapper garçon-là.   Mo sé frapper li.
Nous sé frapper garçons-yé.   Mo sé frapper li.
Nous sé frapper garçons-yé.   Nous sé frapper yé.

The *passé composé* (I have beaten, I beat the boy.):

Mo frappé garçon-là.   Mo frappé-li.
Nous frappé garçons-yé.   Nous frappé yé.

The *pluperfect* (I had beaten the boy.):

Mo té frappé garçon-là.   Mo té frappé li.
Nous té frappé garçons-yé.   Nous té frappé yé.

The future perfect (I will have beaten the boy.):

Mo sa frappé garçon-là.   Mo sa frappé li.
Nous sa frappé garçons-yé.   Nous sa frappé yé.

The conditional perfect (I would have beaten the boy.):

Mo sé frappé garçon-là.   Mo sé frappé li.
Nous sé frappé garçons-yé.   Nous sé frappé yé.

As could be expected, the *passé simple* does not exist in Creole, any more than it does in Acadian.

It is safe to conclude that relaxation in pronunciation and reduction, leveling and simplification of syntax and grammar are found in the three varieties of French spoken in Louisiana, but the phenomena are more common in Acadian French than in Louisiana and more in Creole than in Acadian.

Phonetic Symbols

1. Consonants

b--bon
č--English *chop*; Acadian *queue*: /k/ plus /eú/, /y/ and Acadian *tiens*: initial /tj/ plus vowel.
d--donner
f--in
g--gros
h--English *hot*; Acadian *haut*
ź--joli
Ž--English *jury*; Acadian *gueuler*; /g/ plus /eù/ or /eú/
k--col

l--lire
m--mère
n--non
ng--English *long*; Acadian *longue*
p--père
r--rat (dental trill *r*)
R--English *ride*
s--sa
š--chat
t--ta
v--va
z--zone

2. Semi-consonants and semi-vowels

j̰--bien, ail

j̃--Acadian *oignon, campagne, panier, gagner*

y--lui

w--Louis

3. Vowels

a--intermediate sound between /a/ of *patte* and /â/ of *pâte*

ã--blanc

ǎ--English *cap*; Acadian *mère*: /è/ plus /r/

é--(closed e) *été, aller*

è--(open e) *belle, bête*

ẽ--(nasal open e) *vin*

ẽ́--(nasal close e) Acadian *semer* /smé/

i--(close i) *pris*

î--(open i) English *ill*; Acadian *lire*

î̃--(nasal open i) English *sing*; Acadian *ligne*

ó--(close o) *gros*

ò--(open o) *porte*

õ--(nasal o) French, Acadian *bon*

ò̃--(open nasal o) Acadian of Abbeville *bon*

eũ--(close eu) *bleu*

eu--(open eu) *pleure*

eu-le

eu--(nasal open eu) un

u--*doux*

U--English *book*; Church Point Acadian *lourd, courtbouillon:* /u/ plus /r/

ỳ--(close u) *lutter*

y--(open u) Church Point Acadian, French *ulcère*

NOTES

1. The region also includes the parish of East Baton Rouge and the "river parishes," south of Baton Rouge to the Gulf of Mexico.

2. Gayle Calais, "The Acadian French of the Parks (St. Martin Parish), Louisiana, Area," (M. A. thesis, University of Southwestern Louisiana, 1968), p. 3.

3. Ferdinand Brunot, *Histoire de la langue française des origines à 1900* (Paris, 1917), pp. 1072-1073.

4. On is regularly pronounced /ã/.

5. The progressive form of the verb is formed in Creole French, as in Acadian French, by using the appropriate form of the verb *être* plus *après* (pé in Creole French) plus the verb: *Mo té pé frapper garcon-la.* (I was beating the boy.)

Since the present of *être* is not used, the present progressive in Creole French is: *Mo pé frappé li*, or *Mo pé frapper li.* (I am beating him.)

DOMESTIC ARCHITECTURE IN ACADIANA
IN THE
EIGHTEENTH AND NINETEENTH CENTURIES

by R. Warren Robison

Groups of people of a common race, religion, and nationality tend to develop a unique artistic expression which is handed down to succeeding generations to become a point of departure for further development. The French colonists of Acadia (present-day Nova Scotia), exiled in 1755 by the English, were no exception. On their treks in search of a compatible environment, they carried with them their culture which had had its roots in medieval France.

Those Acadians who sought security in the southernmost part of the vast Louisiana Territory discovered that France had ceded the land to Spain. Searching for places of settlement, they made their way up the Mississippi River and, during the subsequent decade of migrations, the Acadians spread out along the rivers and bayous west of the river in the southwestern part of the present state of Louisiana. This move from a rocky North Atlantic peninsula to a swampy land on the Gulf of Mexico was a traumatic experience. They found Southwest Louisiana to be an alien environment wherein the climate, topography, flora and fauna were almost opposite to that which they had known. Moreover, their culture was different from that of the French colonists already in Louisiana and it contrasted with those of the German and Spanish inhabitants among whom they first settled. All this brought about cultural changes which were manifested in their architectural endeavors.

The Acadian immigrants found that in Southwest Louisiana there are two distinct seasons--winter and summer. The passage from one to the other is so abrupt that autumn and spring are hardly discernable seasons. The winters are short and mild but wet; the summers are long, hot, and wet. At times the sunrays are fierce. Along the bayous and in the swamps was to be found luxurious plant growth heavily draped with Spanish moss. There were vast stands of cypress trees. The open prairies and marshes were thick with various grasses. There was no rock nor stone, but there was plenty of clay.

The Acadians were devout Roman Catholics who were honest, industrious, and ingenious. They reared large, close-knit families in the Acadian tradition, a heritage so strong that no other culture could absorb it. In general, they were modest people of limited means. In harmony with their background and the new environment, some of the new settlers became trappers, moss gatherers, and fishermen, others became small farmers and cattlemen. They prospered and spread across Southwest Louisiana which today is referred to as *Acadiana*.

156

Given such a cultural background and the peculiar geographic and climatic conditions, the early Acadians developed a basic house type which satisfied their needs and which was compatible with the environment. Thus, they unwittingly developed their own peculiar style of folk architecture which is generally referred to as the Cajun Cottage.

The Acadian Cottage

The humble Acadian Cottage has perhaps become as symbolic of Southwest Louisiana as the Eiffel Tower is of Paris. The Acadian immigrants built their own houses with the help of their neighbors. The principal material used to build these primitive structures was cypress wood which was discovered to be straight grained, relatively free of knots, easily worked, little affected by moisture, and insect resistent.

Seasoned logs were rived and sawed by hand into long planks of varying widths while other logs were adzed into such structural members as joists, posts, braces, beams, rafters, and purlins. The first four elements were sized, tenoned, and mortised, then assembled to form a frame which was fastened with wooden pegs. Such a timber frame, except for the type of wood used, was almost the same as that used in faraway Acadia. This Louisiana version of timber frame was raised off the ground by ranges of two-foot-high cypress log segments. This innovation was in response to the demands of a flood-prone, insect-ridden site. In addition, it allowed a cooling breeze to flow beneath the structure.

Instead of infilling the walls with stone, plentiful in Acadia but nonexistent in Louisiana, the Acadians used a mixture of clay and Spanish moss (bousillage) which had been used by previous French builders in the Mississippi River Valley. This concoction was an effective insulating material. The infill was held in place by closely spaced, horizontal slats let into the corresponding centers of the posts and braces. Such a raw clay mixture would not withstand the rains: therefore, the walls were protected on the outside by a sheathing of wide, overlapping cypress planks. Since the front wall was protected by a porch overhang, materials and labor were saved by plastering and whitewashing.

Openings into the frame consisted of front and rear doors at the center of the respective walls. The double doors were of solid boards held together by dovetailed battens. They were mounted on wooden or homemade strap hinges of iron, and swung outward to conserve inside space.

Each side wall was pierced by one or two window openings filled with solid wood casements constructed similarly to the doors. The use of expensive and hard-to-get iron was limited to window and door hinges. No glass was used. Inside or outside the frame, a chimney and fireplace of sticks, clay, and moss was

constructed against one of the side walls. This was used for heating and sometimes for cooking.

A high, steep-pitched gable roof was constructed to cover the almost square
frame along with an added porch. The effect was that the porch, which served
as an open living area, was built in. Ranging across the outside of the porch
were four square posts to support the outer edge of the overhanging roof.

The tall roof, with high colar beams connecting the rafters, provided un-
encumbered space for storage or sleeping. It was reached by a steep ladder-like
stairway located at one end of the porch. Finally, the roof was covered with

An Acadian Cottage

hand-split cypress shingles pegged to the purlins. No nails were used in these
early structures.

Cypress wood which weathered to a natural gray did not require paint
which, like glass and metal, was beyond the means of these poor farmers.

This very primitive house became the progenitor of many larger and more
sophisticated Acadian Cottages.

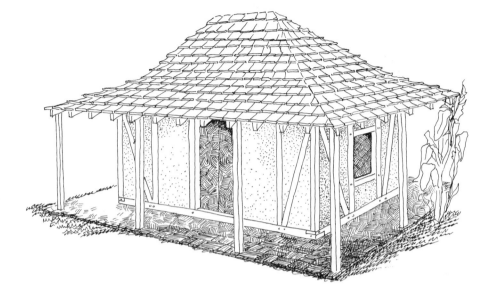

Creole Cottage

The Creole Cottage

A house similar to the Acadian Cottage was developed in and around New Orleans by the French long before the arrival of the Acadians. Its plan and structure was not unlike that of the Acadian Cottage except that it had a hipped roof that covered the basic building, including its veranda. It ranged in plan from a single gallery at the front or a gallery at front and rear to an encircling gallery. It rested on a series of pillars and it is said to have features derived from the West Indies. This early Louisiana structure is generally referred to as a Creole Cottage, and, like the Acadian Cottage, it developed into the raised cottage type of Plantation House.

The Plantation House

There are several historical house types in rural Acadiana which are far less common than the humble Acadian Cottage. They are usually larger, comparatively more expensive, and are identified by several terms. These are the house types that many present-day residents of Southwest Louisiana prefer to identity with because, to them, such houses symbolize the mythical luxurious life of the bygone aristocratic plantation owners.

The Plantation House evolved during the colonial era. It is a classic example of fine architecture in the grand tradition. It possesses ageless qualities in that

Acadian Plantation House

its forms are as vital today as when first built. The building satisfied the human needs of its occupants. It was the result of a sensitive use of materials, and the most advanced technology of the time was incorporated in the structure. But most important, it was a statement of ideas and values cherished by its builders.

The Raised Cottage

The most indigenous style of the plantation house is the Raised Cottage. It grew from the ground up to become an organic structure, existing in perfect harmony with its environment. No designer would dare to conceive of a sub-surface basement in an area where the water table was only a few feet below the surface, where year-round rainfall was more than abundant, and where flooding was not unknown. Basement space was necessary on a plantation to satisfy the needs of certain activities which were beyond the living requirements of the family. The logical answer to these needs was to construct the basement above ground.

Creole Raised Cottage

The ground floor of a raised cottage was typically a structure of solid brick walls seven-to-eight feet high and sixteen-to-twenty inches thick, resting on in-ground footings. Such strength was necessary to support the superstructure. The on-grade brick floors were only inches above the ground. The rectangular plan was divided into a single work or storage area at each side with an open passageway between. The exposed joists and the underside of the flooring of the frame structure above constituted the ceiling of the ground floor.

Appropriately sized square, rectangular, or round brick piers or sometimes columns were positioned to support the outer edges of the gallery above. The handmade, low-fired brick did not withstand the elements; therefore, the outside walls and all piers were coated with a thick plaster and were whitewashed.

Above this strong masonry foundation rested a heavy cypress frame which was constructed in the same manner as that of the Cajun Cottage. All walls that were protected on the outside by an overhanging gallery roof were plaster-ed over with the same material used on the masonry structure below. Where there was no gallery, walls were sheathed with clapboard.

In a time before mechanical air conditioning, the designers sought ways to counteract destructive elements by providing the basic shelter with a wide gallery to capture the natural breezes and shield the walls of the house from pounding rains and fierce sunrays.

The simplest Raised Cottage had a gallery only on the front. Others had a gallery at front and rear, and with some, the gallery ran all around the house. The gallery was a functional element of the house. In the spring and summer it was used for recreation, entertaining, and sometimes for sleeping.

The earlier plan of the rectangular second level, which contained the family living space, was two or three rooms side by side, each opening onto the wide veranda. The eight-to-ten-foot-high walls of the interior were plastered and painted or boarded over with wood.

Openings onto the porch were inward swinging, glazed double doors protected from the outside by solid wood shutters swinging outside against the wall. Windows were either multi-light sash or hinged single or double casements with shutters. Each set of two rooms was heated by back-to-back fireplaces with one inside chimney. Ceilings were of exposed joists revealing floorboards above, or they were lathed and plastered. Expert joiners produced fine mantlepieces, paneling, moulding, and trims from cypress.

The whole house was covered by a gable roof, hip roof, or a French hip roof where the steep pitch was broken into two planes by a less steep prolongation extending outward to cover the entire eight-or-nine-foot-wide gallery. The outer edge of the roof was supported by cypress colonettes corresponding to the piers below. A balastrade ranged between the columns. Shingles were rived from cypress logs and were fastened down with wooden pegs or by nails. In some cases, well-proportioned dormers pierced the roof to provide light for the attic space which was sometimes used for living quarters.

In essence, the fully developed Raised Cottage was a two-story, rectangular form capped by a large, high-pitched, hipped roof which overhung all around to form an open, colonnaded, two-story veranda running entirely around the house. This organic structure was an outgrowth of its natural environment and reflected a deep reverence for nature. The form of the building and the material of which it was constructed was the result of the local environment.

Greek Revival

During the first half of the nineteenth century, the plantations of Southwest Louisiana prospered sufficiently to allow landowners to construct dwellings which reflected their economic station in life. Such buildings were commodious, constructed of quality materials by skilled craftsmen, and they were duly appointed. Aesthetics was a prime consideration. While some of the plantation houses were reminiscent of the Georgian style of architecture, most were in the Greek Revival style.

The American style of Greek Revival architecture drifted into Southwestern Louisiana where it encountered various forces which drastically modified it. The subtropic climate with its hot, humid summers and mild, rainy winters made its imprint. The flat, fertile, flood plains, with luxurious plant growth, made its demands. The variegated history of French, Spanish, and American domination, with its potpourri of customs, was quite influential. In concert,

Greek Revival Plantation House

these and other strong influences modified the Greek Revival movement to evolve a Classical architecture peculiar to Southwest Louisiana.

The Louisiana Greek Revival style of architecture is renowned. It synthesized a variety of forms each based on a near square but more often on a rectangular plan. One was a two-story frame or brick structure capped with either an overhanging gable or hip roof, sometimes with dormers to light the attic. The roof was supported on the outside by a colonnade of Tuscan columns rising from the ground to the roof and supporting, at midway, a balcony which, sometimes, completely encircled the building. The symmetrical plan was rectangular, being wider than its depth. An ample hall ran completely through the center separating two magnificent rooms of equal size on each side. This plan was repeated on the second floor. Vertical circulation varied; however, stairs in the central hallway are most prevalent. On the other hand, there are a number of plans that located the stairs on the veranda. The effect seems to be to have large rooms arranged to allow for the best possible ventilation through a most handsome interior.

A variation of this basic design was the same rectangular structure capped with a gable roof which overhung the front side only. The outside edge of the overhang was supported by a range of four to eight columns. These columns supported a balcony let into the columns at mid-height. The balcony ran the entire width of the house. Instead of a central hallway, the plan called for three side-by-side sets of back-to-back rooms. The three front rooms opened directly onto the gallery. All rooms were interconnected. Access to the second floor was via an outside staircase on the veranda and a small, closeted stair at the rear.

Another variation was simply to attach a Greek Temple front complete with columns, architrave, and pediment to the center of a two-story structure. A few of the later Greek Revival plantation houses were of monumental scale, containing up to seventy-five rooms in an asymmetrical plan, with porticoes of tremendous fluted columns of plastered brick topped with six-foot-high Corinthian capitals of carved cypress. Such a structure was the epitome of the Classic Revival in Louisiana.

The Shotgun House

There is another folk house type in Southwest Louisiana that carries the disparaging name "Shotgun." On the surface "Shotgun" may seem to be an incongruous name for a house type. However, the logic behind the name is the assumption that a charge from a shotgun fired into the front door opening would pass through the entire house and out the rear opening without hitting a thing.

A Shotgun House is the simplest type of multiroom dwelling. Though it is distinctly New Orleans French, it probably had its origin with the thatched huts of Haiti; or, the form might have derived, in part, from the long thatched huts of the Gulf Coast Indians.

The earlier, fully developed Shotgun was a narrow, off-ground, ten-by-twenty-foot wood-frame structure. It was a single-story, rectangular box which rested on ranges of brick pillars. The outside of the frame was covered with horizontal, wood sheathing. It was divided with transverse walls to form two or three successive rooms with all doors on a single axis. Typically, there was

Shotgun House

one window on both sides of each room. An interior, brick chimney was located at the center of the transverse wall to serve back-to-back fireplaces, one in each room. The front room served for sleeping. The kitchen and toilet facilities were originally placed behind the house and were unattached.

The shingled roof was a gable which extended forward to cover a shallow porch which stretched across the entire width of the house. The outer edges of the gable end of the roof were supported by thin, square posts. An alternative to the roof extension was a lean-to shed attached to the gable in such a manner as to cover the porch. By the turn of the century, Victorian opulence influenced the decoration of the porch which was "tricked up" with a balustrade of turned, candlestick-like banisters, overhead ranges of wooden spindles and filigreed, wooden brackets at the top sides of the turned wooden posts.

Shotgun Houses which were built to accommodate low-income families were constructed on the back streets of the towns and villages of Acadiana. Because of its small size and simple shape with unbroken walls and roof, it was not costly to build. This type was often adopted by lumber, sugar, and rice mills to serve as "company houses."

The Open Passage House

American immigrants began to construct the Open Passage type of dwelling

in the northern part of the state shortly after Louisiana was admitted to the
Union.   Very few such dwellings are extant.   Though the Open Passage House
was quite popular among the hill farmers in the piney woods of North Louisiana and other Southern states, it was not so numerous in Southwestern
Louisiana where the Acadian Cottage type of house prevailed.   The Open Passage House was facetiously referred to as a "dog-trot house" simply because
dogs ran at will through the open, central passageway.

The form of this house evolved from the log-pen type structure built on the
ground in two equal parts separated by an open passageway and covered with a
single, low-pitched, gabled roof which in turn was covered with rough-barked
planks.   A stick chimney of mud and straw was sometimes attached to the outer
ends of both segments.   There was a door opening on the passageway for each
room, but there were few if any windows which were unglazed though shuttered
with rough boards.   There was no paint or whitewash anywhere, and the floors
were the natural hard-packed dirt.

The further developed Open Passage House, built as the farmers became
more prosperous, consisted of two wooden frame structures placed at each end
of a rectangular plan with a wide, unenclosed passageway between them.   The
single floor and gabled roof were continuous.   The whole rested on a series of

Open Passage House

brick pillars. Each unit was divided into two equal rooms, each with a door opening onto the open hallway.

A porch about nine feet deep was attached to the front side of the house. It extended almost the entire width of the front and was covered by a low-pitched, lean-to roof attached to the eaves of the house. It was supported by a range of four or more square posts at the outer edges. The gabled roof was neither steep nor shallow. It was covered with hand-split cedar or cypress shingles.

Two inside, brick chimneys for back-to-back fireplaces served the two rooms of each unit. The stock frame of mill-cut lumber was sheathed with horizontal clapboards. Each room boasted an ample number of glazed, multi-pane, sash windows. The openings onto the porch extended from the floor almost to the ceiling.

The two rooms of one segment served as bedrooms, while the opposite rooms were the parlor and dining room. The kitchen was a separate or attached building at the rear of the house. If it was within the means of the builder, the house was painted white or yellow, and the crowning glory was a set of fancy lightning rods with a weather vane.

As time went on, the builders enclosed the open passage to form a commodious hall running from front to back. Others closed in and dormered the attic space to form a living area entered by a simple staircase in the hall. This latter stage in the evolution of the Open Passage House was popular throughout Southwest Louisiana, and many fine examples still exist.

The Midwestern House

A type of house which was alien to the Acadian culture developed on the prairies of Southwest Louisiana during the latter part of the nineteenth century. This was a wood-frame structure built by immigrant farmers from the Midwest who came to Louisiana to raise rice and cattle. The earlier Midwestern-type buildings were simple, box-like structures of two stories capped with an unbroken gabled roof. The front and back were the long sides of the rectangular plan which contained a central hall which separated the single rooms on each side. The second floor echoed the first floor. There was a smaller wing, usually one story, attached at a right angle to the rear center. A small porch covered with a lean-to roof protected the entrance. The whole house was raised two or more feet off the ground by a series of brick pillars.

These austere structures reflected no historic building style. They were almost completely devoid of ornamentation. While their builders were assimilated into the Acadian culture, the extant buildings still remain distinctive.

Midwestern House

Victorian Architecture in Acadiana

The Classic tradition in domestic architecture survived in Acadiana until the Civil War which accelerated the decline of classicism nationwide. Around the turn of this century a style of domestic architecture appeared in Acadiana that was alien to the region. Whereas the older Plantation Houses and Acadian Cottages were conceived in the light of the local environment, the new style was by no means a product of the locale. Rather, it flourished in Northeast and Midwest America and quickly spread to the West Coast and on to the South, including the bayou country of Southwest Louisiana. Victorian-style houses were built in Acadiana without significant regional variations dictated by geographic and climatic conditions, available materials, local skills and tecniques, and the sociological background of the people. Such houses in Rhode

Victorian House

Island, Illinois, California, and Crowley, Louisiana, differed little, except for detail.

This new style of domestic architecture in Acadiana was a wooden structure with a design based on the final and declining stages of the American Victorian Period which, in turn, had its roots in the English architecture of the Victorian Age (1837-1901).

By the time Victorian architecture became prominent in Acadiana during the last decade of the nineteenth and first decade of the twentieth centuries, purveyors of architectural styles were spreading their influence with numerous copybooks containing instructions and drawings that an ordinary carpenter would have no difficulty in following.

Designers of the time who were attracted to the Victorian style no longer concerned themselves with historical accuracy. They used the Victorian style as a point of depature. In their quest for novelty, they turned to a form of extreme eclecticism. In general, they managed to congest elements of various historical styles along with motifs of their own invention into buildings which were often referred to as "fussily ugly" and "ostentatiously ornate." As a result, there is no such thing in Louisiana as a "pure" example of Victorian architecture. Instead, there are numerous individual variations which differ in plan, exterior profile, proportion, and decorative treatment.

The house in Louisiana which displayed Victorian opulence was a massive wooden building of irregular plan and shape. Its structural system was a relatively new invention (1830s) called the balloon-frame. This system was quite a departure from the medieval-type frame of the older Plantation House and the Acadian Cottage. This revolutionary, balloon frame was made up of small-dimensioned, mill-manufactured lumber cut to standard sizes and put together as studs and plates with mass-produced, metal nails. Such light and simple construction eliminated the need for the skilled wood craftsman of the past. The carpenter with his hammer and saw took his rightful place in the construction trade. A few such tradesmen could construct a balloon-frame house within a relatively short time at a surprisingly low cost. The flexibility of the construction system allowed the designer to depart from the rigid symmetry of the Classical design. Such a system led to the fanciful late-Victorian style by fostering a certain license of architectural imagination.

The typical extant Victorian house in Acadiana is a large, three-story, steep-gabled structure which sits on a partially above-ground basement. The asymmetric plan of this commodious and comfortable structure was light and airy. There was, more often than not, a secondary facade with its porch at the side of the house. The dominating feature of the building was a strategically placed tower of several stories. The plan of the tower was round, octagonal, or square and was capped with a corresponding steeple, though many were topped with round, pointed, or onion-shaped domes.

In a single building the window shapes varied. They took the shape of vertical rectangles, circles, ovals, half-rounds, lozenges, and the pointed Gothic. Transoms over the entrance door were horizontal rectangles, segmental or four-pointed arches. Much of the exterior glazing was in colored glass. The exterior doors of wood were lightened by decorative panels of leaded, stained glass or beveled, clear glass.

The porches were covered with a low-pitched, lean-to roof connected to the house just above the top of the first floor. Its overhang was extensive. The roof was supported by widely spaced, slender, wooden posts which had been turned on a lathe to produce a graceful, curvilinear contour. Resting on blocks a few inches above the floor and ranging between the posts was a wooden balustrade with a wide handrail supported by a range of closely spaced candelabrum-shaped banisters.

The overall interior plan of a Victorian House was convenient and roomy. It was laid out so as to accommodate the needs of a large family including the activities of servants. The first-floor plan was usually an arrangement of high-ceilinged rooms for specific functions pertaining to the activities of the family circle, the entertainment of visitors, along with food storage, preparation and service.

During the 1920s and '30s, the Victorian style was looked upon with disfavor. It was considered to be a vulgar imitation of Gothic. Now that we are from seventy-five to a hundred years away in time, we have come to appreciate the Victorian style.

Queen Anne House

The Queen Anne Style

A relative of the Victorian style of domestic architecture is the Queen Anne style which originated in England during the early nineteenth century. There, it was generally executed in brick and was characterized by the use of sash windows and a hipped roof that was almost obscured by parapets. Compared to its contemporary, the restless and congested High Victorian, the Queen Anne House was calm and well proportioned.

The Queen Anne label was loosely applied to a style of domestic architecture that flourished in Southwestern Louisiana during the last quarter of the nineteenth century. Compared to the exuberant Victorian style of the same period, which utilized a broad range of historical sources, the Queen Anne House was a relatively unpretentious style which was well suited to the taste of the developing middle class in Southwest Louisiana. In this area, this convenient and comfortable house was most often a wooden, balloon-frame structure with sash windows, a gabled or hipped roof, and a commodious porch. Elements of bygone styles were used with discretion. Its sensible plainness was attractive. This style is evident in the urban and rural areas of Acadiana.

Conclusion

The Acadian and Creole Cottages along with the antebellum Plantation Houses have largely disappeared with the changing socio-economic systems. New building materials, techniques, and services have replaced the old and respected manner of building. The balloon frame replaced the timber frame. Factory-made insulation replaced the mud-and-moss infill. Cypress wood became scarce while brick became expensive. Mechanical air conditioning replaced the fireplace and chimneys.

Each year a few more of the historic structures fall to the elements or the wrecking ball; however, a few are being maintained for posterity while new building traditions continue to develop in Acadiana.

BIBLIOGRAPHY

Kniffen, Fred B. "Louisiana House Types," *Annals of the Association of American Geographers*, XXVI (1935), 179-93.

—————. *Louisiana, Its Land and People*. Baton Rouge: L. S. U. Press, 1968.

McDermott, John Francis, ed. *The French in the Mississippi Valley*. Urbana: University of Illinois Press, 1965.

Post, Lauren C. *Cajun Sketches, From the Prairies of Southwest Louisiana*. Baton Rouge: L. S. U. Press, 1962.

Robin, C. C. *Voyage to Louisiana*. Trans. by Stuart O. Landry, Jr. New Orleans: Pelican Publishing Co., 1966.

THE POLITICS OF THE ACADIAN PARISHES

by Perry H. Howard

The pervasive French influence in state affairs is apparent whenever a scholar assembles a list of variables to explain the behavior of Louisianians, be it in agriculture, industry, politics, or recreational pursuits.[1] This point was demonstrated recently when an attempt was made to explain "the Edwards victory," the election of the first "Cajun" governor during the twentieth century.[2] Urban-Republicanism, racism, and Catholicism were found to be the most important underlying tendencies in Louisiana politics in the1970s.

The most impressive finding of all, however, turned up when these three dimensions were used to delineate political and ecological areas among the parishes. A French-Catholic area appears as the most homogeneous of parish clusters. A North Louisiana Anglo-Protestant cluster is considerably less important since this region divides into delta and hill parishes. The borders of the French-Catholic cluster follow the western edge of the Mississippi River from Avoyelles to, but not including, Jefferson Parish, and the western limits of Evangeline, Jefferson Davis, and Vermilion parishes. These boundaries coincide almost exactly with those of Acadiana as delineated by scholars throughout the years. The French-Catholic area is made up of some parishes closer to the Mississippi--including the parishes of Pointe Coupée, St. Landry, West Baton Rouge, Iberville, St. Martin, St. John, St. James and Assumption--the others south and west, including the parishes of Avoyelles, Evangeline, Jefferson Davis, Acadia, Vermilion, Iberia, St. Mary, Terrebonne, Lafourche, St. Charles, Ascension, as well as Lafayette Parish, which had appeared in the initial cluster as an urban place. To study the political tendencies of the South Louisiana parishes, the parishes of Cameron and Calcasieu were added for a total of 22 parishes, almost identical with what the Public Affairs Research Council has called Acadiana in its publications.

Today, culture (primarily language and religion) rather than ethnic origin identifies what has become known as South Louisiana.[3] It is difficult to distinguish the people of colonial French background from those of Acadian origin. The French population of colonial Louisiana was augmented from 1764 on by the homeless Acadian exiles who established themselves on the "Acadian Coast" (St. James and Ascension parishes). These *petit habitants*, bypassing the great Atchafalaya basin, settled on small parcels of land along the smaller

174

waterways, especially Bayou Lafourche and Bayou Teche, in the Attakapas district and the Opelousas district of the upper Teche and the prairie borders. To this day these parishes have a high density of rural population.

Professor D. L. A. Hackett's study of Louisiana in the Jacksonian period shows how these settlement patterns evolved in the early nineteenth century.[4] In 1840, the parishes with the largest proportion of French families were St. Charles (94.4 percent); St. John (92.6 percent); St. James (89.7 percent); Ascension (84.3 percent); Assumption (77.7 percent); Lafourche (73.9 percent); St. Martin (83.0 percent); and Lafayette (89.3 percent). (See map.) In 1940 a Frenchman writing his Master's thesis at L. S. U.,[5] Claude Jean Roumagnac, used lists of French names and Catholic religious affiliation to pinpoint the areas of Acadian influence. By then the predominantly French area had shifted westward, and its core was composed of the parishes of Avoyelles, St. Landry, St. Martin, Lafayette, Iberia, Assumption, Terrebonne, and Lafourche. We should not be surprised to find French influence persisting, for, as we have been told, Acadians have assimilated foreign elements in the southern part of the state, infecting all with their *joie de vivre*.[6]

Despite the apparent homogeneity of the region, the politics of the Acadians cannot be easily analyzed because it must be viewed in the context of its historical experience and its relations with the rest of the state. One must take into account the French colonial beginnings and the tradition of centralized authority institutionalized in the state constitution by creating a strong chief executive; the predominance of one staple (sugar) as the main cash crop of the southern parishes, and the subsequent policy preference for a protective tariff; the isolation of the Cajuns; and the problem of political participation by the *petits habitants des bayous* versus apathy and indifference toward affairs of state. The analysis is further complicated by the fact that the data available on most of these questions is recorded on the parish level, thus allowing only general inferences.

Down to 1860, Louisiana history celebrates what has been called the French Ascendancy.[7] When Louisiana entered the Union it preserved the French judicial system, with Spanish modifications, which has remained the basis of state law to this day. Debate in the legislature could be conducted either in French or English, and state laws were published in both languages until 1898. Of the thirteen elected governors before 1860, three were of French background, two were Acadians (see pictures), and one had a French mother.[8]

The earliest electoral skirmishes took place between French and American "parties," which soon became Whig and Democrat. The predilection of the Louisiana French for Whigdom is not hard to explain if we assume that politics is based to a large extent upon economic needs. Such policies as a national bank, internal improvements and protective tariff readily appealed to South

Paul O. Hébert

Alexandre Mouton

Louisiana at election time when voters chose their party nominee, a "gentle-
man," which usually meant a wealthy sugar planter.

The parish records reveal the preference of the French area for the Whigs.
In the period 1834 and 1852, nearly three-fourths of the Acadian parishes voted
Whig while close to two-thirds of the rest of the state recorded Democratic
majorities.[9]   Voter participation was quite high statewide, as Hackett has
shown,[10] but it is difficult to estimate actual voter turnout on the parish level.
More research must be undertaken to obtain a representative notion of the
"civic virtues" in antebellum Louisiana. But we analyzed presidential turnout
on the parish level for 1840. The number of white males 21 years of age and
over was estimated for each parish and divided by the number of popular votes
cast in the presidential election of that year. This procedure yielded a turnout
level below estimations based upon numbers of qualified voters, but the results
were all the more telling. We found that in 1840 the statewide turnout of
voters of voting age was only 41 percent, but in the Acadian parishes it reached
68 percent. Of course, South Louisiana was then the more settled area of the
state, and one would expect lower turnout in the North Louisiana "frontier"
parishes. Surprisingly enough, Acadian parishes with the largest number of
"planters" recorded a turnout fifteen percent lower than the "bayou" parishes
with more *petits habitants*.

By the time Louisiana faced the coming of the "irrepressible conflict,"
Acadians had begun to vote like the rest of the state. With the Whig party's
demise in the 1850s, the proportion of Acadian parishes supporting the Democrats matched that of the rest of the state in the gubernatorial elections. But,
in the presidential election of 1860, the parishes in the rest of the state were
decidedly more Southern Democrat than South Louisiana, where there was a
Union sentiment, reflecting the heavy investment in sugar. Yet, an equal proportion of Acadian and other parishes voted in favor of secession.

During Reconstruction, South Louisiana participated in the power struggle
which pitted Republican against Democrat, North Louisiana against South, and
white against black. No definitive study we know of has explained why the
Acadian parishes became a seat of radical Republicanism.[11] South Louisiana
was occupied by Federal troops earlier and, of course, was always concerned
over tariff and therefore tended toward Union sentiment. In the election for
ratification of the Constitution of 1868, the sugar parishes favored ratification
although a substantial opposing minority could be found among the relatively
numerous small landholders in Lafourche, Terrebonne, and St. Mary parishes.
Blacks were granted the franchise; Henry Clay Warmoth was elected governor;
and Reconstruction was in full swing.

Perhaps the most important influence was simply numbers. From 1876 to
1898 black registrants outnumbered white in 27 parishes, 12 of which were

Acadian: Pointe Coupée, West Baton Rouge, Iberville, St. Martin, Iberia, St. Mary, Assumption, Ascension, St. John, St. Charles, and Terrebonne (the heart of the sugar bowl). In the six presidential elections held during this period, the Acadian parishes voted a Republican majority on the average of 3.66 times, while 15 other parishes with a black majority voted Republican 4.86 times. In gubernatorial elections, the averages were 3.42 and 0.66 respectively. Apparently it was one thing to vote Republican in a presidential election, but in local contests former Confederates preferred to support the Democratic party in order to retain control of the state house.

With the election of Rutherford B. Hayes in 1876 and the end of Reconstruction, the Bourbon Democrats became intent upon creating counterrevolution.[12] In 1896, the threat of the Populist-Republican fusion was vanquished, and Murphy J. Foster, the Democratic candidate, was elected. Ironically enough, the Fusion candidate, John Newton Pharr, was, like the victor, a resident of St. Mary Parish (which went for Pharr). In this election, 53 percent of the Acadian parishes (10 of 19) voted with 49 percent of the rest of the state (18 of 37), mainly farmer parishes in the hills, in support of the Fusion. The Fusion, like Longism later, bridged North and South Louisiana.

The triumph of the Bourbon Democrats resulted in the Constitution of 1898, the disfranchisement of most black voters, and a lowering of voter turnout figures for a generation. The Fusionists tried once more for the governorship in 1900, fielding another of St. Mary's illustrious sons, Donelson J. Caffery, Jr. In this election, the Democratic majorities followed the classic distribution of predominately black parishes along the Mississippi and Red rivers where now only the white man voted. In South Louisiana, however, no planter parish with a predominantly black population went Democratic. Three parishes, Cameron, Ascension, and St. James, recorded Republican pluraities, while in six parishes—Lafayette, Iberville, St. Mary, Assumption, Terrebonne, and Lafourche—the Republican vote was above the state average of 18 percent. In Acadia and St. Landry also, the votes were above the state average—but for the People's party.

The voter turnout decreased sharply in the elections after 1898. The decline showed first in the presidential elections: for six elections the total vote was less than the 114,054 cast in 1892 until 1920 the total reached 126,396. Voter participation continued in the gubernatorial contests until 1896 when 206,354 votes were cast, but declined thereafter until 1924 when 239,529 votes were cast. In 1892, the presidential vote represented 42.7 percent of the registered voters; in 1920 the figure was 48.5 percent; and in the six elections between it averaged 46.3 percent. Gubernatorial turnout was 73.7 percent in 1896; 74.0 percent in 1924; and 62.2 percent as an average for the intervening elections. Except for the spirited election of 1928, which brought about larger participation, the presidential turnout began to approximate the gubernatorial turnout only in the 1960s. South Louisiana voters turned out in numbers well above the state average in the presidential elections of 1896, 1920, and 1928: 76 percent as against 74 percent, 58 percent as against 55 percent, and 87 percent as against 82 percent, respectively. In gubernatorial elections the South Louisiana average was lower than that for the state: 27 percent as against 36 percent, 43 percent as against 48 percent, and 55 percent as against 61 percent, respectively.

In 1920, the Republican party championed the tariff issue nationally and, predictably, in the presidential election of that year fourteen Acadian parishes recorded Republican majorities ranging from 52 percent in Evangeline and Acadia to 78 percent in Assumption Parish. The Republican tradition remained strong in French Louisiana through 1956 while, at the same time, the state's urban parishes were beginning to show Republican tendencies. In 1956, even the slogan on campaign buttons--"Moi, J'aime Ike"--failed to move all Acadian voters as only twelve French parishes gave the Republican majority support.

Republicanism in contemporary Louisiana has resulted from growing Democratic disaffection and, paradoxically enough, the center of Democratic support since 1944 has been consistently in the southern parishes. Thus, in the elections of 1960, 1964, 1968, and 1972, only eight parishes--Beauregard, Iberia, Lafayette, St. Mary, and Terrebonne (twice each), and Jefferson Davis, Lafourche, and Vermilion (once each)--have had Republican totals above the state average.

The sensitivity of voters in French parishes was revealed in 1928 by their support of Roman Catholic Democratic candidate Alfred E. Smith. There was no doubt that among states of the "Solid South," Louisiana would stay in the Democratic fold (76 percent Smith). This higher percentage was produced, however, by an average 72 percent in North Louisiana to 78 percent in South Louisiana. Between the 1924 and 1928 elections northern parishes increased their total by 58 percent, but the French parishes' increase was 85 percent. The modern era presidential politics began in 1944 with widespread voter disaffection and, in the nine elections which followed, the Democratic candidate carried the state only three times (1952, 1960, and 1976). As North Louisiana Democratic support decreased in 1944, South Louisiana parishes voted Democratic 5 percent more than the state average. When John F. Kennedy carried Louisiana by 50 percent in 1960, two-thirds of the French parishes had cast a majority of the votes for their fellow Catholic.

In the 1920s an Acadian son appeared, who, but for the almost simultaneous appearance of Huey P. Long, may have one day become governor of the "gret stet." Dudley J. LeBlanc's colorful career included a stint as representative from Vermilion Parish in the same primary which saw Huey Long lose his first bid for the governorship.[13] LeBlanc's reputation as a man of the people never decreased after the successful passage of his first bill, the "horse and wagon refund," which required a refund of any monies previously collected in an area where this mode of transportation was still quite characteristic and to levy taxes on it was felt to create hardship. The happy impact of this was felt by many voters. LeBlanc's career included a stint as representative, Public Service commissioner, state senator and president pro-tem of the upper chamber.

LeBlanc did not succeed in becoming governor, probably more because of forces beyond his control than because of any personal shortcomings. As T. Harry Williams has made clear,[14] Huey P. Long became the mass leader and leading edge of reform tendencies of the little people of Louisiana, frustrated and pressed down by the Bourbon oligarchs. Huey could carry the votes of Protestant North Louisiana red-neck farmers, but he could also carry those of the Catholic South Louisiana Cajuns. In fact, in 1928 Long gained majorities in three-fourths of the Acadian parishes but in only half the North Louisiana parishes. LeBlanc probably could not have accomplished the reverse. "Coozan Dud" kept trying, but the die was cast as Longism became strongly entrenched in Cajun as well as red-neck country. In 1936 only West Baton Rouge and West Feliciana parishes failed to give majorities to the Long candidate. Acadian parishes supported Sam Jones in 1940 after the Louisiana Scandals, but in 1948 every French parish gave a majority to Earl Long, and in 1956 all but two repeated that performance.

The 1950s, however, saw the rise of race and religion as issues that would polarize state politics in the 1960s.[15] Blacks had begun to register again after 1944, first swelling the rolls in New Orleans and other urban parishes and, by the 1950s, finding their reenfranchisement acceptable in the rural Acadian parishes.[16] The black bloc vote and desegregation became the focal points of the 1960 primaries as the urbane Catholic mayor of New Orleans, "Chep" Morrison, squared off against the opposition. The coalition built by the Longs was broken up by the race issue and the distribution of candidate support divided the state into north and south. Despite (or more likely because of) Morrison's moderate stand and French-parish support for his candidacy, Jimmie Davis won his second term as governor. The pattern was clear. Over three-fourths of South Louisiana parishes supported Morrison while over four-fifths of the North Louisiana parishes went for Davis. The pattern was repeated in 1964 except that John J. McKeithen, half a Long anyway, made inroads among the Cajuns and carried over one-third of the Acadian parishes. This is difficult to explain, for, at the same time, voter participation in the French parishes decreased: 78 percent of the registered voters cast ballots in the state, but only 56 percent bothered to vote in the Acadian parishes. This phenomenon is worthy of further research, particularly since the presidential election of 1960 brought out more Acadian voters than Louisianians in general--72 percent as

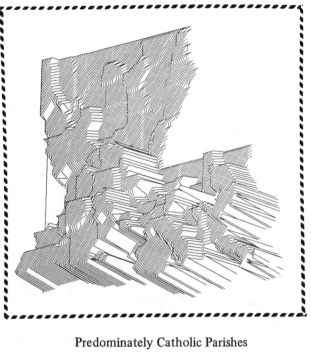

Predominately Catholic Parishes

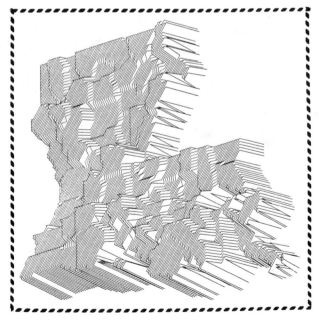

Parishes Carried by Edwards, 1972

Edwin Edwards
Cajun Governor of Louisiana,
1972-1980

against 70 percent. Did Acadians like JFK more and DSM less?

The elections of 1972 showed the consequences of black voter registration after the 1965 civil rights acts. Black Political Equality is measured by dividing the proportion of blacks registered by the proportion of black population in a unit. The Acadian parishes led the way with percentages ranging as high as 80 percent or more. The Black Political Equality for the state as a whole reached 73.6 percent of parity. What would happen if a candidate could build a coalition on "black power" and "Cajun power?" The answer came in 1972 when black voters everywhere chose Edwin Edwards, and the rural parishes, which had been rather unenthusiastic toward Chep Morrison, gave over 80 percent of their votes to Edwards in the second primary election. It was this Cajun support which gave Edwards the razor-thin edge over Senator J. Bennett Johnston statewide.

Sample surveys have increased our understanding of Acadian politics. A study of political culture has been made of two towns, Mansfield and Breaux Bridge, selected as representative cities for northern and southern Louisiana subcultures.[17] Political culture consists of public knowledge of government, beliefs about government and politics, and estimates of how government theoretically works and how it actually works. The two rural communities were compared as to sense of citizen duty, faith in people, and feelings of political efficacy. Statistical analysis of the data showed that both acceptance of democratic principles and faith in people were significant for the French community. Race was the more significant variable, however, as in every case blacks scored at lower rates, suggesting that the real sub-cultural division may be between black and white, rather than between north and south. On the other hand, the study gave support to the general belief that in South Louisiana Catholic faith and practice provide a more congenial setting for the exercise of citizenship by blacks. In both presidential and gubernatorial elections, Breaux Bridge whites showed a decidedly higher rate of voter turnout than Mansfield whites, and, though black rates in both towns were lower than white, the blacks in the French town were more involved in the political process than their North Louisiana counterparts.

The Louisiana electorate has been subjected to analysis on the aggregate ecological (parish) level for almost three decades so that there is great interest in the 1968 statewide sample survey of individual Louisiana voters undertaken as part of the Comparative State Election Project of the Institute for Research in Social Science at Chapel Hill.[18] This study, the first of its kind as far as we know, shows that on the national level, the non-voters of the 1968 fall election were chiefly young, high school graduates, manual workers, and low income. There were 10 percent more non-voters in the Louisiana sample, but distributed somewhat differently: rural blacks, young, and Catholics. On the sub-regional level, the survey showed more non-voters in North Louisiana and in Southwest Louisiana parishes. When asked their main reason for not voting, 45.6 percent of the Louisiana respondents answered "not registered"; 15.7 percent "too busy"; 14 percent "ill"; and 10.7 percent said they "never voted."

Historical accounts of demographic and political tendencies have enabled us to identify Louisiana's most likely populist and racist constituency. In the CSEP study, we sought to define this constituency in terms of attitudes. Five policy statements were used to build a "populism index": "the government ought to help the common man"; "the county needs more jobs and better wages"; "Social Security benefits ought to be increased"; "the government should stop spending money on welfare programs"; and the "government ought to help big business." "Populists" would be expected to endorse the first three items and reject the latter two. Similarly, three items were used to build a "racism index": "I favor letting Negroes move into white neighborhoods"; "the government ought to help Negroes"; and a question about the rapidity of integration in Louisiana. "Racists" would oppose the first two statements, and would feel that integration was proceeding "too rapidly."

The resulting indexes of populist and racist views were cross tabulated with race and with religion. Black respondents, as one might expect, were almost unanimously (91 percent) low in the Racism Index and high (64 percent) in the Populism Index. A bare majority (51 percent) of whites could be classed as "racist" (high), and white Catholics were significantly less likely to be racist (40 percent Catholics to 60 percent Protestants). Catholics were found more likely to be "populist" than Protestants (high 37 percent and 24 percent, respectively).

Two-thirds of our state sample identified with the Democratic party and close to half revealed conservative leanings. Yet the Democratic tradition remained so strong among many whites (despite their disaffected votes in the face of the recent civil rights liberalism of the national Democratic party) that 30 percent of all Louisiana respondents considered themselves to be both Democrats and conservatives. To be sure, Louisiana Republicans are more likely to call themselves conservatives than are Democrats; but the modal identification of Democrats is also conservative. When we check the relationship between the respondents' positions along the conservative-liberalism contimuum and the degree of their populism and racism, we discover a significant association. Conservatives were more than twice as likely to score high on the Racism Index (56 percent) than liberals (26 percent). Conversely, a majority of liberals (53 percent), but only about one-fifth of the conservatives, are to be found in the low racist category. Of course, among Louisiana respondents, only 10 percent had said they were liberals (roughly the same as the national sample but significantly larger than for the Deep South as a whole). While liberals were disproportionately Catholic.

Louisiana's conservative and racist dispositions were obvious in the presidential elections of 1968 and 1972. Less obvious was the fact, derived from the CSEP sample survey, that only 13 percent of the state's white voters supported the Democratic candidate in 1968 while the bulk of the black voters voted Democratic. Among whites, Catholics voted for Nixon 31 percent, Humphrey 23 percent, and Wallace 46 percent, but Protestants voted 26 percent for Nixon, 6 percent Humphrey, and 68 percent Wallace. These dispositions within the electorate are reflected in the votes recorded on the parish level. The existence of more populist or conservative trends in the 1968 and 1972 presidential elections may be found in the overwhelming Wallace (48 percent) and Nixon (64 percent) victories in Louisiana. Wallace ran ahead in all areas of the state, gaining majorities in 40 parishes and pluralities in 21 more parishes. In 1972, Nixon carried every Louisiana parish but West Feliciana.

By averaging the percentage support in the top six Democrat, Republican, and Wallace parishes in the Acadian unit, we confirm that Democrat support is highest in parishes where black voter registration is highest. Most Republican and Wallace votes are taken to be white votes.

1968	STATE AVE.	ACADIAN AVE.	IN 6 HIGHEST ACADIAN PARISHES		
			DEMO.	REP.	WALLACE
Democrat	29.0	30.0	(41.0)	26.7	24.0
Republican	23.0	19.0	13.0	(27.0)	28.0
Wallace	48.0	49.8	50.0	45.0	(58.0)
Black Registration	19.7	20.3	39.8	19.3	16.5

DEMOCRATIC: St. Landry, Pointe Coupée, West Baton Rouge, Iberville, St. James, St. John
REPUBLICAN: Jefferson Davis, Lafayette, Iberia, St. Mary, Terrebonne, Lafourche
WALLACE: Cameron, Vermilion, Acadia, Evangeline, Avoyelles, Ascension

Acadian and State averages, as well as Black Registration, are quite similar in the aggregate. But, suggestive that contextual effects are at work, distinct clusterings are discovered for each set of six highest parishes. The highest Acadian Democrat parishes follow the Mississippi River, where many parishes possess high black voter registration. Republican parishes skirt the Gulf of Mexico, whereas high Wallace parishes follow a line northward from Cameron and Vermilion to Avoyelles Parish. Even in the high Democrat and Republican parishes we can conclude that, when white voters have a choice, more choose the populist Wallace than the conservative Nixon. In evidence of the stability of these parish vote patterns, the 1972 vote for the Democrat, George McGovern, and the Republican, Nixon, produces similar parish profiles. Five of the six high parishes in the previous election maintain those positions for both

Democrat and Republican. Taken together, Louisiana parish results trace the continuation of the Democrat disaffection in favor of more populist or conservative leaning candidates on the part of whites and continued Democrat support by blacks.

Kevin Phillips[19] in 1969 had predicted the beginning of an emerging Republican majority in the American party system. 1972 appeared to clinch the argument (with Louisiana in the forefront), except that after the Watergate affair, electoral enthusiasm for the Republicans was dampened. Writing in response to the present budgetary impass encountered by the "conservative" Reagan administration, Phillips finds neither "liberal" nor "conservative" positions promise positive solutions.[20] We are informed, rather, that the contemporary "new right" includes many people whose families were associated with the old Southern populist tradition together with elements of the old Northern working class. While these categories voted for Reagan, many of them favor government economic support for rural and blue collar interests, all quite compatible with the populism that had been displayed by George Wallace. If much of what has gone down as conservatism the past decade and a half is in fact populism, this sentiment is readily visible in the county vote for presidential candidates in what Phillips had first labelled the "Sun Belt" in 1969. Indeed he now goes on to say: "One can easily enough imagine the Sun Belt as the launching pad of a powerful conservatism--based on communication and on high corporate technology, frequently plebisictary and intermittently populist."[21] That Louisiana has become part of this Sun Belt, and that the Acadian parishes reflect some of its leading characteristics, may become clear in reading the remaining few pages.

Toward the end of Edwin Edwards' second term, won handily with over 60 percent of the votes cast in the first primary of 1975, there were Cajun challengers all over the place vying for the governor's chair. There was Edgar Mouton, state senator from Lafayette, Paul Hardy, secretary of state from St. Martin, and Louis Lambert, Public Utility Commissioner, from Ascension. There was also Republican David Treen, U. S. congressman from Jefferson, whose Third District consisted of the five Acadian parishes of St. Charles, Lafourche, Terrebonne, St. Mary, and Iberia. Rounding out the list of candidates were James Fitzmorris, secretary of Department of Commerce and Industry, from New Orleans, and E. L. Henry, a state representative from Union Parish.

This was to be the first serious test of Louisiana's new open primary law in which both Democrat and Republican candidates run for office in the same election. As some observers had surmised would happen with such an arrangement, the Republican candidate, Treen (nominated previously in a state convention), led the field with 21.8 percent of the vote, while the intense Democrat competition in the open primary ended with Lambert and Fitzmorris virtually in a dead heat for second place. The results are listed in ascending order in the State Vote column and beside it the percentage support in Acadian parishes as well as that in each candidate's home and surrounding parishes. It is plain to see that the Cajun candidates were supported with higher percentages here than statewide, whereas Henry, Fitzmorris, and Treen were proportionally stronger outside the Acadian parishes. Each candidate scored well among his friends and neighbors, with Mouton and Lambert found to be the most popular when one compares State Vote and that in Home and Contiguous Parishes. The latter did astonishingly well in ascension and surrounding parishes.

CANDIDATE	STATE VOTE	ACADIAN VOTE	HOME AND CONTIGUOUS PARISHES
Mouton	9.1%	13.0%	25.0%
Henry	9.9	3.7	28.0
Hardy	16.6	24.0	27.0
Fitzmorris	20.6	14.2	34.0
Lambert	20.7	25.0	50.0
Treen	21.8	18.0	30.0

After the charges of first primary vote stealing were settled, Treen and Lambert squared off and the former gained a razor-thin margin of 9,551 votes to become the first Republican governor in over 100 years. Out of a total 1,371,825 votes, Treen gained 50.3 percent and Lambert 49.7 percent. These

CANDIDATE	STATE VOTE	ACADIAN VOTE	HOME AND CONTIGUOUS PARISHES
Edwards, 1972	50.2%	68.0%	74.0%
Treen, 1979	50.3	44.0	59.0 (3rd Dis.)
Lambert, 1979	49.7	56.0	70.0

returns can be usefully compared with the even closer margin of Edwin Edwards in 1972 when he bested J. Bennett Johnston by 4,518 votes, 50.2 percent to 49.8 percent. While both Edwards and Lambert scored well among friends and neighbors, Edwards' Acadian vote overall was substantially better. To some extent, Lambert was competing with Treen in South Louisiana. Treen's vote in the Third District parishes was 15 percent greater than his average Acadian parishes support and, thus, his most substantial support was elsewhere, 53.1 percent, in fact, in the urban areas of the state.

The presidential elections which took place less than a year after these gubernatorial primaries warrant comparison. The votes for Democrat and Republican presidential candidates in both 1976 and 1980 were also extremely close, 52.8 and 47.2 percent, respectively, in the former, and just the opposite in the latter. Turnout of electorate voting age increased in the 1980 election for the state of Louisiana. Our attention falls on the increased presidential turnout

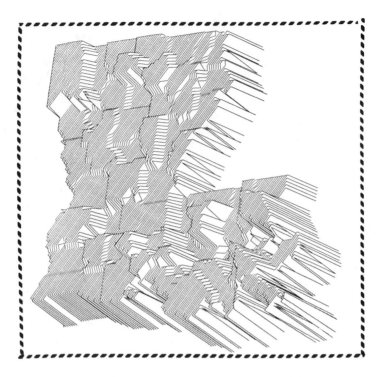

Parishes Carried by Treen, 1979

GUBERNATORIAL	1975	1979
Voting Age	2,500,000	2,700,000
Vote	1,203,004 (48.1%)	1,371,825 (50,8%)
PRESIDENTIAL	1976	1980
Voting Age	2,532,000	2,780,000
Vote	1,251,395 (49.4%)	1,501,306 (54.0%)

in 1980. It turns out that of a total increase in votes 1980 over 1976 of nearly 250,000, there was a Republican surge of 201,786 votes, or 80.7 percent of the total increase. Two categories of voters have been found to contribute most to the 1980 Republican increase–urban parishes (43.3 percent) and Acadian parishes (25.6 percent).

Reference may be made to the maps which provide visual evidence of the tendencies being discussed. Looking across the state from southeast to northwest, the lines are set to record the percentage value for each parish of the characteristic being mapped. Thus, it is clear that the highest proportion of

Catholics is to be found in St. Martin Parish, which appears to arise like a mountain peak in the center of the state. Except for a few Catholics in Caddo, Lincoln, and Ouachita parishes, North Louisiana looks like a flat plain reaching toward the Arkansas border. The 1972 Edwards vote would be expected to reveal a similar profile, except, of course, Edwards gained support in North Louisiana within parishes with high proportions of black population, along the Mississippi, and up the Red River Valley. The relative lack of urban support can also be seen, as, for example, in the low spot representing East Baton Rouge Parish. By comparison, the Treen 1979 map reveals a high percentage of urban support throughout the state. Apart from his Third District parishes and Lafayette support, Treen vote distribution traces a low profile in Acadian parishes.

Support of Democrat candidates among the parishes is quite similar in both the 1976 and 1980 elections. The maps show greatest Democrat support peaking in the Acadian parishes, especially on the eastern side, with high percentage black populations. The low spots mark the urban parishes where, of course, the Republican tendency is strongest. Only eleven parishes shifted support from Carter 1976 to Reagan 1980. This can be seen in the Democrat 1980 map as a ditch in front of an escarpment to the west, dividing the state. It includes the parishes of Vermilion, Acadia, Evangeline, Rapides, Grant, Winn, and Jackson. It is difficult to determine what led to the shift in these parishes as they cut across several of the political ecological areas of the state (Acadian, Urban, North Louisiana Hills). A check of percentage change between 1976 and 1980 does give a clue, however, as at least we know that a considerable increase in Republican support (51.9 percent) was accompanied by a decrease in Democrat support (-7.4 percent). This set of parishes contributed 16.2 percent of the statewide Republican surge. It was the only parish category yet found to record *less* Democrat votes in 1980 than in 1976. Acadian voters in Vermilion, Acadia, Evangeline, and Avoyelles parishes are volatile, each of these parishes having recorded votes above the state average for McGovern, among the top-six Acadian Wallace parishes, among the top-eight Acadian Kennedy parishes in 1960, high in support for Thurmond in 1948, and above the state average Longism support, 1928-1956.

We propose, now, to couple the electoral analysis just made with parish distributions of several key demographic characteristics, to show how the Acadian parishes may have begun to differ among themselves. A total of 20 items are used including 13 parish vote distributions and 7 demographic characteristics. In addition to Urban Population, Black Population, Black Registration, and Catholic, three employment categories to get at potential change were included. Added were percent of labor force employed in Farming, Oil and Gas production, and Industrial manufacturing.[22] Dramatic change has taken place in the past decade both statewide and within the Acadian parishes in the

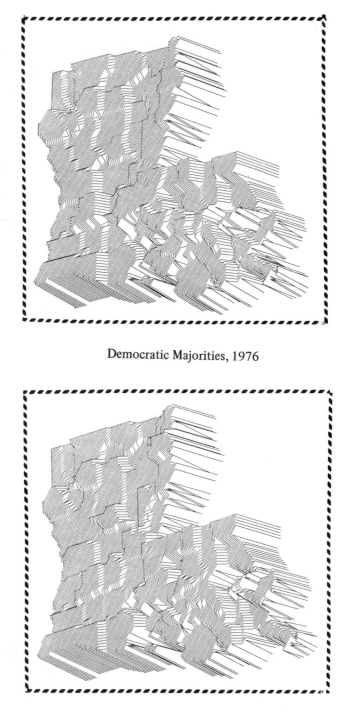

Democratic Majorities, 1976

Democratic Majorities, 1980

Louisiana version of the "Sun Belt". Percent employed in Farming decreased decidedly for both state and Acadian parishes (-38.0 percent and -33.0 percent, respectively). Employment in Oil and Gas related jobs increased over 100 percent, nearly double the rate for the state. Industrial employment increased by 100 percent, also, five times greater than that for Louisiana as a whole.

Republican Treen and Democrat Carter received nearly equal support in parishes with high proportions of Farming, since this category of employment is widespread in the area. There is clear difference in predominant support of candidates within Oil and Gas (Treen) and Industrial parishes (Democrat), however, indicative of varied, ecological contexts. This finding led us to apply statistical techniques to identify potential clustering of Acadian parishes.[23] The results, using both 64 parish state and 22 parish Acadian units, showed a continuation of tendencies described above, together with some new findings. Three distinct factor dimensions were found, quite similar on both state and Acadian parish levels, with hints of the perpetuation of the Urban Republican,

	STATE FACTOR DIMENSIONS			ACADIAN FACTOR DIMENSIONS		
	1	2	3	1	2	3
DEMOCRAT	+			+		
BLACK POPULATION	+			+		
FARMING	+					+
EDWARDS '72		+			+	
BLACK REGISTRATION		+				+
CATHOLIC		+			+	
HARDY			−		+	
MOUTON			−		+	
OIL & GAS			−			−
REPUBLICAN	−			−		
URBAN POPULATION	−			−		
TREEN	−			−		
LAMBERT			+			+
INDUSTRIAL			+			+

black and Catholic tendencies in the early 1970s. The presence of the additional data, however, changes the clusterings, such that the Urban-Republican tendency appears on one end of a dimension oppositely headed by a Black-Democrat tendency, on both state and Acadian levels. Also, one dimension on both levels profiles the Edwards-Catholic-Black power tendency. Notice that on the Acadian level, the Cajun candidates, Hardy and Mouton, join this dimension, displaying the affinity of their voter support. Finally, one finds on both levels a dimension which includes Lambert and Industrial, opposite Oil and Gas.

On the state level the Cajun candidates cluster with this characteristic, while on the Acadian level, Farming and Black Registration join the Lambert tendency.

Factor Scores for each parish have been determined which show its value on each of the three dimensions discussed. In doing so we discover the manner in which Cajun parishes have begun to differ, while still reflecting a distinct difference from the remaining 42 parishes of the state. We have tentatively identified three such sets of parishes:

REPUBLICAN-OIL
(Lafourche, Terrebonne, St. Mary, Iberia, Lafayette, Vermilion)

Less Black	Majority Catholic	More Republican

DEMOCRAT-INDUSTRIAL
(Pointe Coupée, West Baton Rouge, Iberville, Ascension, Assumption, St. James)

More Black	Less Catholic	More Democrat

EDWARDS-CATHOLIC
(St. Martin, St. Landry, Evangeline, Acadia, Jefferson Davis)

Medium Black	More Catholic	Varied Democrat

Recall that, historically, Acadian parishes lining the Mississippi River were devoted to Plantation agriculture. They continue to count relatively large black and farm populations. Now, however, a vast build-up of industrial plants has taken place and these parishes have become less Catholic. While these parishes supported Edwards by over 60 percent in the 1972 run-off, Industrial parish (his home base) support for Lambert in the run-off approached 75 percent.

The interior Acadian parishes, remaining the most Catholic, a quarter black and relatively high in percentage of farm employment, gave Edwards his greatest support. Of course, he was at home in Acadia Parish. Democrat support had remained high through 1976, but in 1980 the Democrat vote fialed to reach a majority by eight-tenths of one percent. Republican support here had increased nearly 15 percent. Time will tell whether this trend was temporary. Since Edwin Edwards ended up endorsing Carter, the effect of this on Edwards' potential bid for a third term as governor in 1983 remains to be seen.

Finally, Acadian parishes bordering the Gulf of Mexico and characterized by a large build-up of oil and gas related activities, have become the most difficult within which to depict tendencies. Majority Catholic, they are also the least industrialized and black, and lowest in the category of farm employment. They supported Edwards heavily, but two elections later provided Treen with 60 percent of their vote. This category overlaps with Treen's former congressional district, of course. Reagan gained his highest Cajun-parish support in these parishes. The Republicans had promised to further deregulate oil and gas production.

Analysis of voting and demographic data has made clear that, while, statewide, Acadian parishes remain an important entity in Louisiana affairs, distinct changes are taking place among them. It seems apparent, though, that whatever tendencies develop in Louisiana politics, the Acadians will continue to play a large part in shaping that development.

NOTES

1. Perry H. Howard, "Louisiana," *Encyclopedia Britannica*, 15th ed. (Chicago, 1974); Perry H. Howard, *Political Tendencies in Louisiana* (Baton Rouge, 1971); Mark T. Carleton, Perry H. Howard, and Joseph B. Parker, *Readings in Louisiana Politics* (Baton Rouge, 1975).

2. Charles E. Grenier and Perry H. Howard, "The Edwards Victory," *Louisiana Review*, I (1972), 31-42. The statistical technique of factorial ecology was used to search for interrelated patterns among 36 such variables as percent Black, Catholic, and Democratic vote.

3. T. Lynn Smith and Homer L. Hitt, *The People of Louisiana* (Baton Rouge, 1952); Fred B. Kniffen, *Louisiana: Its Land and People* (Baton Rouge, 1968).

4. D. L. A. Hackett, "The Social Structure of Jacksonian Louisiana," *Louisiana Studies*, XXI (1973), 324-353.

5. Claude Jean Roumagnac, "A Demographic Analysis of Selected Characteristics of the 'Acadian' Population of Louisiana, 1940," (MA thesis, Louisiana State University, 1952).

6. T. Lynn Smith and Vernon J. Parenton, "Acculturation Among the Louisiana French," *American Journal of Sociology*, XLIV (1938), 355-364.

7. Howard, *Tendencies*.

8. Miriam G. Reeves, *The Governors of Louisiana* (Gretna, La., 1972).

9. Howard, *Tendencies*; all data in this paper is derived from secondary analysis of book and personal files.

10. Hackett, "Jacksonian Louisiana."

11. But see J. Carlyle Sitterson, *Sugar Country: The Cane Industry in the South, 1753-1950* (Lexington, Ky., 1953); see also Joe Gray Taylor, *Louisiana Reconstructed, 1863-1877* (Baton Rouge, 1974).

12. William Ivy Hair, *Bourbonism and Agrarian Protest: Louisiana Politics, 1877-1900* (Baton Rouge, 1969).

13. Floyd Martin Clay, *Coozan Dudley LeBlanc: From Huey Long to Hadacol* (Gretna, La., 1973).

14. T. Harry Williams, *Huey Long* (New York, 1970).

15. William C. Havard, Rudolf Heberle, and Perry H. Howard, *The Louisiana Elections of 1960* (Baton Rouge, 1963).

16. John H. Fenton and Kenneth N. Vines, "Negro Registration in Louisiana," *American Political Science Review*, LI (1957), 714.

17. Elizabeth Levin Peneguy, "Elements of Political Culture in Rural Louisiana," (MA thesis, Louisiana State University, 1972).

18. David M. Kovenock, James Prothro and Associates, *Explaining the Vote: Presidential Choices in the Nation and the States, 1968*, 2 vols. (Chapel Hill, 1973). See chapter there on Louisiana by Perry H. Howard, Maxwell E. McCombs, and David M. Kovenock.

19. Kevin Phillips, *The Emerging Republican Majority* (New Rochelle, N. Y., 1969).

20. Kevin Phillips, "Post-Conservative America," *New York Review of Books*, May 13, 1982.

21. *Ibid.*, 32.

22. The percentages were derived from Wage and Salary Employment by sector. Farm percentages are calculated from the base Total Employment. Industrial and Oil and Gas percentages were calculated on the base Private Non-Farm Wage and Salary Employment by industry. The title "Oil and Gas" was given to the general employment category, "Mining." The title "Industrial" was given to "Manufacturing."

23. Statistical analyses at the L. S. U. System Network Computer Center made use of the Statistical Package for the Social Sciences (SPSS) software. "Discriminant Analysis" derived the "best" set of discriminating variables with which to characterize and set boundaries of the Acadian parishes. "Factor Analysis" contributed to data-reduction of the arrays of correlation coefficients for the set of 20 items described herein. Underlying patterns of relationships were derived confirming and extending the discriminant analysis.

CAJUN MUSIC:
ITS ROOTS AND DEVELOPMENT

by Barry Jean Ancelet

Cajun music is a Louisiana hybrid, a blend of cultural influences with an identity which accordian maker and musician Marc Savoy of Eunice describes in culinary terms: "It's a blend of ingredients, like a gumbo in which different spices and flavors combine to make a new taste." Indeed, like Cajun cooking and culture in general, Cajun music blends American Indian, Scots-Irish, Spanish, German, Anglo-American, and Afro-Caribbean influences with a base of western French folk tradition. Ethnomusicologists and tourists alike invariably note that this music differs greatly from the traditional music of its sister cultures in Quebec and Acadia. The merging of elements which produced Cajun culture also created a new musical form which is now called Cajun music.

The Acadians took few possessions into exile in 1755, but they carried with them a rich cultural heritage from their former homeland. Derived from western French origins (primarily northern Poitou), their culture had been influenced by neighboring American Indian tribes, such as the Micmac and Malecite, since their establishment in 1604 and by contact with their English and Scots-Irish administrators after the Treaty of Utrecht in 1713. Their music and songs reflected their European origins. In some songs the Old World versions survived relatively intact. For example, in the 1930s, Irene Whitfield Holmes collected a Louisiana version of "Malbrough s'en va-t-en guerre" which is identical to the song still popular among French school children, though somewhat shorter.[1] More often, the lyrics underwent change, often to a considerable degree. Play songs and round dances such as *Trois jeunes tambours, La Fête printanière (La Fête du village), Cadet Roussel, Mon petit mari, Mon beau château*, commonly found in French tradition were sung by the Acadians with changes in lyrics or tune, and sometimes both. The traditional French version of *Cadet Roussel*, for example, usually begins:

Cadet Roussel a trois maisons (bis)
Qui n'ont ni poutres ni chevrons. (bis)
C'est pour loger les hirondelles.
Que direz-vous de Cadet Roussel?

Ah, ah, ah oui, vraiment, } (bis)
Cadet Roussel est bon enfant.

195

In a version collected by Irene Whitfield Holmes,[2] there are slight vocabulary and grammar changes:

> Cadet Rousselle a une maison qui n'a ni poteaux, ni chevrons,
> C'est pour loger les hirondelles, qui croyez-vous de cadet Rousselle?
> Ha! Ha! Ha! Oui, vraiment, Cadet Rouselle c'est un bon garçon.

These changes reflect a difference of language and the *poteaux-en-terre* building technique used in New France and Acadia. A version that Harry Oster collected in 1973 from Isom Fontenot[3] shows further modification:

> Cadet Rousselle, c'est un bon jeune homme,
> Cadet Rousselle, c'est un vaillant bougre.
>
> Cadet Rousselle, il a des chiens que le roi n'a pas de si bons,
> Un aux lapins et l'autre si bête que quand il l'appelle, il se sauve.
> Ah, oui, vraiment.
>
> Cadet Rousselle, il a une habille que le roi n'a pas de si belle.
> Elle est doublée de papier gris, elle est cousue de la ficelle.
> Ah, oui, vraiment.
>
> Cadet Rousselle, il a des chevaux que le roi n'a pas des si bons.
> Ils sont si gras que les os percent la selle.
> Ah, oui, vraiment.
>
> Cadet Rousselle, il a-t-un clos que le roi n'a pas des si grands.
> Il est si grand, il monte une face, il crache sur l'autre.
> Ah, oui, vraiment.
>
> Cadet Rousselle, c'est un bon jeune homme.
> Cadet Rousselle, c'est un vaillant bougre.

Le Pont de Nantes, a well-known French folksong, survived the Atlantic crossing under several titles: *Au Pont des vues, Au Pont du nord,[4] Le Pont du Nane,[5] Bonjour, Hélène.[6] Mon petit mari*, which in the French version typically combines rather gruesome lyrics concerning the devouring of the diminutive husband by the housecat with a joyous tune, keeps basically the same storyline in the Acadian version, but the melody is altered to a more suitable, plaintive style.[7] This transformation from gay, lilting ditties to mournful *complaintes* occurs commonly in Acadian tradition.

In some cases, only the kernel of the story survives. *Grand Dieu, que je suis a mon aise*, a well-known French folksong, loses most of its direct references to European wars in the New World version. Compare this excerpt from the French version,

> Grand Dieu, que je suis à mon aise
> Quand j'ai ma mie auprès de moi, auprès de moi,
> De temps en temps, je la regarde
> Et je lui dis, «Embrasse-moi.»
>
> «Comment veux-tu que je t'embrasse,
> Quand on me dit du mal de toi, du mal de toi?
> On me dit que tu pars pour la guerre,
> Chez les Flamands, défendre le roi,»

with the following Louisiana version, sung by Odile Falcon.[8] Note that it has retained the theme but generalizes the references to the war:

> Oh, Grand Dieu, comme je suis-t-à mon aise
> Quand je la vois, elle assise auprès de moi.
>
> «Temps en temps je vous regarde, ma douce aimée,
> Oh, ma douce aimée, embrasse donc moi.»
>
> «Oh, cher amant, comment tu veux moi, je t'embrasse
> Quand on me défend de t'aimer tous les jours.
>
> Un petit mot qui me monte à l'oreille
> C'était de me faire faire un petit portrait,
>
> Un petit portrait de ta ressemblance
> Et cent fois par jour, je l'embrasserai.»
>
> «Qu'est-ce que tes amis diraient de toi,
> Te voir embrasser ce petit portrait?»
>
> «Je leur dirai que c'est le portrait,
> Que c'est le portrait de ma bien aimée,
>
> Que j'avais quittée d'un si grand regret
> Pour partir servir sur l'armée régulière.
>
> Oh, maman, elle vena me souffler un petit mot à l'oreille
> En me disant que j'étais parti,
>
> J'étais parti pour servir le grand roi
> Servir le grand roi sur l'armée régulière.»

Another popular French song tradition transplanted to Acadia and Louisiana was the drinking song, called in the New World *la chanson de bamboche*. The universally known *Chevaliers de la table ronde* is echoed in *Fais trois tours de la table ronde*,[9] which retains the essential elements of the pre-Arthurian fisher king legend with a medieval tune structure transformed to fit the blues.

Oh, fais trois tours de la table ronde,
Fais trois tours de la table ronde.
Allons en chercher, chercher, chercher, chercher.

Oh, c'est quoi, se divertir, c'est comme des camarades,
C'est quoi, se divertir, c'est comme des camarades.
Allons en chercher, chercher, chercher, chercher.

Un de nos plus grands de nos ivrognes était au lit malade.
Mettez lui couché en bas d'une table de vin.
Allons en chercher, chercher, chercher, chercher.

Tous les temps en temps quittez une goutte dégoûter,
Tous les temps en temps quittez une goutte dégoûter.
De leur quitter une goutte dégoûter, c'est pour les satisfaire.

French songs were often adapted to new styles or recent events. *La Veuve de sept ans,* originally a *complainte* about two lovers separated during the Crusades, became in Acadia a song about the Seven Years War:[10]

J'avais une maîtresse, un jour y avait longtemps.
J'ai reçu une lettre, «en guerre il faut aller.»

Ma pauvre petite maîtresse ne fait que brailler
Toute la nuit et toute la journée.

«En guerre j'm'en va ma belle, j'reviens dans une semaine
Attendrir nos amours.»

Ça bien duré sept ans, pendant ma vingtième année
J'suis rentré en Acadie.

J'ai été voir ma belle qui pouvait pas me regarder.
Oh! la grande misère.

J'ai été voir ma mère, ma mère qui braillait,
Mon père est mort, mes frères sont morts, ma terre ruinée
Ma belle mariée à cause de la maudite guerre.

Ecoutez-moi bien, jeunes gens,
Partez jamais à la guerre.

J'ai perdu mon père, perdu ma famille,
Ma terre est toute ruinée
A cause de la maudite guerre.

In Louisiana, the girl was put in a convent, a fate worse than death for the anticlerical Acadians.[11]

C'est une fille de quatorze ans
Voilà Grand Dieu la plus belle brune
Un soir elle dit à son papa,
«Papa, je veux me marier.»
«Oh, tais-toi, fillette, jeunette,
Toi qui n'as pas encore quinze ans.»
Elle prend un seul petit frère,
Le seul pour la reconsoler.
«Reconsole-toi, mon cher coeur,
Papa, te mettra dans un couvent,
Dans un couvent des orphelines
Où on y prie Dieu bien trop souvent.»
Son beau galant revient le soir,
Après sept ans de temps passé.
En revenant de sa révolte,
Il court au logis de sa belle.
«Bonsoir, bonsoir, les beaux yeux noirs,
Je voudrais les voir encore une fois.»
Ils lui ont dit, «Ta belle à toi,
Elle n'est pas ici pour te voir.
Oui, elle est morte et enterrée,
Ça fait quatre jours, y a pas longtemps.»
Je me ferai une grande crêpe noire,
Que tout le ciel je tiendrai dedans.
Bonsoir, bonsoir, les beaux yeux noirs,
Je voudrais les voir encore une fois.
Bonsoir, bonsoir, les beaux yeux noirs,
T'es dans ta tombe, mais je t'aime toujours.

Another Louisiana version presents the dilemma of the woman who, believing herself a widow, remarries only to have her first husband return on her wedding day:[12]

Dessus le premier jour des noces, il y a été venu un commandement,
Il y a été venu un commandement, oh, un commandement de guerre.
«C'est à la guerre il faut aller, c'est à la guerre il faut partir.»
Oh, quand la belle a entendu ça, elle se mit à se désoler.
«Ne pleurez pas autant la belle, ne versez pas autant de larmes.
Oh, ma campagne serait pas longue, six semaines à deux mois le plus.»
Oh, ma campagne, elle a bien été belle, elle a été belle et belle et longue.
Oh, ma campagne, elle a bien duré, oh, regarde, elle a duré sept ans.
Au bout de la septième année, oh, quand j'ai pu me retirer,
C'était revenir chez moi, c'était trouver la mariée.
C'était trouver ma bien aimée, qui sortait d'être épousée.
Elle s'est tournée à sa mère, «Oh vierge, vierge, douce vierge,
Quoi ce qu'en deviendra de moi?
Regards donc sept ans je me croyais veuve, et me voilà avec deux maris.»
«Courage, courage, courage, ma fille,
Que le premier choix de l'homme lui appartiennent à lui ses droits.»

From Acadia, the exiles brought an instrumental tradition based primarily on violin or fiddle tunes, though it is doubtful that any instruments survived the deportation. As *La Chanson de la cuillière* points out:

> Les violons tout attristés
> Sont restés sur le quai.[13]

Their western French heritage had included brass and reed instruments such as the biniou or cabrette (instruments of the bagpipe family found in Celtic and southwestern French traditions) and trumpets (widely used in Poitou). These instruments fell into disuse in America, but the stringed-instrument tunes retained a distinctive drone. The French *vielle à roue*, with its characteristic *bourdon* drone, was too complicated and delicate to survive frontier conditions, but early fiddles, played in open tuning, achieved a similar effect. By the time of the exile, English and Scots-Irish reels, jigs, hornpipes, and contredanses had already enriched the Acadians' repertoire of dance music.

When instruments were unavailable or, at times, such as Lent, when instrument music was forbidden, the Acadians managed to dance anyway, producing music with their voices, clapping their hands, and stamping their feet for percussion. If the repertoire of round dances became stale, they simply hummed dance tunes to produce a *reel à bouche*. Descriptions of the Acadians at the time of the Dispersion invariably mention their insatiable love of dancing. In a letter to his intendant dated March 12, 1764, Saltoris described a communal wedding and baptism blessing ceremony among the Acadians in Saint-Domingue: "They did not eat until every one had given his toast. They danced, the old and the young alike, all dancing to a fast step...."[14]

The Acadians who began arriving in Louisiana in 1765, wanted to recreate their society on French territory. They were surprised to find themselves under Spanish rule, Louisiana having been ceded to Spain in 1762. Spanish language and culture, however, prevailed only at the highest administrative level; everyday life in the colony continued essentially in French. The Acadians settled along the banks of the Mississippi River, Bayou Lafourche, and in the lands west of the Atchafalaya Basin near the Poste des Attakapas and Poste des Opelousas. In all three areas they lived in relative isolation and addressed themselves to the huge task of reestablishing their society in Nouvelle Acadie. Though songs about the exile experience do not seem to have survived, the upheaval did affect their music. The sufferings they had endured endowed their songs with a preoccupation with death and lost love and their instrumental music with a mournful quality.

In Louisiana, the Acadians continued to sing old songs and create new ones. Their self-imposed isolation in the bayous and southern prairies did not preclude selective contact with other cultures, when they needed, or wanted, to learn something from their neighbors. They learned agricultural techniques from the local Indians and from the Alsatian/German community along the German Coast, fishing techniques from the Anglo-Americans, cooking techni ques from the black slaves. Even the Spaniards, generally believed to have influenced only New Orleans architecture and the colonial political scene, con-tributed to the civilization of the frontier-minded Acadians, especially through the churches. The steady trickle of French immigrants in the late nineteenth century brought some changes in language and customs.

The Acadians' contact with these various cultures also contributed to the development of new musical styles and repertoire. From the Indians, they learn-ed wailing singing styles[15] and new dance rhythms; from the blacks, they learn-ed the blues, percussion techniques, and improvisational singing; from the Anglo-Americans, they learned new fiddle tunes including Virginia reels, square dances, and hoedowns. The Spanish contributed the guitar and even a few tunes, including the melody to *J'ai passé devant ta porte* (used in a concerto by the eighteenth-century Spanish composer Fernando Sors). Refugees and their slaves who arrived from Saint-Domingue at the turn of the nineteenth century brought with them a syncopated West Indian beat. The Jewish German immi-grants began importing diatonic accordians (invented in Vienna in 1828) when Acadians and blacks became interested in the instruments toward the end of the nineteenth century. They blended these elements to create a new music just as they were synthesizing the same cultures to create Cajun society.

At the turn of the twentieth century, Cajun music entered a highly creative period. Dances included old world waltzes, contredanses, varsoviennes, polkas, mazurkas, and cotillions as well as two-steps, one-steps, baisse-bas, lalas, and breakdowns developed to accompany the contemporary musical styles. In this formative period, some of the most influential musicians were the black Creoles who brought a strong, rural, blues element into Cajun music. Musicians such as Adam Fontenot and Amédé Ardoin developed new ways of making music with the recently acquired accordion. Ardoin's innovative, syncopated style made him a favorite at both black and white dances, but it was his powerful and highly creative singing that attracted the attention of early recording scouts. He was among the first of a group of Louisiana French musicians to record, immediately following Joe Falcon's pioneering *Allons à Lafayette* in 1928. These early recordings, which the black Creole singer and accordianist made with white Cajun fiddler Dennis McGee, were immensely popular and influ-ential. In the 1930s, his style became increasingly introspective. Because he recorded alone in this later period, his creative genius unbridled, and he com-posed songs which quickly became part of the classical Cajun music repertoire. His percussive accordian style also influenced the parallel development of zydeco music, later refined by Clifton Chenier. Some of Ardoin's most important compositions include the *Eunice Two-step* (called today *Jolie Catin*), *La Valse à Abe* (*La Valse de quatre-vingt-dix-neuf ans*), *Tante Aline* (*Chère Alice*), *Blues de la prison* (*Two-step de la prison*), *La Valse à Austin Ardoin* (*La Valse de l'orphelin*), and *Madame Etienne* (*La Robe barrée*): An example of Ardoin's work is found in the following:

MADAME ETIENNE[16]

Malheureuse, quoi t'as fait, oui, avec moi?
Tu me fais du mal chaque fois je te regarde,
    malheureuse.
Quoi t'as dit, mais chère Jouline, tu me fais du
    mal.
Quoi faire t'as fait, mais tout ça t'as fait si long
    avec moi?

Je vas m'en aller, je vas m'en aller, mais dans la
    maison,
Je vas m'en aller, mais dans la maison sans toi,
    Jouline.

Malheureuse, regardez donc, mais quoi t'as fait
    à ton petit coeur.
J'ai pas pu juger ton histoire rapport à toi.
Ta bonne histoire est aussi bonne que tes
    bonnes paroles.
Ça tu m'as dit, toi, Jouline, ça m'a fait du mal.

Chère Jouline, je suis pas sûr d'être capable de
    m'en aller,
C'est rester pour espérer que tu t'en reviens.

Oh, Jouline, comment je vas faire, tu me fais du
    mal.
Je suis content pour toi, Jouline, toi, mon cher
    petit monde.
T'aurais pas du de me dire ça, mais joli coeur.

Dis ton idée, je suis pas comme ça, toi,
    malheureuse

Chaque fois je dis oui, je vas rentourner, mais à
    la maison,
Mon coeur fait mal juste assez pour moi pleurer.

In the early part of the twentieth century, commercial recording companies like RCA Bluebird and Decca began recording ethnic music throughout America in an effort to sell record players to members of the ethnic groups. In South

(Photo by André Gladu)

Sady Courville, Dennis McGee, Revon Reed and Angelas LeJeune

(Photo by Steen Neilsen)

Kenry Fontenot and Bois-sec Ardoin,
1977 Tribute to Cajun Music Festival, Lafayette

Louisiana, this effort captured the end of Cajun music's formative period. The
first record to be released was Joe Falcon's *Allons à Lafayette* and *La Valse qui
m'a porté en terre*. *Allons à Lafayette*, a two-step, was typical of the changes of
the times, being a relatively new song adapted from an older tune, *Jeunes gens
de la campagne*.

> Allons à Lafayette, mais pour changer ton nom.
> On va t'appeler Madame, Madame Canaille Comeaux.
> Petite, t'es trop mignonne pour faire ta criminelle.
> Comment tu crois, mais moi, je peux faire, mais moi tout seul.
> Mais toi, mais joli coeur, regarde donc mais quoi t'as fait.
> Si loin que moi, je suis de toi, mais ça, ça me fait pitié.[17]

Fiddlers such as Dennis McGee and Sady Courville, Ernest Frugé, the
Connors, the Aguillards, and the Walkers still composed tunes, but the accordian
was rapidly becoming the mainstay of traditional dance bands. Limited in notes
and keys, it simplified Cajun music as songs that it could not play faded from
the scene. Fiddles were often relegated to playing a duet accompaniment or
a percussive second line below the dominant accordian's melody lead.

New songs were composed often utilizing very ancient themes from French
tradition. *Les Barres de la prison*, for example, Kenry Fontenot's classic song
based on Douglas Belair's original blues tune, recalls the old French *chanson de
Mandrin*.

> Good-bye, chère vieille mam,
> Good-bye, pauvre vieux pap,
> Good-bye à mes frères
> Et mes chères petites soeurs.
> Moi, j'ai été condamné
> Pour la balance de ma vie
> Dans les barres de la prison.
>
> Moi, j'ai roulé,
> Je m'ai mis à malfaire.
> J'avais la tête dure,
> J'ai rentré dans le tracas.
> Asteur je suis condamné
> Pour la balance de ma vie
> Dans les barres de la prison.
>
> Ma pauvre vieille maman,
> Elle s'a mis sur ses genoux,
> Les deux mains sur la tête,
> En pleurant pour moi.
> Elle dit, «Mmmmmm,
> Cher petit garçon,

Moi, je vas jamais te revoir.
Toi, t'as été condamné
Pour la balance de ta vie
Dans les barres de la prison.»

J'ai dit, «Chère vieille maman,
Pleure pas pour moi.
Il faut tu pries pour ton enfant
Pour essayer de sauver son âme
De les flammes de l'enfer.»[18]

Compare *La Chanson de Mandrin*:[19]

Nous étions vingt ou trente
Brigands de vieille bande
Tous habillés de blanc,
Mes compagnons, vous m'entendez?
Tous habillés de blanc
A la mode des marchands.

La première volerie
Que je fis dans ma vie,
Ce fut de goupiller
La bourse d'un curé.

— — —

Ces messieurs de Grenoble
Avec leurs longues robes,
Et leurs bonnets carrés,
M'eurent bientôt jugé.

Ils m'ont jugé à pendre,
Dieu, que c'est dur à entendre!
A pendre et étrangler
Sur la place du Marché.

Debout sur la potence
Je regardai la France
Je vis mes compagnons,
A l'ombre d'un buisson.

«Compagnons de misère,
Allez dire à ma mère
Qu'elle ne me verra plus!
Je suis un enfant perdu!»

Musicians continued to enlarge the repertoire, recording recently developed songs into the mid-1930s. *Jolie Blonde* was first recorded in 1928 by Joe

Falcon's brothers-in-law, Amédé, Ophé, and Cléopha Breaux.[20]

> Jolie blonde, regardez donc quoi t'as fait,
> Tu m'as quitté pour t'en aller,
> Pour t'en aller avec un autre, oui, que moi,
> Quel espoir et quel avenir, mais, moi, je vas avoir?
>
> Jolie blonde, tu m'as laissé, moi tout seul,
> Pour t'en aller chez ta famille.
> Si t'aurais pas écouté tous les conseils de les autres
> Tu serais ici-t-avec moi aujourd'hui.
>
> Jolie blonde, tu croyais il y avait juste toi,
> Il y a pas juste toi dans le pays pour moi aimer.
> Si je peux trouver juste une autre, jolie blonde,
> Bon Dieu sait, moi, j'ai un tas.

Angelas Lejeune recorded *La Valse de la Pointe Noire* (*Kaplan Waltz*) and *Bayou Pom Pom* as early as 1930. The recordings of Mayus Lafleur and Leo Soileau, Moise Robin, Nathan Abshire, the Walker Brothers, among others, were regional successes as Cajuns began to acquire Victrolas.

The advent of radio further enhanced the popularity of certain performers who had the good fortune to have access to the broadcast media. Like the phonograph player, radio, which broadcast records and live performances, lent importance to the most popular trends. It also introduced into South Louisiana music from the music centers emerging in Nashville, New York, and the West Coast. The early surge of musical creativity carried over into this new period as Cajun performers adapted tunes they heard on the radio. Nathan Abshire's classic waltz *La Valse de Bélisaire*, for example, was based on Roy Acuff's *A Precious Jewel*, and Leo Soileau's *Dans ton coeur, tu aimes un autre* was a translated version of the traditional *Columbus Stockade Blues*.

By the mid-1930s, Cajuns were reluctantly, though inevitably, becoming Americanized. The French language, native to them and their music, had been banned from schools throughout South Louisiana as America, caught in the "melting pot" ideology, tried to homogenize its diverse ethnic and cultural elements. In South Louisiana, speaking French was not only against the rules, it became increasingly unpopular as Cajuns attempted to escape the stigma attached to their culture. New highways and improved transportation opened the previously isolated area to the rest of the country, and the Cajuns began to imitate their Anglo-American neighbors in earnest.

The social and cultural changes of the 1930s and 1940s were clearly reflected in the recorded music of the period. The slick programming on radio and later television inadvertently undermined the comparatively unpolished traditional sounds and forced them underground. The previously dominant accordian faded from the scene completely, partly because the old style music had lost popularity and partly because the instruments, hitherto manufactured in Germany, were unavailable.

As the western swing and bluegrass sounds from Texas and Tennessee swept the country, string bands which imitated the music of Bob Wills and the Texas Playboys and copied Bill Monroe's high lonesome sound sprouted across South Louisiana. Among the early leaders in this new trend were the Hackberry Ramblers (with Luderin Darbonne on fiddle) who recorded new, lilting versions of what had begun to emerge as the classic Cajun repertoire, such as *Jolie Blonde*. They also performed new compositions such as *Une Piastre ici, une piastre là-bas*, a song which shows what it means to live in a money-based e-conomy caught in the throes of a depression:

> Quand j'ai eu vingt-et-un ans
> Mon père m'a dit que j'étais dedans.
> «C'est l'heure que t'arrêtes de dépenser
> Un piastre ici, une piastre là-bas.»[21]

Freed from the limitations imposed by the accordian, string bands readily absorbed various outside influences. Darbonne's Ramblers were the first to use electrical amplification systems. Dancers across South Louisiana were shocked in the mid-1930s to hear music which came not only from the bandstand, but also from the opposite end of the dance hall through speakers powered by a model T idling behind the building.[22] The electric steel guitar and trap drums were added to the standard instrumentation as Cajuns continued to experiment with new sounds borrowed from American musicians. Amplification made it unnecessary for fiddlers to bear down with the bow in order to be audible, and they developed a lighter, lilting touch, moving away from the heavy, mournful earlier styles.

Undoubtedly the most popular Cajun musician of his day, Harry Choates, was born near Rayne, in Acadia Parish, but like so many of his countrymen, moved to East Texas with his family to work in the ship building and oil boom of the 1940s. This move greatly influenced his music. In songs such as the *Austin Special* and the *Port Arthur Blues*, he developed the "tu m'as quitté pour t'en aller au Grand Texas" theme which was to become ubiquitous in modern Cajun music. Choates also sprinkled his songs like *Louisiana Boogie* with English lyrics to reach a larger audience.

> Tu m'as quitté pour t'en aller,
> Pour t'en aller, mais chère, si loin,
> C'est pour faire le boogie-woogie,

Faire le boogie-woogie,
Après faire le boogie-woogie,
Je connais ça sera pas pour longtemps.

Tu honky-tonk ici, tu honky-tonk là-bas
Tu honky-tonk, tu honky-tonk, tu honky-tonk tout le temps,
T'es après faire le boogie-woogie,
Après faire le boogie-woogie,
Après faire le boogie-woogie
Je connais ça sera pas pour longtemps.[23]

His popularity carried him as far west as Austin, in the heart of Anglo-Texas, on regular weekend dance jobs, and his simplified interpretation of *Jolie Blonde*, not only a regional hit but a national success, became the standard version performed by bands throughout South Louisiana.

Other bands recorded bilingual songs, reflecting a gradual gravitation toward the English language. In 1947, for example, the Oklahoma Tornadoes released *Dans la prison*:

Well, I left from Louisiana about a year ago,
Going to Texas, travelling with a show.
I landed in old Houston doing mighty fine,
Until I met that woman, and now I'm doing time.

Dans la prison, la hell avec ça.
Moi, je connais ça sera longtemps.
Dans la prison, la hell avec ça.
Moi, je m'en reviens dans vingt-quatre ans.[24]

Darbonne's group, which had recorded French swing tunes as the Hackberry Ramblers, recorded English country tunes under the name the Riverside Ramblers, featuring the singing of Joe Werner on regional hits such as *Wondering* (which predated Webb Pierce's version by a few years). The transition was nearly complete; recorded Cajun music showed increasing discomfort with the French language and traditional sounds. Even Joe Falcon's wife Cléoma joined the move away from the roots, recording *Hand Me Down My Walking Cane* in 1947.

By the late 1940s, the music recorded by commercial producers signalled an unmistakable tendency toward Americanization. Yet, an undercurrent of traditional music persisted which would surface with the music of Iry Lejeune, a young accordian player and singer from Pointe Noire in Acadia Parish. Greatly influenced by the early recordings of Amédé Ardoin and by the music of his own uncles and cousins, among them Angelas and Steven Lejeune, he tagged along with the Oklahoma Tornadoes in 1948 to record *La Valse du Pont d'Amour*, in the turn of the century Louisiana style and in French.

> Hé, 'tite fille!
> Moi, je me vois
> Après partir
> Mais m'en aller donc te rejoindre.
> Oh, chère 'tite fille,
> Quand même tu voudrais
> T'en revenir, petit monde,
> 'garde donc, je veux plus te voir.
>
> Hé! Tu m'as dit.
> 'tite fille, criminelle,
> Tu sais toi, tu voulais plus
> M'aimer, malheureuse.
> Tu connais, 'tite fille,
> Que moi, j'ai pris ça dur,
> Pris ça assez dur
> Que moi, j'ai pris les grands chemins.[25]

Skeptics wondered at his forsaking current trends, but the recording, an unexpected success, presaged a revival of the earlier style. Iry Lejeune became a pivotal figure in a revival fueled by the return of homesick GIs seeking to immerse themselves in a hot, cultural bath. Dance halls providing traditional music flourished, and musicians such as Lawrence Walker, Austin Pitre, and Nathan Abshire brought their abandoned accordians out of the closet and once again performed old-style Cajun music. Local recording companies picked up the slack left by the national producers who had turned exclusively to widely known performers. Though bearing the marks of Americanization, Cajun music was making a dramatic comeback just as interest in the culture and language quickened before the 1955 Acadian bicentennial celebration.

In the early 1950s, many dance bands performed as often as seven and eight times a week. The groups developed a tight, well-orchestrated, dance-band style, keeping the successive instrumental "rides" learned from swing and bluegrass music.[26] Groups incorporated palatable elements from various new styles, including early rock-and-roll, to develop new sounds. Some began performing on local radio stations; others, such as Aldus Roger and the Lafayette Playboys and Happy Fats Leblanc and the Mariné Band, were featured on area television. Most bands were composed of musicians who made a living from other regular jobs, but a few, such as Doug Kershaw, became professionals who quickly realized that they should perform in English if they were to attract an audience large enough to support them. Kershaw based his English songs on traditional Cajun tunes and developed a small national cult, even appearing on the immensely popular "Ed Sullivan Show." Cajun music was again straying far

(Photo by Elemore Morgan, Jr.)

Nathan Abshire

afield from its traditional sources. Deliberate efforts would be necessary if traditional Cajun music was to survive.

The needed impulse came from the national level. Alan Lomax, a member of the Newport Folk Foundation, had become interested in Louisiana French folk music during a field trip he made with his father in the 1930s. In the manner prescribed by activist ethnomusicologist Charles Seeger, Lomax sent "cultural guided missiles" to document and encourage the preservation of the music during the 1950s. Harry Oster, a professor of English at Louisiana State University in Baton Rouge, recorded a musical spectrum which ranged from unaccompanied ballads to contemporary dance tunes, especially in Evangeline and Vermilion parishes. His collection, which stressed the evolution of Cajun music, attracted the attention of local activists such as Paul Tate and Revon Reed.

The work of Harry Oster and Alan Lomax caught the imagination of the Newport board, and fieldworkers Ralph Rinzler and Mike Seeger were sent to find Cajun musicians for the festival. Cajun dance bands had played at the National Folk Festival in the 1950s, but little echo of these performances reached Louisiana. Rinzler and Seeger, seeking the gutsy roots of Cajun music, invited Gladius Thibodeaux, Louis "Vinesse" Lejeune, and Dewey Balfa to represent Louisiana at the 1964 Newport Folk Festival. There they performed the turn-of-the-century, unamplified music which made the Louisiana cultural establishment uneasy. These unrefined sounds embarassed the upwardly mobile Cajuns who barely tolerated the more polished sounds of popular dance bands and considered the music chosen for the Newport festival crude, "nothing but chanky-chank." The Newport organizers, however, were intent on showing the beauty and impact of root music.

Their instinct proved well founded as huge crowds gave the old-time music standing ovations. Two members of the Louisiana group were impressed, but the third, Dewey Balfa, was so moved that he returned to Louisiana determined to bring the message home. He began working on a small scale, among his friends and family in Mamou, Basile, and Eunice. Rinzler, who continued his fieldwork through the 1960s, urged him on. The Newport Folk Foundation, under the guidance of Lomax, routed money and fieldworkers into the area through the new Louisiana Folk Foundation. Financial support and outside approval brought a gradual change on the inside. Local activists such as Paul Tate, Revon Reed, Catherine and Ed Blanchet, Milton and Patricia Rickels, and, of course, Dewey Balfa, became involved in preserving the music, language, and culture. Traditional music contests and concerts were organized at local events such as the Abbeville Dairy Festival, the Opelousas Yambilee, and the Crowley Rice Festival. Eventually, Dewey Balfa convinced Swallow Records, a local company, to release a recording of traditional Cajun music alongside its

Dewey Balfa

(Photo by Philip Gould)

more modern listings. *La Valse du bambocheur,* one of the songs that had attracted Rinzler's attention to the Balfa Brothers sound, proved popular among the heritage-minded Cajuns of the late 1960s, and led to several albums on Swallow and other labels.

LA VALSE DU BAMBOCHEUR

Hé, yaïe! Depuis l'âge de quatorze ans,
Je suis après rouler manche à manche,
Après rouler avec ma bouteille dans la main,
Après essayer d'en trouver, d'en trouver-z-une autre comme toi,
Mais t'es la seule mon coeur désire.

Hé, bébé! Chaque fois je pars de la maison,
Pap et mam se mettent à pleurer.
Ça me suit jusqu'à la porte de court
En disant, «Toi, bonrien,
Fais pas ça. Reviens donc nous rejoindre.»

Oh, yé yaïe! Moi, j'ai toujours dit,
Toujours dit à mon vieux pap et ma chère vieille bonne maman, yaïe,
«Moi, je connais, je suis bonrien, mais je suis bonrien pour moi-même.
J'ai jamais fait rien à personne.»

Hé, yaïe! Aujourd'hui, n'importe ayoù,
N'importe ayoù moi, je peux passer,
Blanc et noir, ça me pointe au doigt, chère,
En disant, «Regarde-le là, regarde-le là, grand vaurien,
Le rouleur et le bambocheur.»

Hé chère! Aujourd'hui je suis condamné,
Condamné à rouler
Ma brouette sur ma planche de six pouces
Quatre-vingt-dix-neuf ans.

Quatre-vingt-dix-neuf ans, c'est la limite d'un bonrien.

Ça, c'est triste dans ma vie
Aussi loin de tout ça moi, j'aime.

Quand moi, j'étais petit, moi, je braillais pour des patates,
Et quand je suis devenu moyen, moi, je braillais pour ma bouteille.
Asteur moi, je suis grand, je suis après brailler pour les petites veuves.
Je serais content de m'en avoir une,
Et de l'amener à ma maison.

In 1968, the state of Louisiana officially recognized the Cajun cultural revival which had been brewing under the leadership of the music community and political leaders such as Dudley Leblanc and Roy Theriot. In that year, it created the Council for the Development of French in Louisiana (CODOFIL) which, under the chairmanship of James Domengeaux, began its efforts on politicial, psychological, and educational fronts to erase the stigma Louisianians had long attached to the French language and culture. The creation of French classes in elementary schools dramatically reversed the policy which had barred the language from the schoolgrounds.

Domengeaux's efforts were not limited to the classroom. Influenced by Rinzler and Balfa, CODOFIL organized a first *Tribute to Cajun Music* festival in 1974 with a concert designed to present an historical overview of Cajun music from its origins to modern styles. The echo had finally come home. Dewey Balfa's message of cultural self-esteem was heard by over 12,000 enthusiastic participants, and was heard again and again as the festival became an annual celebration of Cajun music and culture.

The festival not only provided exposure for the musicians but presented them as cultural heroes. Young performers were attracted to the revalidated Cajun music scene, and local French movement officials, realizing the impact of the grassroots, began to stress the native Louisiana French culture. Balfa's dogged pursuit of cultural recognition carried him farther than he had ever expected. In 1977, he received a Folk Artists in the Schools grant from the National Endowment for the Arts to bring his message into elementary school classrooms. He became a regular on the national folk festival touring circuit along with many other of his colleagues.

Young Cajuns, discovering local models besides country and rock stars, began to perform the music of their heritage. Yet, they did not reject modern sounds. Michael Doucet incorporated jazz and classical music into the carefully researched sound of his group "Beausoleil." Zachary Richard, who brought country and pop music trends into his renditions of traditional music and into his own compositions, discovered new outlets in Quebec and France to support a career as a professional musician singing in French. Young performers, such as Tim Broussard, Ricky Bearb, and Wayne Toups, are gradually making their presence known on the Cajun music scene, replacing older musicians on the regular weekend dance hall circuit and representing traditional Cajun music at local and national festivals.

Thus, Cajun music seems likely to live for another generation. The renewed creativity within the tradition (as opposed to the simple imitation of outside styles) makes earlier predictions of imminent disintegration seem hasty. Recent compositions by musicians such as D. L. Menard and Belton Richard continue to enlarge the stock repertoire of contemporary dance bands. Menard's *La Porte d'en arrière*, which has already become a modern classic, reiterates the *l'enfant perdu* theme encountered in *Les Barres de la prison*, but treats it in a humorous vein.

Fiddlers' Convention, 1981 Festival de musique acadienne

(Photo by Philip Gould)

Beausoleil (Michael Doucet second from left),
Paris, 1976

(Photo by Radio France)

Moi et la belle, on avait été z-au bal,
On a passé dans tous les honky tonks,
On s'en a revenu le lendemain matin,
Le jour était après se casser.
J'ai passé dedans la porte d'en arrière.

Après-midi, moi, j'ai été z-au village
Et je m'ai soûlé que je pouvais plus marcher.
Ils m'ont ramené back à la maison,
Il y avait de la compagnie, c'était du monde étranger.
J'ai passé dedans la porte d'en arrière.

Mon vieux père, un soir quand j'ai arrivé,
Il a essayé de changer mon idée.
Je l'ai pas écouté, moi, j'avais trop la tête dure.
«Un jour à venir, mon nègre, tu vas avoir du regret.
Tu vas passé dedans la porte d'en arrière.»

J'ai eu un tas d'amis tant que j'avais de l'argent.
Asteur j'ai plus d'argent, mais ils voulont plus me voir.
J'ai été dans le village et moi, je m'ai mis dans le tracas.
La loi m'a ramassé, moi, je suis parti dans la prison.
On va passer dedans la porte d'en arrière.

Purists who would resist new instrumentation and styles neglect to consider that change and innovation have always been an integral part of Cajun music. Those who want to freeze the tradition at any point necessarily miss the mark. The same approach would have barred the introduction of the accordian in the late nineteenth century, the adding of other instruments in the 1950s, the influence of the blues, the addition of swing and rock sounds along the way. As Dewey Balfa points out, "When things stop changing, they die. The culture and the music have to breathe and grow, but they have to stay within certain guidelines to be true. And those guidelines are pureness and sincerity."[29] European record producer Sam Charters also notes the life and change in Cajun music optimistically:

> Occasionally, there are articles published saying that the music is dying out, or that it's losing its traditional style, but the writers obviously haven't been to Opelousas or Lafayette or Crowley recently, for the music here is alive as ever. There are, of course, changes; it is a music that is growing and adapting new instruments and styles all the time, but the basic sound of Cajun music is still there. . . . It's obvious now—with all of the recent developments—that Cajun music is going to have a future that will be as vigorous as its past.[33]

The blending and cultural fusion at the heart of the development of Cajun culture continue to be essential to its music.

NOTES

1. Irene W. Holmes, *Louisiana French Folk Songs* (1939; reprint ed., Eunice, La., 1981), pp. 61-63.

2. *Ibid.*, p. 47.

3. Oster Collection, Folklore Archives, University of Southwestern Louisiana, Lafayette, Louisiana; hereinafter cited as FA, USL.

4. Holmes, *Folk Songs*, pp. 59-60.

5. As sung by Odile Falcon, 1976, Lafayette, La., Ancelet Collection, FA, USL.

6. As sung by Inez Catalon, 1975, Kaplan, La., Elizabeth Brandon Collection and Ancelet Collection, FA, USL.

7. As sung by Lula Landry, 1977, Abbeville, La., Ancelet Collection, FA, USL.

8. 1976, Ancelet Collection, FA, USL.

9. As sung by Kenry Fontenot, 1977, Ancelet Collection, FA, USL.

10. As sung by Pierre Robichaux, "La maudite guerre," *1755*, Presqu'île Records, New Brunswick, Canada.

11. As sung by Zachary Richard, *Bayou des Mystères*, Kébec disc, Canada.

12. As sung by Mme. Agnes Bourque, Ron and Fay Stanford Collection, *J'étais au bal*, Swallow Records, Ville Platte, La.

13. Jacques Savoie, *Beausoleil Broussard*, Le Tamanoir Records, New Brunswick, Canada.

14. Gabriel Debien, "The Acadians in Santo Domingo," *The Cajuns: Essays on Their History and Culture*, ed. by Glenn R. Conrad (Lafayette, La., 1978), p. 46.

15. Alan Lomax developed this idea during his keynote address at the 1980 Louisiana Folklore Society meeting, Lafayette, La.

16. From a reissue of Ardoin's early 78 recordings on Arhoolie Records.

17. From *Louisiana Cajun Music*, Volume I, Old Timey Records, (reissues of earlier 78 recordings).

18. 1977, Ancelet Collection, FA, USL; see also, *Bois Sec*, Melodean Records.

19. From an interview with Mathé Allain, 1982, Lafayette, La.

20. From *Louisiana Cajun Music*, Volume 5, Old Timey Records.

21. From *Louisiana Cajun Music*, Volume 3, Old Timey Records.

22. From an interview with Luderin Darbonne, 1982, Lake Charles, La.

23. From *Harry Choates*, Arhoolie Records. This album contains reissues of earlier 78 recordings.

24. From *Louisiana Cajun Music*, Volume 4, Old Timey Records.

25. From Iry LeJeune, *The Greatest*, Goldband Records.

26. A musical ride features a lead instrument for an eight-bar phrase. The pattern of rides in Cajun music is typically as follows: accordion lead, vocal break, steel guitar lead, fiddle lead, accordian lead.

27. From *The Balfa Brothers Play Traditional Cajun Music*, Swallow Records.

28. From D. L. Menard, *The Back Door*, Swallow Records.

29. Barry Jean Ancelet, "Dewey Balfa: Cajun Music Ambassador," *Louisiana Life*, I (Sept./Oct., 1981), 84.

30. Liner notes, *Cajun Paradise: Wayne Toups and the Crowley Aces*, Sonet Records.

THE FOLKLORE OF THE ACADIANS

by Patricia K. Rickels

The announcement of a federally funded program of Ethnic Heritage Studies by the Department of Health, Education, and Welfare in 1974 made official what had been apparent for some time: the myth of the American melting-pot has been replaced by the concept of pluralism. As emerging disciplines such as sociolinguistics turned their attention not just to far-off "primitive" tribes but to minority groups in the United States, and as the bicentennial spirit motivated a search for the cultural roots of our peoples, the significance of regional ethnic cultures like that of the Louisiana Acadians became increasingly clear to all students of American culture, including folklorists.

The late Richard M. Dorson, one of the most distinguished of American folklorists, has pointed out that those countries where folklore studies have flourished most vigorously--for example, Finland, Ireland, Japan--"possess the tidiest of cultural histories."[1] In contrast, the facts of American history create problems for the folklorist, who will hardly be able to discover an American folklore in this polyglot, multi-ethnic, and sprawling nation. But, as Dorson suggests, various kinds of folklore research can be undertaken with profitable results for the understanding of American civilization.

> A regional folk-culture complex offers the American folklorist one of his most inviting targets. A spectacular variety of regional folk cultures confronts the American folklorist. He thinks at once of German Pennsylvania, the bayou country of the Louisiana Cajuns, the Spanish-Mexican Southwest, Mormon Utah. . . . Such regions and pockets stand in contrast to the general American mass culture of urbanization, industrialization, and other-direction. The folklorist is particularly qualified to investigate these shadowy corners of American life.[2]

In his anthology of regional literature in the United States, *Buying the Wind*, Dorson devotes one of the seven sections to "Louisiana Cajuns,"[3] thus underlining his assessment that the regional folk culture of southern Louisiana is a significant one.

The study of Louisiana French folklore is, in fact, nearly as old as formal folklore studies in the United States. Alcée Fortier, one of the founding members of the American Folklore Society, a Professor of Romance Languages at

Tulane University, began to read papers on Louisiana French folklore topics at meetings of the Modern Language Association as early as the 1880s. Elected president of the American Folklore Society in 1894, Fortier had two years earlier founded the New Orleans branch of that organization. In 1895, as the second volume in its Memoirs series, the American Folklore Society published a bilingual edition of Fortier's *Louisiana Folk-Tales.* Fortier's major interest was in the language of Creole (black French) folktales, but he did valuable work on other aspects of Louisiana French history, language, and folklore. After his death, the New Orleans branch became inactive, and it was not for several decades that formal collecting and publication of Louisiana French folklore was revived and that particular attention was devoted to the folk traditions of the Acadians.[4]

Several Acadians who were not folklorists did record observations about their own culture which are valuable because of their early dates. In 1901, an educated and articulate Acadian, tentatively identified as the Honorable Joseph A. Breaux, chief justice of the Louisiana Supreme Court, completed work on a manuscript in which he had recorded observations about Acadian life, character, and folkways going back to the 1840s. Judge Breaux bequeathed the manuscript to the Louisiana State Museum in New Orleans, where it has since been lost. Fortunately, however, before its loss the manuscript was edited by Jay K. Ditchy of Tulane's French Department and published in Paris in 1932 under the title *Les Acadiens louisianais et leur parler.* To make these valuable materials more readily available, George F. Reinecke of the University of New Orleans translated and published extracts from the Breaux manuscript in the *Louisiana Folklore Miscellany* for 1966 under the title "Early French Life and Folklore." The fascinating wealth of information contained in the Breaux manuscript may be judged from this list of section titles in the Reinecke edition: "Character of the Acadians;" "Early Courts;" "Peddlers and Storekeepers;" "Rural Schooling;" "Clothing;" "House, Farm, Food, and Drink;" "Customs Through the Years;" "Courtship and Marriage;" "Death and Funerals;" "*Les Veillées;*" "The *Sabbat* and *Feu-Follet;*" and "Superstitions."

In 1907 Judge Felix Voorhies of St. Martinville published a small volume entitled *Acadian Reminiscences,* consisting of information reportedly transmitted by his 100-year-old grandmother in the late 1840s. The grandmother, herself one of the exiled Acadians, had entertained her grandchildren with stories of the older and, to her, better times. The chapter called "Acadian Manners and Customs" is of particular interest to the folklorist.

In 1880, noted New Orleans author and self-taught folklorist George Washington Cable was commissioned by Colonel George E. Waring to research the Acadians and prepare a report for inclusion in the United States census. Cable, who had already spent some time in the Acadian country, traveled widely

Alcée Fortier

Justice Joseph A. Breaux

through the area again, spending considerable time in some communities, particularly New Iberia. He observed closely, asked questions, made extensive notes about the economic, social, linguistic, and other aspects of Acadian life. The compilers of the *Tenth Census* decided not to include his material, but his notebook survives and is deposited in the Manuscript Division at Tulane University Library. Cable incorporated parts of his Acadian material into three stories: "Carancro (*sic*)," "Grande Pointe," and "Au Large," collected for book publication in 1888 as *Bonaventure: A Prose Pastoral of Acadian Louisiana.*

In 1927, the *Journal of American Folklore* published a collection of 1,585 superstitions collected by Hilda Roberts in Iberia Parish. Considering its date, Miss Robert's introduction to the collection is perceptive, especially in its discussions of the relationship between the superstitions of blacks and whites and of the relation between South Louisiana superstitions and those found in Europe in other parts of the United States.[5]

The publication in 1939 of Irene Thérèse Whitfield's book, *Louisiana French Folk Songs,*[6] with a fifty-eight page collection of, and commentary on, "Cajun Folksongs," marked the beginning of a flourishing period of scholarship on Acadian folklore. In the 1940s, Calvin Claudel began publishing a series of folktales of his native Avoyelles Parish in the *Southern Folklore Quarterly*, stories of Foolish John, Bouki and Lapin animal tales, and *märchen*. In the same decade two students at Laval University were at work on doctoral dissertations on Louisiana folklore, Corinne Saucier studying the traditions of Avoyelles Parish and Elizabeth Brandon those of Vermilion Parish.[7]

In 1956, the Louisiana Folklore Society was established, and, given direction by folklorist and musicologist Harry Oster, then a member of the Louisiana State University English faculty, it began publication of the *Louisiana Folklore Miscellany* and issued a series of field recordings. The society and its publications continue to flourish, and a growing number of articles, theses, books, and documentary films on Acadian folkore and the other folk cultures of Louisiana is being produced.[8] As evidence of institutional commitment to folklore studies, the University of Southwestern Louisiana established in 1974 a Center for the Study of Acadian Folklore and Culture.

Within the area of Louisiana French folklore, the student who wishes to confine his attention to Acadian culture may find himself involved in complexities of definition and demarcation. Every step of the way he will be reminded of Dorson's warning that "regions are dynamic not static" and that "regional folk culture is not a simple tableau but must be studied in depth and in process."[9] The inevitable questions arise: What do we mean by an *Acadian* or *Cajun*, and who is the authentic bearer of the Acadian folk heritage? Not every person descended from the Acadian exiles is a bearer of the folk culture. Culturally and linguistically all the Acadians belonged to a minority group, significantly separated from the American mainstream by geography and religion as well as language. Yet, among the Acadians, from early in their Louisiana residence, there was an educated class which constituted what might be termed the Acadian Establishment. These families provided members of the professions and political and economic leadership--indeed, they continue to do so. Their high culture is of interest to the student of American intellectual and religious history, but less so to the folklorist, who is concerned with the unofficial culture of a people, that not transmitted by the authorized institutions like church and school but learned by imitation and example through the oral traditions and customs of the folk community. Cable recognized the dichotomy in Acadian society, as shown by an entry in his notebook: "The lower class is very superstitious."[10]

On the other hand, persons not descended from the original Acadians must be considered authentic bearers of their folk traditions when they have been absorbed into Acadian folk culture. In this sense octogenarian Dennis McGee of Eunice is correct when he calls himself a Cajun and insists that "Dennis McGee is a Cajun name."[11] His language, his life style, his values, and the music he plays are Cajun. It has often been pointed out that many settlers of St. Martinville were not Acadians but later arrivals from France or the West Indies. Likewise, Ville Platte was not settled by Acadians but by veterans of the Napoleonic Wars. Yet the folk culture of these communities is basically Cajun. This use of the term *Cajun* sees the folk heritage in the perspective called for in Dorson's phrase "dynamic not static." It rejects what Alan Dundes has called "The Devolutionary Premise in Folklore Theory,"[12] the idea that the folklorist is concerned with an idyllic pastoral culture, transplanted to Louisiana two centuries ago, where it was essentially preserved until recently, but which has now suffered encroachment, degeneration, and decay so that only a few precious remnants can now be discerned. Rather, it defines Cajun folk culture as a vigorously thriving American culture, developed on Louisiana soil by the descendants of the Acadian exiles and other groups whom they interacted with and culturally absorbed. It is in this sense that people who call themselves Cajuns usually understand their own culture and that they are perceived by others. One example might be cited: Texans speak of "the Acadian colonies of the Beaumont-Port Arthur-Orange triangle," also known as Cajun Lapland, "because that's where Louisiana laps over into Texas."[13] Explaining that most of the Cajuns came to the Golden Triangle during the two World Wars to work in defense industries, one Texas writer characterizes their culture by the Cajuns' fondness for crayfish bisque, shrimp gumbo, and jambalaya.[14] In fact, these dishes are all of multi-ethnic origin and all of them evolved in Louisiana. Today, they are considered by both Cajuns and outsiders to be typically

Cajun, as is accordion music, actually a nineteenth-century German contribution to Cajun culture.

There is a core which folklorists and other perceptive observers have agreed in finding central to and persistent in Louisiana Acadian culture: a strong attachment to the Catholic Church, to the land, and to the family; gregariousness, conviviality, and a hearty enjoyment of the pleasures of the flesh. These attitudes and values lie at the heart of Cajun folklore and account for its essential difference from that of Anglo-Saxon Protestant Louisiana.

It would be difficult to overestimate the influence of the Catholic Church on Acadian folklore. Its sacraments and sacramentals, rituals, festivals, and observances of the ecclesiastical year, as well as its doctrines (sometimes imperfectly understood), provide a rich source of folkloric belief and custom. All aspects of life are permeated by this influence: the stages of life from birth to death, household routines and culinary practices, planting and weather lore, folk medicine, superstitions and taboos.[15]

Attachment to the land and to the family have insured a stable, conservative cultural environment where there is every opportunity for folk traditions to be passed on. Family gatherings are the occasion for young women to learn kitchen customs and hear pregnancy and child-care lore from older wives, for men and boys to exchange hunting and fishing stories, and for children to play traditional games. The persistent custom of evening visits (*les veilles*) provides plenty of opportunity for talk and storytelling. The lack of puritanical religious strictures has fostered, as an accompaniment and an encouragement to Cajun gregariousness, a festive tradition, one emphasizing the enjoyment of food, drink, music, dance, and the excitement of contests on which money is wagered--card games, horse races, and cock fights.

Certain types of Acadian folklore collected in past years strongly persist today, others not at all or in a markedly changed form. Folktales like those collected by Fortier, Saucier, and Claudel are no longer really a living part of Acadian culture. Many old people know *marchen*-like "Ti-Poucette," some Jean Sot stories, or tales of Bouki and Lapin, but they never tell them unless a folklorist comes around collecting. The grandchildren, their natural audience, do not like to hear such old things when they could be watching television and, despite ambitious bilingual programs in the schools, they would probably not be able to understand the stories in French. Today the joke has replaced the folktale as the flourishing form of oral narrative.[16] Cajun jokes are ubiquitous, told in French, in English, and in comic amalgamation of the two. They deal irreverently with sex, race, politics, religion, and the peculiarities of the "Cajun character." Many are jokes in general American circulation, given a local setting and a dialect style.

The Acadians loved dancing, even before the exile, and were reputed to excel in the art. Until about a generation ago, the dance was the favorite social recreation for all ages. But the last twenty years have seen a sharp decline in dancing. House dances are seldom held, only once in a while at weddings. The old round dances are virtually never performed, and even public dances with couples dancing to Cajun music are becoming rare. One fiddler who played for dances sixty years ago can still play the fiddle tunes for dances nobody knows how to do anymore--mazurkas, polkas, jigs, reels, cotillions, lanciers, handkerchief dances.[17] Only the two-step and the waltz survive, and those among the old folks. Young people prefer modern dances and rock music. Instrumental music which was the occasion for dancing will not long survive out of its social context. Cajun songs, as they are the subject of another essay in the present collection, will not be discussed here.

In the areas of custom, belief, and superstition, students in folklore courses at the University of Southwestern Louisiana have been systematically collecting for the past twelve years, using a finding list organized into eight categories, on the pattern of the Frank C. Brown Collection of North Carolina Folklore.[18] The collection now includes about 3,500 items. A study of the kinds of folklore most frequently and less frequently collected reveals some interesting patterns. In descending order of importance, the eight categories are The Human Body and Folk Medicine; the Life Cycle; Domestic Economy and Social Relationships; Animals, Birds, and Fish; Seasonal Beliefs and Practices; Plants and Plant Husbandry; Weather; and Witchcraft, Ghostlore, Spirits, and Voodoo (Hoodoo).

The Human Body and Folk Medicine accounts for nearly half the items in the collection, the great majority dealing with folk medicine. Home remedies are very numerous, including poultices, teas, ointments, and religio-magic rituals for both man and beast. Another important part of folk medicine is the *traiteur*, a folk healer who has power passed down to him/her from another *traiteur* to cure through prayer, sometimes assisted by magic and perhaps the administration of herbs or other substances. The institution of the *traiteur* persists strongly in Cajun culture, in spite of the general availability of good medical facilities.

The Life Cycle is another very large category. In it, more space is devoted to birth, infancy, and childhood than to courtship and marriage, death and funeral practices, and all other subjects combined. An elaborate system of taboos and customs still surrounds pregnancy, infant care, baptism, and child-rearing. In addition, a large part of the folk medicine material deals with complaints of babies and children. Cajuns have traditionally had large families. Their continuing concern with bearing babies and rearing children is strongly reflected in the material collected. In many families customs are those of the folk tradition with little dependence on the pediatrician or the child psychologist.

Domestic Economy and Social Relationships is also a large section, reflecting the home and family orientation of Cajun culture and its emphasis on gregariousness. Kitchen customs and culinary practices are included in this category, but food recipes are not recorded. If they were included, this section would be much larger, for cooking is one of the most important aspects of Cajun life. Gumbo lore alone would make a sizeable category. In this section and the ones outlined before it, women predominate as informants. In the remaining categories men and women are about evenly represented, except that men predominate as informants on Animals, Birds, Fish, Plants, and Plant Husbandry.

Animals, Birds, and Fish is a rather small section. The folk beliefs and practices which do survive may be traced to the Acadians' traditional occupation as cattlemen, their continued pleasure in horses, and their knowledge of hunting, trapping, and fishing. Fewer Cajuns engage in cattle raising or trapping than in past generations, but hunting, and especially fishing, are very popular pastimes.

Seasonal Beliefs and Practices deals with both the natural and the ecclesiastical year. It is a section of modest size, but strikingly dominated by the Easter Season, including in that designation Mardi Gras. The celebration of Mardi Gras still maintains some folkloric elements, though each year the influence of New Orleans crowds country customs further back. The community of Mamou has preserved a tradition of "running Mardi Gras," with horsemen riding from farm to farm begging and dancing for chickens to make a big gumbo. However, this celebration attracts so many television cameras, scholars from the Smithsonian, and folklorists from Nebraska that not much spontaneity can be expected to survive.

In some other communities which have escaped the scholarly and popular spotlight, there are still survivals of ritual begging by children and, among men, real masquerading with the intent to disguise identity. Besides the male Cajun *courir de Mardi Gras* in Mamou, there are black groups and women's groups in some communities.[19]

It is Holy Week, and especially Good Friday, which has the largest number of folkloric practices and taboos attached to them. The custom of planting parsley on Good Friday and the taboo against breaking the ground on that day are still nearly universally respected by Cajuns.

In Catahoula and the surrounding rural area, the once widespread custom of breaking the Good Friday fast before noon with a feast of sweet pastries persists. Some families call Good Friday "Pie Day" and insist on the celebration in defiance of clerical disapproval.

Marcia Gaudet has recently studied a number of calendar customs in St. John the Baptist Parish, most notably the tradition of Christmas Eve bonfires on the levee. Introduced by French priests in the mid-nineteenth century, this seasonal practice has become a flourishing folk custom among families on the Acadian Coast.[20]

Plants and Plant Husbandry is a small section. Farming is a declining occupation for Cajun families, and those who do farm or make gardens tend to be guided by the advice of the county agent. Some older folks do remember how to plant by the moon, and a few rely on the *Farmer's Almanac*. In Cajun gardens, there is almost always, besides the "general American" vegetables, a section of okra, and plenty of green onions and parsley, indispensable ingredients in many traditional dishes.

Weather Lore is a very small section, concerned largely with rain, fog, and wind. Since hurricanes are the most dramatic weather phenomena in South Louisiana, it is not surprising that folklore and legends have developed concerning the major storms. Patricia Perrin has collected and analyzed such traditions in "Storm Lore About the Hurricanes of 1893 and 1915 in the Coastal Areas of Lafourche and Jefferson Parishes."[21]

The smallest category is Witchcraft, Ghostlore, Spirits, and Voodoo (Hoodoo). Among black informants in the same geographical area this is a very significant category, with many supernatural tales in oral circulation, but Cajuns seem to have fewer such traditions. Most of them know stories of the *Feu-Follet* and the *Loup-Garou* (usually pronounced *Fee-Follet* and *Roo-Garou*), but these spirits are believed in mostly by children. Indeed, adults find it convenient to frighten children into obedience by threats of these and other supernatural beings. *Gris-gris* (a word of African origin, noun: an object or symbol to cause or prevent evil; verb: to cast a spell over) is a term everyone knows, though few take it seriously. Some Cajuns do consult black practicioners of folk medicine and magic, and the line dividing fortune teller, *traiteur*, and voodoo doctor is a fuzzy one in communities where both blacks and whites share a French Catholic folk culture. Very few Cajuns have even heard of *cauchemar*, a night-riding spirit almost universally familiar to black Creoles in Acadiana and deeply feared by many.[22]

In summary, Acadian folklore as of today reflects a culture in transition from rural to urban life, rapidly becoming dependent on the canned entertainment of American popular culture, but still traditionally oriented toward family life and child-rearing, attached to the rituals and sacramentals of Catholicism, spiritually inclined in that they feel illness and trouble have spiritual rather than merely physical causes, but not afraid of the supernatural in the form of ghosts and spirits after they leave childhood, lovers of hunting and fishing and of cooking and eating what they bring home.

As noted early in this essay, there is a great deal of scholarly interest in Cajun culture at the present time. Hardly a week passes at the University of Southwestern Louisiana without a visit from a folklorist, ethnomusicologist, or sociolinguist from France, Canada, U.C.L.A., or the University of Michigan, hot on the trail of informants. But, this professional research aside, there are four trends or developments involving Louisiana Acadian folklore which merit comment.

The first is the "fakelore"[23] being concocted by tourist bureaus and civic clubs for commercial gain. It is harmless enough, though irritating to the purist and misleading to visitors because of the historical inaccuracies introduced and because of its cultivation of the quaint and the picturesque. In this category belong spurious legends about the origin of the crayfish, the custom of dressing up in "Evangeline costumes" for public occasions, the staging of *gris-gris* rituals, and the practice of putting imitation medieval armor on the riders in the Ville Platte *tournoi*. All this is window dressing for the sale of "colorful Acadiana" as a tourists' paradise.

Second, not to be confused with "fakelore," are the attempts of know-ledgeable people to preserve dying folk traditions, or at least the knowledge of them, usually by teaching them in the schools. Such projects include Jeanne and Robert Gilmore's collection of Louisiana French folk songs designed to combine the teaching of elementary school French and music.[24] Another example is the Acadian Assembly, a group formed at the Blanchet School in Meaux, under the direction of Catherine and Edward Blanchet. The young people in this ensemble learn and perform authentic Louisiana folk dances, some of which the Blanchets learned from the last survivors who knew them. Collections of beliefs and superstitions published recently by students suggest other areas where the schools might foster an interest in high school and college and knowledge of the local folklore of the recent past.[25]

Outside the schools, the Louisiana Native Crafts Festival, held annually at the Lafayette Natural History Museum since 1972, gives an opportunity for experts to demonstrate their traditonal skills in cooking, basketry, blacksmith-ing, soap-making, net-weaving, making folk toys, and many other areas. This festival deserves partial credit for reviving interest in learning the arts of quilting, spinning, and hand-weaving. Since 1981, story telling in the folk tradition has been included and has drawn large audiences. Organizers of the Cajun Days celebration in Church Point began in 1975, and plan to continue each year, the custom of offering generous cash prizes to the winners of an accordion-playing competition. The contest is open only to young people, who must play an old Cajun waltz and a two-step, in traditonal style. The hope of the sponsors of the competition is that these young Cajuns will be motivated to learn the old ma-terials and techniques from their grandparents.

The third and fourth developments involve forces or elements diametrically opposed to one another and co-existing in a mood of considerable tension. The two groups might be labelled: "Genteel Acadians" and "Just Plain Coonasses."

The Genteel Acadian position is strongly influenced by the image of Golden Age virtue, tranquility, and piety presented in Longfellow's *Evangeline* and Voorhies' *Acadian Reminiscences.* Spokesmen for this view reject any suggestion that elements of rudeness, earthiness, ignorance, violence, or impiety are present in "authentic" Acadian culture. Fiercely respectable, they resent, for example, the depiction of Cajun life in Les Blank's prize-winning documentary film "Spend It All." They find the scenes of a rough country pig-butchery and of a family barbecue with lots of beer drunk straight from the can offensive and cannot identify with them. "We are Cajuns." they say, "but our families never acted like that." This was the group referred to earlier as the Acadian Establishment, mostly families with a long history of education and privilege, keepers of the cult of "Evangeline Enshrined,"[26] centering around the Evangeline Oak and the "grave of Evangeline" in St. Martinville. For them, only polite traditions, traceable back to the earliest times, qualify as authentic Cajun.

The group of Cajuns who refuse to be included in this mystique, finding it "emasculated and phoney," in the words of one college student, have seized with delighted irreverence on the term "coonass." This interesting word, of disputed origin but indisputedly vulgar connotation, is an abomination in the ears of the Genteel Acadians but is defiantly blazoned forth on bumper stickers, T-shirts, and record albums by those who proclaim themselves "Proud Coonasses," or "Registered Coonasses," with a number of other, sometimes obscene variations on the theme. Their attitude toward those whose refinement seems pretentious is illustrated by the following remark attributed to one Martin Delahoussaye, formerly of Lafayette, now living in Texas:

> Cajuns are trying to establish a new image. They want to overcome the idea that they are crude or profane; they want to use sophistication. They, therefore, do not say 'coon ass' anymore when they refer to a country Cajun; they say 'cooh ahss.'[27]

Although it is only one facet of a complex culture, the folklorist finds much to support the position that there has been, at least since the mid-nineteenth century, a strong tradition of drunkenness, fighting, blood sports, and malicious practical jokes in the folk culture of male Cajuns. Richard Slotkin's study of American mythology suggests that the psychology and world view of the anti-Genteel Acadian party is the result of the American historical experience and in general parallels the development of the American "national character," with its "frontier psychology" and its emphasis on disorder, destruction, and violence.[28] According to Slotkin, the image of New World culture as pastoral, orderly, Christian and sublime was a European invention with roots in the arcadian myth of the Greeks.[29] The experience of American settlers, however, did not harmonize with the ideal. Their experience was of wildness and a savage struggle with nature, Indians, and each other.

> On the level of universal human psychology, this tension between the two patterns expresses the dilemma of all men coming of age, inheriting their parents' world, and replacing their sires as the shapers of that world. In particular context of colonial history, it expresses the alternatives open to the American generations: (a) to be reconciled with Europe and the culture of the first founders, or (b) to acculturate, to adapt to the Indians' wilderness. The earlier generations . . . clung to their heritage, . . . later generations . . . tended toward acculturation.[30]

Eventually, in Slotkin's dark view, "the myth of regeneration through violence became the structuring metaphor of the American experience."[31]

Whatever the sources of the wild and unruly element in Cajun culture, it is those who refuse to deny or relinquish it who maintain the most vigorous folk life. They are, for example, the perpetuators of a folk music tradition, though they offend traditionalists by absorbing country and western styles and racists by preferring Clifton Chenier's black Creole Zydeco music to "J'ai passe devant ta porte." They are the regular patrons of Fred's Bar in Mamou, who gather every Saturday morning for lively Cajun music and racy Cajun stories. They are the informants the folklorist needs to record if he is to study a dynamic culture in process.

NOTES

1. Richard M. Dorson, *American Folklore and the Historian* (Chicago, 1971), p. 28.

2. *Ibid.*, pp. 441-442.

3. Richard M. Dorson, *Buying the Wind* (Chicago, 1964), pp. 229-288.

4. Calvin Claudel, "New Orleans Branch, American Folklore Society (The Louisiana Folklore Association)," *Journal of American Folklore*, LIX (1946), 488-489.

5. Hilda Roberts, "Louisiana Superstitions," *Journal of American Folklore*, XL (1927), 144-208.

6. Irene Therese Whitfield Holmes, *Louisiana French Folk Songs* (Baton Rouge, 1969).

7. Both collections were published in part, Saucier's as *Traditions de la Paroisse des Avoyelles en Louisiane* (American Folklore Society Memoir No. 47, 1958), and *Folk Tales from French Louisiana* (Baton Rouge, 1962), and Brandon's as "La Paroisse de Vermillon: Moeurs, Dictons, Contes et Legendes," serially in the journal *Bayou*, Nos. 64-69 (1955-1957).

8. To cite a few examples, Lauren Post, *Cajun Sketches: From the Prairies of South-west Louisiana* (Baton Rouge, 1962); Anna M. Boudreaux, "A Profile of the Folklore and Idiomatic Expressions of the French Language of the Kaplan Area in Vermilion Parish," (MA thesis, University of Southwestern Louisiana, 1969); Catherine B. Blanchet, "Louisiana French Folk Songs Among Children in Vermilion Parish, 1942-54," (MA thesis. University of Southwestern Louisiana, 1970); Malcolm L. Comeaux, *Atchafalaya Swamp Life* (Baton Rouge, 1972); Jon L. Gibson and Steven L. Del Sesto, eds., *The Culture of Acadiana: Tradition and Change in South Louisiana* (Lafayette, La., 1975); Films: Les Blank's "Dry Wood," "Hot Pepper," "Spend It All;" Stephen Duplantier's "D. L. Menard, Cajun Musician," "Vivre Pour Manger."

9. Dorson, *American Folklore*, p. 41.

10. *Ibid.*, p. 111.

11. Videotaped interview conducted by the author, June 24, 1974.
Some blacks of French culture have objected to being included in the term "Cajun" and have recently organized an "Un-Cajun" movement. The question of clutural relations and influences between Cajuns and black Creoles has interested scholars as far back as Cable, recently Harry Oster, "The Acculturation of Cajun Music," *McNeese Review*, X (1959), 12-24; Nicholas Spitzer, "Cajuns and Creoles: The French Gulf Coast," *Southern Exposure*, V ((1977), 140-155; Steven Del Sesto, "Cajun Music and Zydeco," *Louisiana Folklore Miscellany*, IV (1976-1980), 88-101; Andre Prevos, "Anglo-French Spirituals about Mary Magdalene," *Louisiana Folklore Miscellany*, IV (1976-1980), 41-53.

12. Alan Dundes, "The Devolutionary Premise in Folklore Theory," *Journal of tne Folklore Institute*, VI (1969), 5-19.

13. Francis E. Abernethy, ed., *The Folklore of Texan Cultures* (Austin, Tex., 1974), p. 58.

14. *Ibid.*, p. 49.

15. For a full discussion with many examples, see Patricia Rickels, "Folklore of the Sacraments and Sacramentals in South Louisiana," *Louisiana Folklore Miscellany*, II (1965), 27-44.

16. Barry Ancelet has collected about 1,000 stories, 118 of them animal tales, fairy tales, tall tales, and legends, the rest shorter anecdotes. See his Indiana University M. A. thesis (1977); "Talking Pascal in Mamou: A Study in Folkloric Competence," *Journal of the Folklore Institute*, XVII (1980), 1-24.

17. Dennis McGee, see note 11 above.

18. This continuing project is under the general auspices of the *Dictionary of American Popular Beliefs and Superstititions,* directed by Wayland D. Hand of U. C. L. A.'s Center for the Study of Folklore and Mythology.

19. Susan Théall, " 'Sauce for the Gander': The Women's Mardi Gras Run in Basile," (Unpublished research paper), presented at the April 1980 meeting of the Louisiana Folklore Society, University of Southwestern Louisiana, Lafayette.

20. "The Folklore and Customs of the West Bank of St. John the Baptist Parish," (Ph. D. dissertation, University of Southwestern Louisiana, 1980). See also her "Mississippi Riverlore and Customs," *Louisiana Folklore Miscellany*, V, (1982), 26-33.

21. M. A. thesis, University of Southwestern Louisiana, 1977. See also her "Oral Accounts of the Storms of 1893 and 1915 from the Chenier Caminada Area," *Louisiana Folklore Miscellany*, IV (1976-1980), 54-60.

22. See Patricia Rickels, "Some Accounts of Witch Riding," *Louisiana Folklore Miscellany*, II (1961), I-17.

23. Dorson coined this word in 1950. See his *American Folklore* (Chicago, 1959), p. 4.

24. *Chantez, La Louisiane!* (Lafayette, La., 1970).

25. *Mais, Jamais de la Vie! A Collection of Folklore from the Parish of Acadia*, 2 Parts (Crowley, La., 1976-1977); Erath High School, "C'est La Vie," (1979-1980). Students of Xavier University, *Legacy: The Documenting of Louisiana Traditions and Folk Life* (New Orleans, 1979).

26. The name of a little shop in St. Martinville, where for many years Andre Olivier sold copies of *Evangeline*, souvenirs, and general store merchandise.

27. Abernethy, *The Folklore of Texan Cultures*, pp. 49-50.

28. Richard Slotkin, *Regeneration Through Violence: The Mythology of the American Frontier, 1600-1860* (Middletown, Conn., 1973), pp. 3-5.

29. As an embodiment of the arcadian myth, consider Longfellow's *Evangeline: A Tale of Acadie*, which Newton Arvin has analyzed in "Acadian Idyl," Chapter VI of his *Longfellow: His Life and Work* (Boston, 1962). Arvin discusses the bland tone of the poem, emphasizing its decorousness, tameness, and serenity, the lack of indignation or wrath over the maltreatment of the Acadians. "It is largely wanting, too, despite its subject, in effects emphasizing the Eden-like quality of the Louisiana environment, and the 'bucolic peace and contentment' in which the people spend 'their innocent lives.' " *Ibid.*, pp. 103-104.

30. Slotkin, *Regeneration Through Violence*, p. 259.

31. *Ibid.*, p. 5.

THE CAJUNS: ETHNOGENESIS
AND THE SHAPING OF GROUP CONSCIOUSNESS

by James H. Dormon

During the fall season of the year 1755, just prior to the onset of the French and Indian War, a group of French-speaking Roman Catholic pas-toralist/fishermen-trappers, between 6,000 and 10,000 in all, fell victim to British geopolitical strategy and military tactics. They were exiled from their homeland in Nova Scotia (formerly French Acadie). Their "grand dérange-ment," as it later came to be known, has supplied the stuff of epic, legend, lore, and endless historiographic controversy, as yet unresolved.[1] Exile also provided the point of origin for a people who would ultimately emerge as one of the most tightly bound ethnic groups the United States has produced. The Acadians' eventual relocation, largely in South Louisiana, inaugurated the ethnogenesis (the *birth* of the group as such) of the people now called "Cajuns." An analysis of their formation into a group, one that has survived to the present time, constitutes the primary concern of this essay.

Socio-cultural processes occur throughout a period of time. An his-torical perspective is usually essential to their understanding, and never more so than in the matter of ethnic group formation and maintenance. Under-standing the dynamics of group development requires familiarity with the group's experiences, experiences that can be comprehended only through longitudinal analysis. In some cases it is necessary to look back far into the past to find a point from which to begin the examination of process, but the precise point of origin is rarely explicit. For the Cajuns we might begin (somewhat arbitrarily) with the advent of the French colony of Acadie in the eastern reaches of Canada, at the time of the earliest French colonization in the New World. The people involved as colonists were largely of peasant French stock. They were ill-equipped for wilderness survival; therefore, they suffered all the hardships typical of early American colonization efforts before developing into self-sustaining and self-perpetuating settlement groups. Although the first Acadian settlement efforts came as early as 1604, nothing resembling a productive colony came into being until the late seventeenth century. The development of a group sufficiently large and homogeneous to be termed an "Acadian people" had to await the early eighteenth century. By 1713 the "Acadians" numbered some 2,500 souls. But in that year their French colonial status shifted abruptly and terminally to that of British

233

colonists. The Treaty of Utrecht ratified English possession of Acadie, which was immediately renamed Nova Scotia.[2]

By the time of their transfer to English control, the Acadians had been forged into group distinctiveness by virtue of their determination to remain "neutrals" in an area much torn by chronic struggle between and among the French, the English (and their Anglo-American colonials, who for years had coveted and indeed claimed the Acadian peninsula), and the local Indians who sided with the French in the struggle. The response of the Acadian population, centered in several villages chiefly on the shores of the Bay of Fundy and the Minas Basin, was to unify, to consolidate in mutual aid and comfort in an effort to protect their villages. Through the years a certain bond had resulted, based on a clear understanding of the need to aid one another for self-preservation. No matter that from time to time their European overlords changed nationality as a result of a military victory or successful occupation; the overriding fact was that the Acadians were determined to protect their own group, to preserve their villages, and to maintain their livelihoods. And so they did, perpetuating and expanding their kinship-dominated clans, pursuing their sustenance by farming, hunting, fishing, and trading with the Indians, professing their Catholic faith despite an inadequate provision of clergy. They were dedicated only to their independence, their self-reliance, and their determination to survive. In relative isolation from the outside world, paying homage to whatever European power assumed temporary control, largely self-sufficient and content in their isolation, they lived, worked, and (to a degree) flourished.

There is remarkable unanimity among the opinions of those who have attempted to characterize the Acadians of the mid-eighteenth century: most agree that they were "simple," rural folk--in Robert Redfield's classic delineation of a "Folk Culture"--homogeneous, hard-working (but only, it would seem, when sheer necessity demanded hard work), largely illiterate, deeply conservative, kinship dominated, dwelling in household units of patriarchal multi-generational families tied closely to the land.[3] Henry Wadsworth Longfellow, in his epic *Evangeline*, characterized the Acadians as perennially optimistic, idyllically content, pious, and virtuous. It is likely that in reality their lot was not altogether idyllic; it was, in fact, a rather hard lot, producing a tough people, at times suspicious, even xenophobic. Without doubt, there was more than a grain of truth in the old Canadian gibe "entêté comme un Acadien" ("pigheaded as an Acadien"). One close student of Acadian history and culture has suggested that by the eighteenth century the Acadians represented a "body of people united by blood ties, common beliefs and common aims for the groups as a whole. . . ."[4] In short, despite the broad dispersion of their communities by 1755, the Acadians had achieved a real sense of their distinctiveness, their "we-ness." They stood quite apart from the "others": French, English, Anglo-American, and Canadian. They had established a group identity by the time of their forced exile at the hands of the British military.

The ultimate test of their initial group solidarity came in the years following their dispersal. And "dispersal" is precisely what the English had in mind as they set about the business of the Acadian exile. British vessels carried small groups of them to all seaboard colonies to the south; others went as prisoners of war to England, ultimately to arrive in France; still others eventually found themselves in Spanish America, and the French West Indies. Yet, by all indications they maintained their Acadian "ethnicity," the measure of their group identity.[5] As a minority element wherever they found themselves, they took on the characteristics of an ethnic group, manifesting a powerful awareness of and attachment to their unique sub-culture. They were also uniformly poor, i. e., of a relatively lower socioeconomic status, thus sharing their adversity as well as their ethnicity. If there is any truth in the view that nations are constituted of people who have suffered together, the Acadians achieved a sort of nationality in the hard years of their odyssey. Moreover, as Professor Griffiths has noted, they believed themselves to have been the victims of acute injustice: they had wanted only neutrality and peace. "This emotional sense of . . . having had unwarrantable sufferings inflicted upon them," writes Griffiths, "was one source of strength for the Acadians in exile, and a partial explanation of the extraordinary capacity for survival which the majority of them showed."[6] The same sense of wrong perpetrated upon them left them with a powerful anti-British bias that would surface soon after their eventual resettlement in colonial Louisiana, when many members of their group would support Spain and France in the struggle against England during the American Revolutionary War. The English, and more broadly English-speakers, were to be suspect and distrusted for generations to come.

That many of the Acadians in exile chose to reestablish themselves as a group in Louisiana is understandable, given the historical circumstances surrounding the affairs of that woebegotten colony. And complex circumstances they were. In brief: the Louisiana colony had been an underfinanced, maladministered, largely unsuccessful colonial effort of France since its founding in 1699. Following the loss of New France at the conclusion of the French and Indian War, the French were only too happy to transfer Louisiana to Spain, which they did, secretly, in 1762. Spain established effective control in 1769, and rather quickly brought life to the moribund little colony. Pursuing politics calculated to increase agriculture and trade and to encourage additional population settlement, the Spanish administration succeeded where the French had largely failed. The results were apparent within a decade: new settlements flourished as population and productivity increased. Indeed, a large measure of the Acadian in-migration to Louisiana came as a direct result of Spanish policy, in that the Spanish offered (in 1784) to transport Acadian refugees from the port cities of France's Breton coast to Louisiana, there to provide them with land, tools, and the necessaries of establishing operational farms. Some 1,600 Acadians accepted the offer and arrived in Louisiana in 1785 to begin life anew after thirty years of abandonment by the French crown.[7]

In reality, however, the Acadian immigration to Louisiana began a decade before the Spanish takeover. A few stragglers were recorded as having arrived as early as 1756.[8] The mid-1760s saw larger groups arriving from the British colonies of the Atlantic seaboard, primarily Maryland and Pennsylvania, as well as from Nova Scotia and French Saint-Domingue. Indeed, in 1765 the parish register of the Poste des Attakapas (later the village of St. Martinville) recorded the arrival of a group of Acadians in an entry signed by Father Jean François, who identified himself as "curé de la Nouvelle Acadie des Attakapas."[9] The group had been dispatched to the Attakapas District by the acting governor of the colony in order that they might take up lands provided for their use by colonial authorities.[10]

It is noteworthy that the Louisiana colony was in a state of considerable flux during the years of Acadian in-migration and resettlement. Not only did the colony change European overlords, but other population groups were arriving along with the Acadian exiles, not the least important of which was the large number of black slaves brought in to work the proliferating indigo plantations of the region. The colony was, of course, centered in New Orleans, but settlement areas extended up and down the Mississippi River from the Crescent City, and isolated outpost settlements (including those of the Attakapas and Opelousas districts) lay to the west. Growing numbers of small villages were beginning to appear along the other waterways of that inordinately fluvial region.

The old families of French "Creoles"[11] dominated the economic and cultural life of the colony, though the Spanish officials, who were sent to govern and defend the area, soon assumed positions of status and authority. Still, the French language prevailed, as did other aspects of French Creole culture. Catholicism was the official and established religion, though the church was understaffed and not altogether effective in function outside the major population centers. Withal, Louisiana manifested a certain Gallic tone most unlike the bustling, burgeoning, now restless Anglo-American states of the Atlantic coast, and the *ancienne population* was more than content to keep it that way.

It was into such a situation that the Acadians arrived to begin their settlement. The details of their initial settlement efforts are complex and still under scholarly contention; they need concern us but little. Suffice it to say that the earliest Acadian settlement sites were along the Mississippi River above New Orleans (the so-called Acadian Coast), at several village sites along the river, to the south on Bayou Lafourche, and most importantly in the Attakapas and Opelousas districts, due west of New Orleans. The Acadian immigrants arrived normally at New Orleans, then moved to other settlement areas with the assistance of the colonial officials in New Orleans. At first, their selection of settlement sites varied, some preferring one area, some another. The officials, of course, guided their selections, and though the land offered was not usually of the most desirable, arable sort, the grants were sizeable: normally a four-arpent frontage on a river or bayou (an arpent being approximately 5/6 of an acre).

As time passed a clear settlement pattern emerged. The Acadians increasingly chose to group together, to seek out and to locate in pre-established Acadian settlements. Anthropologist Eric Waddell, a student of Acadian-American ethnography, has recently suggested that the "basic settlement unit" to emerge was "typically, a closed corporate neighborhood" frequently comprising "extended kin groups."[12] Moreoever, the settlements tended increasingly to be in the interior, relatively isolated areas of the colony made available to the Acadians. The evidence suggests that the Acadians made a tacit decision to avoid the older, Creole-dominated river settlements, and to seek out their own people to the south and southwest. There they could work their small farms and live in close communion with little interference from the outside world. The pull of *ethnos* proved powerful indeed, but it was hardly a mystical force. As *petits habitants,* initially quite poor and dependent upon official largess for their wherewithal, they simply chose not to try to compete with the established, arrogant, and wholly ethnocentric Creole element of the east. It was simply to their advantage, socially, economically, psychologically, to create their own Acadian enclaves in the interior prairie country and on the rivers and bayous to the south and southwest. Though separated by distance they maintained a system of community structure in much the same form as had prevailed in Acadie. They also maintained their sense of group distinctiveness and difference even though they were dispersed geographically over a rather broad area.[13]

Even as the Acadians arrived in Louisiana, and more particularly in the years immediately following their largest single group immigration (from France, in 1785-86), two developments of enormous importance were already in progress. First was the simultaneous in-migration of other population elements, most importantly the Anglo-Americans who began arriving in substantial numbers in the years following the American Revolution. Then came the rapid development of the plantation system, associated particularly (after 1803) with the development of sugarcane cultivation and sugar processing. The discovery that sugar could be produced profitably in the southernmost reaches of the Louisiana colony attracted investment capital to the area, capital that went into land and slaves, thus producing the systematic development of large land holdings and the resulting prestige and power of landed wealth. In the rapidly developing sugar country, a high premium came to be attached to the status associated with land and slave ownership and plantation production. The result was the consolidation of large land holdings utilized in sugar production and worked almost exclusively by slave labor. Most of the new investment capital belonged to the old Creole families and (increasingly) to the *nouveau arrivé* Anglo-American element. Smaller landowners, tempted by sizeable cash offers, frequently chose to sell out and move on, to seek less desirable land elsewhere. This process–it might be termed the "Americanization" of the Louisiana sugar country–actually coincided with the political Americanization that followed the Louisiana Purchase in 1803, and continued long after the Purchase. And in no single area was this Americanization process more in evidence than in the Attakapas District, by the end of the eighteenth century the center of Acadian population concentration.

It should be noted that not *all* of the Acadian *petits habitants* were forced out of their small farms along the bayous by the encroaching Anglo/ Creole planter/bourgeoisie.[14] Some of the Acadians had succeeded rather quickly in adding to their own small holdings, building their own productive potential, buying slaves and cattle, and amassing wealth. As they did so, they often assumed the status and prestige associated with the planter/ bourgeois class, of which more anon. The small Acadian farmers, however, were forced to seek out their subsistence in other areas than the best cane land, or on smaller plots along the waterways and in the lowlands to the interior where they could maintain their farm operations against the encroachments of planter consolidation. Many left their initial settlement sites to go elsewhere, and ultimately to resettle in one of three additional, fairly distinct regions of South Louisiana: the prairie land to the west, the great swamps of the Lafourche and Atchafalaya basins, and the gulf coastal marshes to the south. The forces of plantation consolidation thus brought about the process that William F. Rushton has recently termed the Acadians' "Second Expulsion."[15]

Even slight reflection would suggest that peoples inhabiting ecological environments as different as those occupied following the "second expulsion" would necessarily develop different forms of subsistence and support to accommodate to ecological realities. Such was the case with the Acadian immigrants who moved beyond the reaches of the dominant paths of commercial and social development. Partly by choice, partly by necessity, most of them found themselves relatively isolated and outside the more productive agricultural areas of the region. As the social system that would emerge by the mid-nineteenth century took on its dominant contours, the Louisiana Acadians who could not or would not compete with large landowners and the commercial and proto-industrial bourgeoisie came to occupy, at least in the eyes of the outsiders, a distinctly inferior status in the system. Whether they sought their subsistence as bayou country small farmers, as swamp fishermen and trappers, as prairie farmers and ranchers, or as shrimpers and oystermen of the coastal area, the great majority of the Acadians of Louisiana shared two things: their ethnicity (with all its linguistic, religious, historical, kinship, and other cultural elements) and their relative poverty; *i.e.*, their relative lack of politico-economic power and, inevitably, social status.[16] These factors remained constant, even despite the wide dispersion of their new settlement areas.

But what of the minority that succeeded within the terms of the increasingly dominant Anglo-American values? What of the Acadians who did well in the competition for available resources, those who became large landowners, slaveowners, planter/merchants, professionals, "capitalists?" Naturally, their socio-economic condition and position were somewhat different, especially in the older settlements of the river parishes where the paths of commerce and culture provided diversified contact with the outside world, bringing changes in the patterns of their culture and rendering them more like their Anglo/Creole neighbors than like their rustic cousins to the west and south. Within two generations they found it possible to elevate their status (perhaps by way of an advantageous marriage), acquire the polish and cultivation often (an often erroneously) associated with the planter "aristocracy," join the ranks of the politically notable, and become something very different from their Acadian peasant forebears or their less affluent contemporaries. In the apt phrasing of Professor Patricia Rickels, as they came to look with nostalgia upon their origins, to reflect on their traditions and create their mythologies, they became "Genteel Acadians."[17]

To take a case in point: Consider the history of the Jean Mouton family. Jean, the progenitor of the family in Louisiana, was an early and impoverished immigrant Acadian who had been exiled from Nova Scotia. He found his way to the Attakapas District, where he acquired land and married a cultivated widow of French extraction, Marie Marthe Bordat. As they proceeded to produce a large family, Mouton added to his land holdings by careful management, ultimately founding a village (Vermilionville, later Lafayette) which came to serve as a commercial center for the surrounding region. In time he acquired a degree of cultivation and sophistication, largely through the influence of his wife. The combination of wealth and cultivation and attendant influence provided the foundation for an Acadian-American dynasty that ultimately included a United States senator and governor of Louisiana, two lieutenant governors, several district judges, and a Confederate general.[18] The Moutons were, however, clearly exceptional; The "Genteel Acadians" always constituted a small elite. The less fortunate or aggressive or able or farsighted--in short the vast majority of the Acadian immigrants--became plain "Cajuns."

The term "Cajun," of course, is simply an Americanized version of the French "Acadien"; pronunciation of French has never come easily to Anglo-Americans of the Deep South. Palatization plus a certain laziness of tongue readily converted the French "Cadien" (or "Cadjin") to "Cajun" in English-speaking Louisiana. What is equally clear is that by some time in the mid-nineteenth-century the term "Cajun" had taken on pejorative connotations among those who ascribed certain qualities to the people so designated.[19] There is no way of determining precisely what qualities were so ascribed, at least initially. Given the widespread use of the term Cajun by the late nineteenth century, and the appearance of certain qualities attributed to the Cajuns by descriptive literature even from their earliest arrival, it seems likely that the term bore a fairly specific freight of meaning to outside observers. In addition to the obvious matters of identifying the Cajuns by their linguistic, religious, and family surname distinctions "Cajun" also implied such qualities as poverty, insularity, illiteracy, social inferiority, the absence of culture. On the other hand, Cajuns were also, ascriptively, easygoing (some contended that lazy would be the more appropriate term), unambitious, friendly (if cliquish), fun-loving and pious (at least superficially).[20]

A few examples from the contemporary sources will serve to illustrate the ascriptive qualities associated with the Cajuns in the antebellum years. In 1803 the French traveller Claude C. Robin observed that they "do not show the zeal in their work that their European confreres would...." Rather, "they love to dance . . . more than any other people in the colony . . . . Everyone dances, even *Grandmère* and *Grandpère* no matter what the difficulties they must bear." They danced until late into the night, drank tafia (a poor quality of rum), ate gumbo (apparently the Acadian national dish even as early as this), then departed by pirogue (a small canoe-like craft), or on horseback, or by foot. But, for all their *joie de vivre*, they were poor, "simple" people: "Clean clothes are a luxury for them. . . . They go to the dances barefoot, as they go to the fields. . . . As for learning they don't know what it is. Most of them cannot read."[21] An American traveller, Sargent S. Prentiss, writing to his brother in 1829, described the Cajuns in almost identical terms:

> They are the poorest, most ignorant, set of beings you ever saw--without the least enterprise or industry. They raise only a little corn and a few sweet potatoes--merely sufficient to support life; yet they seem perfectly contented and happy, and have balls almost every day–I attented one and was invited to several others.[22]

And in 1851 a correspondent with *De Bow's Review* was even more direct, branding the Cajuns as "an indolent, uneducated race--oppressed by poverty, and like all poor people, [they] have poor ways."[23]

Needless to say, the "Cajuns" themselves did not use the term to imply such qualities and characteristics--indeed they did not use it at all (though the French equivalent "Cadien" was in common use within the group virtually from the beginning of Acadian self-identification). But the essentially pejorative use of "Cajun" by those outside the group--its use by the "others"-set the group apart, lent it ascriptive qualities, gave it a name, and established what the anthropologist Edward H. Spicer has called a "terminology of opposition."[24] The term represents (in the functional-analytic model established by Frederick Barth) the existence of a "boundary-maker" separating "Cajun" from "Non-Cajun."[25] In perceiving themselves as distinctive and different, and in acting as such, the Cajun population accepted the boundary and marked it from within. The Acadian immigrants were thus well on their way toward division by the end of the second generation, with each major segment distinguished by class factors and by ascription.

Not to oversimplify: nineteenth-century South Louisiana manifested a maddeningly complex social structure, and the Acadian-American element was less clear-cut in character than the "Genteel Acadian" "Cajun" dichotomy would suggest. Between the wealthy, prestigious, cultivated Genteel Acadian and the poor Cajun, subsisting on the bayou or in the swamps or prairies, there existed a spectrum of relative wealth and poverty, though within the Acadian population the spectrum was skewed pronouncedly toward the latter.[26] There were far more Cajuns than Genteel Acadians, even given a mid-range group of indeterminate status. And despite the lack of precision in defining the levels of class division, the class distinction maintains useful, indeed necessary, analytic function in a consideration of Cajun ethnogenesis.

To understand Acadian-American ethnicity in its formative phase further requires making a clear distinction between those groups of Euro-

pean National extraction who were relatively well assimilated into the Anglo-
American dominant culture; *i.e.*, those who acculturated readily to the
norms of the Anglo-dominant socio-economic system and those who did
not.   Most prominent among the latter groups present in mid-nineteenth-
century Louisiana were the Cajuns. Only they could claim their ethnicity
as a primary source of their identity, their status, their life-style, for only
they were, in effect, determined in status and role by the force of ethnic
ascription, by the "others" as well as by themselves. For the Genteel A-
cadian (the 'Cadien *Doré*), ethnicity was a matter of genealogy and nostalgia, perhaps occasionally rendered useful; for example, to be manipu-
lated for social, political, or economic advantage in dealing with others
of Acadian descent.[27]   For the plain Cajun, ethnicity was a tremendously
important day-to-day reality, for he or she was bound to and defined by
it.   To sum up: class status tended to decrease ethnic distinctions among
the gentry elite while sharpening such distinctions among the Cajuns-in-
process.   Class considerations therefore figured prominently in Cajun ethnogenesis and later in the maintenance of the Cajun group.

   This is not to say that the boundary could not be crossed. Barth and
others have made it clear that boundaries are not barriers. As we have seen,
the Cajuns had some element of status mobility; under certain circumstances,
they *could* gain access to wealth and prestige and join the Anglo-dominant
bourgeoisie.   They could marry "well" (probably exogamously), provide
their children with educational and cultural advantages, and produce in
some cases new dynasties of Genteel Acadians, who might in turn reflect
now and again on what Professor Rickels has called their "image of Golden
Age virtue, tranquility, and piety presented in Longfellow's *Evangeline.* . ."[28]
It is likely, however, that such a metamorphosis would necessitate a move
from the isolation of the original Cajun community into the more accessible
centers of Anglo-dominant culture. The isolation factor was of key significance in the perpetuation of Cajun ethnicity, and by the mid-nineteenth
century the ascriptive category "Cajun" had emerged as a fully articulated
ethnic group, the maintenance of which depended in some measure on
relative separation from the main paths of commerce and culture diffusion.

   It also depended on endogamy, and the evidence is overwhelming that
at least a form of endogamy prevailed among the Cajuns throughout the
nineteenth century and beyond.[29]   I emphasize "a form of endogamy,"
for the Cajun version was by no means absolute. Although the overwhelming
majority of Cajuns married other Cajuns, many of them being relatives within
a single degree of kinship, some did not. The Cajun population showed
a remarkable ability to absorb non-Cajun elements, even quite disparate
elements.   For example, evidence suggests that French, English, Irish, Span-

ish, German, Italian, and American natives often married into Cajun families, proceeded to live in the manner of the Cajuns, produced children who were then raised as Cajuns, and who for all practical purposes came to belong to the group.[30] The gene pool thus greatly expanded; so, of course, did the "cultural pool," though the dominant ascriptive characteristics of the Cajun subculture, however synthetic, apparently maintained a remarkable consistency throughout the antebellum period and into the twentieth century.

Ascription, then, and isolation, and a qualified endogamy all functioned to encourage group maintenance. But there was another powerful influence: the reciprocal effects of ascription, status inferiority, and reaffirmed status ascription. What happened, in effect, was that even as "Cajun" came to imply a lower place in the social order, the Cajuns themselves came to accept their status *as* Cajuns. Many of them simply did not want to become "Americanized," and consequently refused to make the necessary concessions to Anglo-bourgeois ways that would enhance the possibilities of their upward mobility. This is not to say that the larger social system provided much opportunity for status elevation, at least not after ca. 1830. The competition for valuable resources was keen, and Cajuns were hardly favored with advantages in the struggle. Sources of fluid capital were scarce at best; for Cajuns they were virtually nonexistent. The state provided woefully little in the way of educational opportunities for the poor, and particularly for the poor in areas of relative physical isolation. Although the Catholic church technically assumed responsibility for the literacy of its parishioners, fulfillment of that responsibility was pitifully inadequate, as even Catholic sources readily admit.[31] With astonishing speed the English language came to dominate the political and commercial realms of the region as a part of the pervasive Anglo-Americanization process. French monolingualism came increasingly to represent a severe handicap to socioeconomic boundary penetration by Cajuns. Finally, the stigma that came to be attached to the status of "Cajun"--they were disparaged as crude peasants by virtually all "others," including Genteel Acadians--made it extremely difficult to escape from that status, even should an individual choose to make the effort. The boundary was reinforced, then, by the social system. And class considerations continued to weigh heavily, even deterministically, on Cajun ethnic group definition and maintenance.

Up to this point, most of what has been said has reflected a point of view established from a position on the outside of the boundary enclosing the Cajun group. The reason for this perspective--the anthropologists would likely call it an "etic" perspective--is obvious. Ethnohistorical sources proceeding from a dominat, literate culture are more readily available than those from non-literate folk sub-cultures. Indigenous primary sources reflecting the nineteenth-century Cajun experience from a insider's perspective are rare indeed. But the evidence from persistent material culture and folklore can suggest some of the contours of the Cajun value system. And to the degree that we are able to extrapolate certain of their "emic" (i.e., "folk") categories from such sources, it appears that Cajun normative values operated substantially to further inhibit their upward mobility. The boundary was, then, reinforced from within even as it was being bolstered from the outside by external ascription and social-systemic factors.

There is extrapolative evidence, for example, to suggest that Cajuns manifested a substantial sub-culture bias against such "American" values as the work ethic and bourgeois materialism. Cajuns were not, in the American way, aggressively acquisitive; not given to a powerful drive toward amassing material possessions by way of reward for work achievements. It is noteworthy that a close student of Cajun folklore has observed that nowhere in Cajun folk music is there to be found thematic material pertaining to great workers or work achievement; no John Henrys, no Paul Bunyans, no Erie Canal navigation, no "Cotton Needs Pickin'."[32] Their songs are songs of love and courtship, of narrative adventure, of drinking and dancing and the hedonistic pleasures (sometimes pungently earthly pleasures).

Moreover, their value attachment typically was to the land itself, not to land value, or so it would seem from an analysis of their preferred land distribution and agricultural practices. Indeed, there is substantial evidence to suggest that Cajuns did not much care for "Les Américains," whom they viewed as greedy and arrogant and somehow associated with the English, whose role as perpetrator of their derangement was legendary.[33] Profoundly egalitarian among their own, Cajuns were equally anti-deferential: they tended to disparage "aristocracy" or pretension to the same degree that the self-styled "aristocrats" of the plantation system denigrated crude, illiterate peasants. And as the planter-bourgeoisie exercised two kinds of hegemony over the sociopolitical system, it was inevitable that considerable tension would exist between Cajuns and their "betters," including the Genteel Acadians.[34] Spicer might well have had the Cajun experience in mind when he wrote recently of the "oppositional process," suggesting that it may well be "the essential factor in the formation and development of [a] persistent identity system."[35]

Even religion and language, culture elements which, it would seem, Cajuns might share with the Creoles and the Genteel Acadians, provided the stuff of further division. Unquestionably the Cajuns were a pious people, particularly the women, and when church facilities were available to them (by no means always the case), they participated in the Catholic rituals and placed high value on them. But in part due to the inadequacies of formal church instruction, they also practiced a form of religious syncretism by which sacramentals were employed in folk ways suggesting the influence of Afro-Caribbean Voodoo practices.[36] Cajuns of the antebellum period were also, it would seem, somewhat superstitious, a fact attested by their reliance on "gris-gris" (the use of sympathetic magic) in both folk medicine and affairs of the heart. As regards language, the Cajun version of spoken French was different and distinct, and as such was increasingly relegated to the status of a crude and inferior dialect of the dominant European version of the language, thus once again reinforcing the boundaries between themselves and other French speakers of a higher class status.

To the extent, then, that ethnohistorians are ever able to "get inside," we may surmise that there were indeed internal ethnic considerations constantly marking the borders and perpetuating the distinctions. Much in the manner of the old Acadians of Nova Scotia, the Cajuns of mid-nineteenth-century Louisiana maintained their traditional values: the land, family, a form of religiosity, independence and self-reliance, a powerful equalitarianism, the determination to be left alone. Their way, of course, represents a kind of rural-folk conservatism ("folk," again, in the Redfield sense), but is eminently clear that this was the way they wanted things. Such appears to be the case with most folk cultures. The way of the Cajuns, for all its disadvantages within the larger system, was to them a better way; one to be maintained even as the group was maintained, at least for those who by choice or fate lived within the boundaries of the group.

Perhaps the ultimate measure of the distinction between the Cajuns and the others (and the supreme sign of the salience of the boundary) was manifested only with the onset of the American Civil War. As had been the case with their Acadian ancestors of a century before, the Cajuns of 1860-1861 wanted little to do with a world-historical conflict that erupted in the heart of their homeland. The Civil War was not, they believed, their fight. When forced to participate they normally did so. They rarely went by choice, and they often deserted when the paths of war took them near their homes. Sometimes they resisted, or joined gangs of "Jayhawkers," raiding the supply lines of Rebels and Yankees alike, to the horror of their "Genteel" kinsfolk who lent virtually unanimous support to the Confederate cause.[37]

Such was the process, then, by which a unique and distinct group of immigrants, frieghted with cultural baggage and the weight of cruel historical experience, came to be a different but equally distinctive American ethnic group. As the Civil War ended and new socioeconomic and political circumstances emerged, the Cajuns, some 30,000 to 35,000 of them, represented as tightly bounded a group as the United States has ever produced. Their ethnogenesis, initiated by self-segregation and enhanced by geographic isolation, had produced a full-blown ethnic population. As an ethnic group, the Cajuns maintained a continued sense of their "we-ness"--their ethnicity--even as the social system that had nurtured that maintenance dictated the terms of the group's survival, while disparaging Cajuns ascriptively as a rude and illiterate peasantry. The reciprocal effects of social-systemic imperatives and of the group's internalized ethnic values thus contributed to the perpetuation of the group, as did the Cajuns' own sense of identity and belonging, psychic balms that provided certain comfort in a world not otherwise designed to afford much more than mere subsistence to a people it could not or would not assimilate.

. . . .

It has been my contention throughout this essay that class considerations were at the base of the division between Acadian descent groups, and were central to the formation of the Cajun people as an American ethnic group. This thesis has, I believe, been confirmed by the contours of the current Cajun ethnic revival movement. Following a century of lower-class status ascription and increasing denigration by the Anglo-dominant culture (a culture that included their higher-status kinspeople), many Cajuns have opted to pursue the course of 1970's style ethnic revitalization, reaffirming their ethnic qualities and identity, as indeed have the latter-day Genteel Acadians. And even in their revival, a movement inaugurated by the advent of the Council for the Development of French in Louisiana (CODOFIL) in 1968, the class division persists. The Genteel Acadians, representing what they perceive as the revival of the "great tradition," still disparage the Cajuns as crude and rude; the Cajuns, now representing a much earthier and heartier folk revival (perhaps the "little tradition"?) still disdain the pretensions of the 'Cadien Doré, such that (as Dr. Rickels writes), the two groups co-exist "in a mood of considerable tension."[38] No unified Francophone movement appears possible so long as this class division continues, and it seems likely, indeed almost certain, to continue for the foreseeable future.

NOTES

1. For the figures pertaining to the size of the deported group, see Naomi E. Griffiths, *The Acadians: Creation of a People* (New York, 1969), p. 60. The best recent study of the exile and resettlement of the Acadians is Carl A. Brasseaux, "The Founding of New Acadia," (Doctoral dissertation, University of Paris, 1982).

2. The history of the Acadians in Nova Scotia has received substantial scholarly consideration, most notably in Brasseaux, "New Acadia;" Emile Lauvrière, *La Tragédie d'un peuple. Histoire du peuple acadien de ses origines à nos jours* (Paris, 1924); John Bartlett Brebner, *New England's Outpost: Acadia Before the Conquest of Canada* (New York, 1973); Bona Arsenault, *History of the Acadians* (Quebec, 1966); and, most conveniently, in Griffiths, *The Acadians*, and Jacqueline K. Voorhies, "The Acadians: The Search for the Promised Land," in Glenn R. Conrad, ed., *The Cajuns: Essays on Their History and Culture* (Lafayette, La., 1978), pp. 97-114.

3. See Robert Redfield, "The Folk Society," *American Journal of Sociology*, LII (1947), 293-308. The balance of my characterization of the Acadians of Nova Scotia is based on a componential analysis of the descriptive material in Brasseaux, "New Acadia," *passim*; Brebner, *New England's Outpost*, pp. 43-45; Glenn R. Conrad, "The Acadians: Myths and Realities," in Conrad, ed., *The Cajuns*, pp. 1-20; Arthur G. Doughty, *The Acadian Exiles: A Chronicle of the Land of Evangeline* (Toronto, 1916), pp. 83-113; Griffiths, *The Acadians, passim*; Lauvrière, *Tragédie d'un peuple*, I, 178-193.

4. Griffiths, *The Acadians*, p. 16.

5. For the details of the derangement, see Brasseaux, "New Acadia," *passim*; Arsenault, *History of the Acadians*, pp. 141-219; Griffiths, *The Acadians*, pp. 77, 80; Lauvriere, *Tragédie d'un peuple*, I, 441-493; Oscar W. Winzerling, *Acadian Odyssey* (Baton Rouge, 1955), *passim*.

6. Griffiths, *The Acadians*, p. 70.

7. Winzerling, *Acadian Odyssey*, pp. 130-162; Brasseaux, "New Acadia," *passim*.

8. Arsenault, *History of the Acadians*, p. 191.

9. *Ibid.*, p. 195.

10. See Glenn R. Conrad, "The Acadian Story Continues to Unfold," *Attakapas Gazette*, XIII (1978), 89-90. The Attakapas District, along with the adjacent Opelousas District, were military-administrative subdivisions of the Louisiana colony established by the French in the mid-eighteenth century. They lay some 150 miles west of New Orleans in the south-central portion of what is now the state of Louisiana.

11. The term "Creole" in the present context refers to individuals born in a colonial possession of France or Spain, or to the families proceeding from such individuals. For a thorough analysis of the etymology of the term, see Virginia R. Dominguez, "Social Classification in Creole Louisiana," *American Ethnologist*, IV (1977), 589-602. Another useful discussion is that of Larbi Oukada in his *Louisiana French: An Annotated Bibliography* (Lafayette, La., 1979), pp. 3-11.

12. Eric Waddell, "French Louisiana: An Outpost of l'Amérique française, or Another Country and Another Culture?," Document de Travail, *Projet Louisiane* (Quebec, 1979), p. 4.

13. On the emergent settlement patterns, see Arsenault, *History of the Acadians*, pp. 191-208; Conrad, "The Acadians: Myths and Realities," 10-11; Fernando Solano Costa, "The Acadian Emigration to Spanish Louisiana," trans. G. B. Roberts, *Southwestern Louisiana Journal*, II (1958), 2-44; Brasseaux, "New Acadia," *passim*; William B. Knipmeyer, "Settlement Succession in Eastern French Louisiana," (Ph. D. dissertation, Louisiana State University, 1956), *passim*.

14. Contrary to all current usage, I am lumping the "planter/bourgeoisie" to suggest (1) planters were often allied with urban bourgeois interests and were themselves frequently involved in non-agricultural business pursuits, and (2) as elites, planters and upper-bourgeoisie shared their concerns for maintenance of their status as well as their fundamentally Anglo-bourgeois materialist value system.

15. William F. Rushton, *The Cajuns: From Acadia to Louisiana* (New York, 1979), p. 81. The arrival and settlement of the Anglo-Americans (ca. 1793-1820) may be traced in the *American State Papers: Public Lands*, 1st-24th Congress, 1781-1837, 9 vols. (Washington, D. C., 1832-1837), III, 88-123; while the rapid expansion of the slave population (a good index to plantation development) is detailed in the U. S. census reports after 1803. Such sources indicate that from 1800 through 1830 the slave population of what is now the state of Louisiana jumped from some 17,500 to 109,588. Between 1810 and 1820 there was a 99.3% increase in the slave population. See U. S. Bureau of the Census, *A Century of Population Growth, From the First Census of the U. S. to the Twelfth* (Washington, D. C., 1909), pp. 133-134. On the process of plantation consolidation at the expense of the *petits habitants*, see *De Bow's Review*, II (December, 1851), 606; Malcolm L. Comeaux, "Louisiana's Acadians: The Environmental Impact," in Conrad, ed., *The Cajuns*, pp. 142, 147-148; –––––, *Atchafalaya Swamp Life: Settlement and Folk Occupations* (Baton Rouge, 1972), pp. 10-11, 17-18; Lauren C. Post, "Cultural Geography of the Prairies of Southwest Louisiana," (Ph. D. dissertation, University of California, 1936), p. 144, and Table 3 (n. p.); Vernon J. Parenton, "The Rural French-Speaking People of Quebec and South Louisiana: A Comparative Study . . . ," (Ph. D. dissertation, Harvard University, 1948), pp. 333, 342.

16. It should be noted that their "relative poverty" might not have been readily apparent to all of the disadvantaged Louisiana Acadians. Many of them did not, it appears, view their circumstances as disadvantaged. Outsiders viewing them, however, perceived them as constituting a lower class, and most ordinarily poor.

17. Patricia K. Rickles, "The Folklore of the Acadians," in Conrad, ed., *The Cajuns*, p. 251.

18. On the Mouton experience, see William H. Perrin, comp., *Southwest Louisiana, Biographical and Historical* (1891; reprint ed., Baton Rouge, 1971), pp. 238-241; Harry L. Griffin, *The Attakapas Country: A History of Lafayette Parish* (New Orleans, 1959), pp. 186-189; William Arceneaux, *Acadian General: Alfred Mouton and the Civil War* (Lafayette, La., 1972), pp. 7-11.

19. See also George F. Reinecke, trans. and ed., "Early Louisiana French Life and Folklore," *Louisiana Folklore Miscellany*, II (1966), 7; John Guilbeau, "Folklore and

the Louisiana French Lexicon," *Revue de Louisiane/Louisiana Review*, I (1972), 52; Arsenault, *History of the Acadians*, p. 189, note.

20. Although the primary sources alluding to Cajun character are numerous, they must be used with caution. Nonetheless, there is such consistency in their content over the years that the dominant ascriptive qualities are well established. See, for example, Claude C. Robin, *Voyage to Louisiana, 1803-1805*, trans. and ed., Stuart O. Landry, Jr. (New Orleans, 1966), pp. 115, 190-191; Sargent S. Prentiss to William Prentiss, April 9, 1829, in George Lewis Prentiss, ed., *A Memoir of S. S. Prentiss* (New York, 1855), I, 94-95; William Henry Sparks, *The Memories of Fifty Years*, 4th ed. (Philadelphia, 1882), pp. 379-380; Franklin *Planters' Banner*, September 24, 1847; *De Bow's Review*, XI (December, 1851), 66; Frederick Law Olmsted, *A Journey in the Seaboard Slave States*, 2 vols. (New York, 1856), I, 648-650; II, 332-333; ―――――, *Journeys and Explorations in the Cotton Kingdom* (London, 1861), II, 40-45; *New Orleans Daily Crescent*, May 25, 1860. Professor Timothy Reilly has edited and published an excellent collection of primary accounts in English under the running title "Early Acadiana Through Anglo-American Eyes," *Attakapas Gazette*, XII (1977), 3-20, 159-176, 185-194; XIII (1978), 53-71. Despite its earlier pejorative connotations, the term "Cajun" has become the designation of choice in the recent ethnic revitalization movement except on the part of a self-constituted elite. "Cajun" has also been accepted by the scholarly community as well and is in common use in the scholarly literature.

21. Robin, *Voyage to Louisiana*, p. 115.

22. Prentiss, *Memoir*, I, 94-95.

23. *De Bow's Review*, XI (December, 1851), 66.

24. Edward H. Spicer, "Persistent Cultural Systems: A Comparative Study of Identity Systems That Can Adapt to Contrasting Environments," *Science*, CLXXIV (1971), 799.

25. Frederick Barth, ed., *Ethnic Groups and Boundaries: The Social Organization of Culture Difference* (Boston, 1969), pp. 10-28. For an extended discussion of the Barth model, see James H. Dormon, "Ethnic Groups and 'Ethnicity': Some Theoretical Considerations," *Journal of Ethnic Studies*, VII (1980), 23-36.

26. The same social class spectrum of course prevailed for *all* ethnic groups of the region, not just the Cajuns. Indeed, many Louisiana/Acadian descendants were of relatively indeterminate status in the social order, as were many Creoles, Anglos, Spanish, Caribbeans, or whatever. It is impossible to achieve precision in measuring the various levels of class division. But between the uppermost levels and the lowermost the class distinction was a patent and salient feature of the nineteenth century South Louisiana social structure.

27. On the situational manipulation of ethnic identity, see Judith A. Nagata, "What is a Malay? Situational Selection of Ethnic Identity in a Plural Society," *American Ethnologist*, I (1974), 331-350.

28. Rickels, "Folklore of the Acadians," p. 251. On the Louisiana/Acadian acculturation to Anglo/bourgeois norms, see also Vaughan B. Baker, "Patterns of Acadian Slave Ownership in Lafayette Parish, 1850," *Attakapas Gazette*, IX (1974), 144-148; and ―――――, "The Acadians in Antebellum Louisiana: A Study of Acculturation," in Conrad, ed., *The Cajuns*, pp. 115-128.

29. Winston DeVille, ed., *Marriage Contracts of the Attakapas Post, 1760-1803* (St. Martinville, La., 1966), pp. 5-31; Donald J. Hébert, *Southwest Louisiana Records: Church and Civil Records of Lafourche-Terrebonne Parishes*, 7 vols. (Cecelia, La., 1978-1981), *passim*. For a genetic perspective, see Theodore F. Thurmon and Ellen B. De Fraites, "Genetical Studies of the French Acadians of Louisiana," (unpublished paper in possession of the author, for which my thanks to Vaughan B. Baker); see also Thurmon and De Fraites, "Effect of Size of Founding Group on Founder Effect," *American Journal of Human Genetics*, XXV (1973), 80; Comeaux, *Swamp Life*, p. 21.

30. See T. Lynn Smith and Vernon J. Parenton, "Acculturation Among the Louisiana French," *American Journal of Sociology*, XIL (1938), 355. The authors hypothesize that the ability of the Cajuns to absorb others, to transform a "heterogeneous diversity of ethnic elements" into a homogeneous Cajun ethnic unit was based on several factors, chiefly the fact that outsider males tended to marry Cajun women, who then dominated child-rearing and enculturation processes (thus providing another example of the "matrilineal core" of cultural transmission). It appears that the most important single outside group to be so incorporated was the non-Acadian Francophone element of the region, *i. e.*, Creoles, French nationals, and Caribbean Francophones. Increasingly, the evidence is suggesting that the "Cajun" group actually came to comprise what Glenn R. Conrad has termed a "French Synthesis," a coalescence of French speakers subsumed under the rubric "Cajun" and reflecting the Cajun lifestyle even as they influenced the emergent Louisiana/Cajun culture.

31. See, for example, Roger Baudier, *The Catholic Church in Louisiana* (New Orleans, 1939), pp. 322-323; Herman J. Jacobi, *The Catholic Family in Rural Louisiana* (Washington, D. C., 1937), *passim*; Patricia K. Rickels, "The Folklore of the Sacraments and Sacramentals in South Louisiana," *Louisiana Folklore Miscellany*, II (1965), 29.

32. Elizabeth Brandon, "The Socio-Cultural Traits of the French Folksong in Louisiana," *Revue de Louisiane/Louisiana Review*, I (1972), 28.

33. See, for example, Post, "Cultural Geography," pp. 79-80; Brasseaux, "New Acadia," *passim*.

34. There is some evidence that large slaveowners wanted to rid their plantation environs of Cajuns altogether, as the free and independent Cajun farmer served as a bad example to slaves. Olmsted reported (during his 1853 visit) that

> The slaves seeing . . . [the Cajuns] living in apparent comfort, without property and without steady labor, could not help thinking that it was not necessary for men to work so hard as they themselves were obliged to; that if they were free they would not need to work.

Olmsted, *Seaboard Slave States*, II, 332-333.

35. Spicer, "Persistent Culture Systems," 797.

36. Rickels, "Folklore of the Sacraments," 29-42.

37. On the Cajuns' lack of enthusiasm for the Civil War, see U. S. War Department, *The War of the Rebellion: A Compilation of the Official Records of the Union and Confederate Armies . . .* (Washington, D. C., 1880-1901), Series 1, XV, 1092.

Major General Richard Taylor reported of the action near Vermilionville: "Nearly the whole [Lt.-Col. Fournet's] battalion, passing through the country in which the men had lived before joining the army, deserted with their arms, remaining at their homes." *War of the Rebellion*, XV, 393. See also James H. Dormon, ed., "A Late Nineteenth Century View of Acadiana: Charles Dudley Warner's 'The Acadian Land,' " *Attakapas Gazette*, VII (1972), 169; John D. Winters, *The Civil War in Louisiana* (Baton Rouge, 1963), p. 231; and especially Carl A. Brasseaux, "Rebels Without a Cause? Cajuns, Conscription, and the Civil War," (Unpublished article, copy in possession of the author). But, see also, Griffin, *Attakapas Country*, p. 143. It is noteworthy that in claiming broad support for the war among Louisiana's "Acadians," Griffin mentions several examplars of the genteel Acadian class. He says nothing whatever of the Cajuns.

38. Rickels, "Folklore of the Acadians," p. 251.